For Emma

Environmental Law and Regulation

John F. McEldowney

and

Sharron McEldowney

Published by
Blackstone Press Limited
Aldine Place
London
W12 8AA
United Kingdom

Sales enquiries and orders
Telephone + 44-(0)-20-8740-2277
Facsimile + 44-(0)-20-8743-2292
e-mail: sales@blackstone.demon.co.uk
website: www.blackstonepress.com

ISBN 1-84174-114-0
© John F. McEldowney and Sharron McEldowney 2001
First published 2001

British Library Cataloguing in Publication Data
A catalogue record for this book is available from the British Library

Typeset in 10/12pt Palatino by Montage Studios Ltd, Tonbridge, Kent
Printed and bound in Great Britain by Antony Rowe Limited,
Chippenham and Reading

Contents

Preface

This book is intended to explain how the environment is regulated. The main focus of the book is on the use of different environmental standards in regulating the environment. Environmental regulation is heavily dependent on some form of standard to provide best practice for the protection of the environment. The success or failure of the regulatory system depends on how enforceable and achievable those standards are. The explanation and analysis provided inform lawyers and those interested in environmental law how environmental standards are set and developed. Two broad questions are addressed: How effective are environmental standards in protecting the environment?; and Have environmental standards led to improvements in the environment as a whole?

The book is published at a time when there is an increasing awareness of the challenges facing the environment. There is an apparent paradox. While the environment is more carefully monitored and regulated than in the past, public disquiet and concern are at their highest. Public confidence in science and in government is low. In agriculture and land use, the recent BSE crisis, foot and mouth disease, and doubts about Genetically Modified Organisms (GMOs) have contributed to public unease. Concerns exist about satisfactory standards, their observance and enforcement. There are worries about water pollution with the public demanding high standards to ensure pure drinking water and unpolluted bathing water. In the area of transport, car use causing air and noise pollution is a major concern of the government's transport policy. Standards are linked to safety. Society increasingly expects high safety standards and is generally risk adverse. The regulatory system is expected to provide compliance and degrees of accountability unimagined in the past. There is also the potential for conflict between economic performance and safeguarding the environment which lies at the heart of sustainable development.

Regulating the environment through standard-setting places environmental issues within a broad framework. As outlined in the UK's Annual Report, *This Common Inheritance* (Cm 2822, 1995), and reiterated in subsequent white papers, stewardship of the environment requires the setting of environmental goals and objectives. Principles relating to the achievment of such goals and objectives include sustainable development, the precautionary principle and the polluter pays principle. Rectifying environmental damage where it occurs at source is also a key part of the development of an environmental policy and combining these principles into a coherent whole should be at the heart of an efficient regulatory structure for environmental law. At present there is no coherent regulatory system for the environment in Britain though the creation of an Environment Agency has marked a step in the right direction. Nor is there a coherent set of regulatory instruments allowing environmental regulation to be treated as a discrete subject in its own right.

This book attempts to draw together the wide range of controls found in regulating the environment. The focus is on how environmental standards are set, enforced and scrutinized. Almost all environmental controls rely on some form of standard (see, for example, *Environmental Standards — The UK Practice*, London: HMSO, 1995) and the different types of standards are defined and elaborated in some detail in chapter 1. The task of identifying and clarifying standards is made difficult by the diffuse nature of the subject and its cross-disciplinary qualities, which range from the application of economic and fiscal instruments to legal and scientific mechanisms. There is no single body responsible for coordinating all aspects of environmental regulation and, indeed, the subject transcends national boundaries and the legal system of a single state.

There is much uncertainty about how environmental regulation should best be coordinated and this can be seen in the way the environment has been regulated to date. In the United Kingdom, administrative functions are split between centrally organised and locally controlled bodies. In England and Wales the establishment of the Environment Agency has unified a wide number of pollution functions, but even so there remain a number of bodies that retain pollution control functions. These include, for example, the Nuclear Installations Inspectorate and the Health and Safety Executive. Local authorities also have powers over the control of air pollution, statutory nuisances in public health matters and contaminated land, in addition to their powers relating to town and country planning. At the central level, the Secretary of State for the Environment has wide powers to issue guidance to the Environment Agency and the large, multi-tasking Department of Environment, Transport and the Regions (DETR), created in May 1997, oversees environmental and transport matters in England. Devolution in Scotland, Wales and Northern Ireland has created an asymmetrical style of administration with decentralised powers moving to the regions. Very often the regulatory body, be it the Environment Agency or central or local government, is involved in setting the standards that are to be enforced by the regulatory body itself.

The Deregulation and Contracting Out Act 1994, which aims to reduce the burden of unnecessary regulation, provides an additional dimension and there is considerable potential for the extension of this principle in the Regulatory Reform Act.

Finally, there are countervailing tendencies to decentralisation. European Community involvement in the environment favours centralisation and uniformity and this is especially marked following changes introduced by the Treaty of Amsterdam. Article 2 of the Treaty sets the goal of 'promoting a harmonious and balanced and sustainable development of economic activities' and Article 6 requires that environmental protection be integrated into Community policies and activities. The establishment of the European Environment Agency also adds to the considerable influence of the Community in the regulation of the environment. At international level, there are important agreements such as Agenda 21, from the 1992 United Nations Conference on Environment and Development at Rio, which sets general principles for environmental policy.

Regulation of the environment and the setting of standards takes place against this diverse and complex background.

A working hypothesis explored in the book is that far from improving the environment, legal regulation to date may provide a false sense of confidence. The underlying trend might be that the environment has deteriorated and the polluter is able to transfer the costs of waste disposal and bad practice on to others. Perversely, standards — by their apparent objectivity and seemingly universal application — may, in certain circumstances, protect the wrongdoer. They assume compliance. In their non-observance and with weak enforcement they may provide a means to cover up practices that are far below the requirement of the standards. Detection may be prevented if the standards are allowed to be manipulated and used as a means of falsifying the true position.

There is no uniform approach to standard-setting, although it is possible for standards to become adopted in international law. Standards that are universal in application may nevertheless differ in their application at a local level. While standards may be expressed in objective or scientific terms, their practical impact may differ when subjectively interpreted. The global dimension of standard-setting is important. The Royal Commission estimated that $500 billion a year is spent on standards worldwide.

In discussing standards, it is clear that there are differences of approach between the European Community and the United Kingdom. Member states may also differ in the way they implement and regulate standards. Discussion of the EC Environmental Liability proposals is a case in point.

Undoubtedly standards have the potential to set the future agenda for environmental policy. They can provide a wide range of flexible techniques that may lead to real improvements in the environment. Their versatility is seen as advantageous and makes standard-setting attractive for governments and policy makers. Standards are flexible in the range of penalties, from the civil to the criminal law, that may be used for their enforcement. Standards may also apply a range of incentives from licences to fiscal instruments of taxation favouring one process or procedure that is environmentally friendly over any other. Informal and formal means may be used for enforcement strategies. Standards may be used to provide a means to continuously monitor a process or procedure. Equally, by their nature they may be preventative and anticipatory. As the Royal Commission on Environmental Pollution concluded (21st Report, p. 5, para. 1.23): 'Standards are a crucial element in the environmental policy process, and in what has been called "the legal, epistemological and cultural matrix in which environmental politics is conducted".'

Lastly, it is clear that rapid and diverse change is affecting the way society approaches standards. Company accounts may include for the first time environmental accounts. Marketing strategies may adopt environmental standards as a way of selling products and delivering commercial information to the consumer. Internal audit as part of the Eco-management and Audit Scheme (EMAS) may prove an effective means of monitoring and protecting the environment. Competition rules, such as the Competition Act 1998, set new duties on water carriers to monitor water quality. International standards such as ISO 14031 may encourage internal benchmarking in the supply industry to major industrial companies. The countervailing trend in favour of deregulation may encourage self-regulation and self-monitoring. Finally, and with profound implications for the future, sustainable development includes environmental accounting and developing indicators to assess environmental improvement or degradation.

This book is not intended to provide a detailed guide to the vast compendium of regulatory standards. Rather, its primary aim is to provide a framework and conceptual analysis for the understanding and future development of environmental standards. The book is divided into 10 chapters. Chapter 1 sets the scene by explaining how regulation and standards operate in environmental law; Chapter 2 provides an outline of the history of standards and environmental law; Chapter 3 addresses the question of how standards are set and why; Chapter 4 provides an analysis of science and risk assessment; Chapter 5 outlines the main regulators and their role in setting standards for the environment; and Chapter 6 addresses the question of how environmental standards may be enforced. The specific environmental standards for water, land and air are considered in Chapters 7, 8 and 9 respectively and Chapter 10 provides conclusions to the book and draws together some of the themes contained in the earlier chapters.

We owe a great debt to many friends and colleagues who willingly gave of their time and assisted us in numerous ways in the writing of this book. First, our publisher Alistair MacQueen, who was at all times supportive and understanding. The rapid pace of change and new developments in this area set new challenges for publishing. At the University of Warwick, grateful thanks are due to Gavin Anderson, Hugh Beale, Lee Bridges, Julio Faundez, Wyn Grant, Duncan Matthews, Mike McConville, David Ormandy, Eric Pan, Michael Reddish and Ann Stewart. The University provided a period of study leave that helped to lay the foundations of the book. At the University of Nijmegen, thanks are due to Han Somsen. At the University of Westminster, to Jenny George, Bob Scott, Pamela Greenwell and Ann Rumpus. At the University of London, University College, our thanks are due to Professor Richard MacCrory. The library staff at the University of Warwick have also proved to be helpful and supportive in our demands for information.

John and Sharron McEldowney
Warwickshire
30 March 2001

Abbreviations

ACNFP	Advisory Committee on Novel Food and Processes
ACP	Advisory Committee on Pesticides
ACRE	Advisory Committee on Releases to the Environment
AEBC	Agriculture and Environment Biotechnology Commission
AFRC	Agriculture and Food Research Council
BATNEEC	best available techniques not entailing excessive cost
BBSRC	Biotechnology and Biological Sciences Research Council
BOD	biological oxygen demand
BPEO	best practicable environmental option
BPM	best practicable means
BS	British Standard
BSE	bovine spongiform encephalopathy
CFCs	chloroflourocarbons
CFP	Common Fisheries Policy
COPUS	The Committee on the Public Understanding of Science
DETR	Department of Environment, Transport and the Regions
DTI	Department of Trade and Industry
EAC	Environmental Audit Committee of the House of Commons
EC_{50}	concentration of a substance that results in 50 per cent of the maximum response to a chemical under defined conditions
ECs	median effective concentration
ENDS	Environmental Data Services*
EMAS	Eco-management and Audit Scheme
EPSRC	Engineering and Physical Science Research Council

*The ENDS Report, referred to throughout this book, is published on a monthly basis by Environmental Data Services.

ESRC	Economic and Social Research Council
GM	genetically modified
GMO	genetically modified organism
HMIP	Her Majesty's Inspectorate of Pollution
HRI	Horticultural Research International
IMO	International Maritime Organisation
IPC	integrated pollution control
IPPC	integrated pollution prevention and control
ISO	International Standards Organisation
LAQM	Local Air Quality Management
LC_{50} or LC_{70}	percentage of organisms, i.e. 50 per cent or 70 per cent respectively, killed at a given concentration of a chemical under defined conditions
LCs	lethal concentrations
MAFF	Ministry of Agriculture, Fisheries and Food
MARPOL	International Convention for the Prevention of Pollution from Ships
MNRs	Marine Nature Reserves
NAO	National Audit Office
NERC	Natural Environment Research Council
NGOs	non-governmental organisations
NRA	National Rivers Authority
OECD	Organisation for Economic Cooperation and Development
OFWAT	Office of Water Regulation
PEC	predicted environmental concentration
PM	particulates
PNEC	predicted no effect concentration
PPARC	Particle Physics and Astronomy Research Council
PPGs	planning policy guidances
SEPA	Scottish Environment Protection Agency
SERC	Science and Engineering Research Council
SSSI	site of special scientific interest
SWQOs	statutory water quality objectives
TAC	total allowable catch
TCPA	Town and Country Planning Act 1990
UESs	uniform emission standards
vCJD	variant Creutzfeldt-Jakob disease
VOCs	volatile organic compounds
WCA	Waste Collection Authority
WDA	Waste Disposal Authority
WQOs	water quality objectives
WRA	Waste Regulation Authority

Table of Cases

Table of Primary Legislation

Table of Secondary Legislation

Table of International Instruments

Table of European Directives in Force

AIR DIRECTIVES

Directive 70/220 on air pollution from motor vehicles [1970] OJ L76

Directive 72/306 on measures to be taken against the emission of pollutants from diesel engines for use in motor vehicles [1972] OJ L190

Directive 75/116 on the sulphur content of certain liquid fuels [1975] OJ L307

Directive 77/102 on measures to be taken against air pollution by gases from engines of motor vehicles OJ L32

Directive 77/537 on measures to be taken against emission of pollutants from diesel engines for use in wheeled agriculture and forestry tractors [1977] OJ L220

Directive 78/611 concerning the lead content of petrol [1978] OJ L127

Directive 80/779 on air quality limit values and guide values for sulphur dioxide and suspended particulates [1980] OJ L229

Directive 80/1268 relating to the fuel consumption of motor vehicles [1980] OJ L375

Directive 82/884 on a limit value for lead in the air [1982] OJ L378

Directive 84/360 on the combating of air pollution from industrial plants [1984] OJ L188

Directive 85/203 on air quality standards for nitrogen dioxide [1985] OJ L87

Directive 85/581 on limits of lead and benzene in petrol [1985] OJ L372

Directive 87/219 on the content of sulphur in diesel fuel [1987] OJ L91

Directive 88/76 on measures to be taken against air pollution by gases from engines of motor vehicles (amending Directive 70/220) [1988] OJ L36

Directive 88/77 on measures to be taken against emission of gaseous pollutants from diesel engines for use in vehicles [1997] L36

Directive 88/436 on measures to be taken against air pollution from engines of motor vehicles (restriction of particulate pollutant emissions from diesel engines) (amending Directive 70/220) [1988] OJ L214

Directive 88/609 on limitation of emissions of certain pollutants into the air from large combustion plants [1988] OJ L336

Directive 89/369 on the prevention of air pollution from new municipal waste incineration plants [1989] OJ L163

Directive 89/429 on reduction of air pollution from existing municipal waste incineration plants [1989] OJ L203

Directive 91/441 on measures to be taken against air pollution by emissions from motor vehicles (amending Directive 70/220) [1991] OJ L242

Directive 92/72 on air pollution from ozone [1992] OJ L297

Directive 93/12 on air pollution from motor vehicles (amending Directive 70/220) [1994] OJ L100

Directive 93/59 relating to measures to be taken against air pollution by emissions from motor vehicles (amending Directive 70/220) [1993] OJ L186

Directive 93/76 to limit carbon dioxide emissions by improving energy efficiency (SAVE) [1993] OJ L237

Directive 94/12 on measures to be taken against air pollution by emissions from motor vehicles (amending Directive 70/220) [1994] OJ L100

Directive 94/63 on volatile organic compounds (VOC) emissions from storage and distribution of petrol [1994] OJ L365

Directive 96/61 on integrated pollution prevention and control [1996] OJ L257

Directive 96/62 air quality assessment and management [1996] OJ L296

Directive 97/68 on measures against the emission of gaseous and particulate pollutants from internal combustion engines to be installed in non-road mobile machinery [1997] OJ L59

Directive 98/69 on measures to be taken against air pollution from motor vehicles (amending Directive 70/220) [1998] OJ L350

Directive 98/70 on quality of petrol and diesel fuels (amending Directive 94/12) [1998] OJ L350

Directive 99/13 on limitation of emissions of volatile organic compounds due to the use of solvents in certain activities and installations [1999] OJ L35

Directive 99/30 on limit values for sulphur dioxide, nitrogen dioxide and oxides of nitrogen, particulate matter and lead in air [1999] OJ L163

Directive 99/32 on reduction of sulphur content in certain liquid fuels (amending Directive 93/12) [1999] OJ L121

Directive 99/52 roadworthiness for motor vehicles and their trailers [1999] OJ L142

Directive 99/96 on measures to be taken against the emission of gaseous and particulate pollutants from compression ignition engines for use in vehicles, and the emission of gaseous pollutants from positive ignition engines fuelled with natural gas or liquified petroleum gas for use in vehicles (amending Directive 88/77) [1999] OJ L44

Directive 99/102 on air pollution from motor vehicles [1999] OJ L334

Directive 2000/25 action to be taken against the emission of gaseous and particulate pollutants by engines intended to power agricultural and forestry tractors (amending Directive 74/150) [2000] OJ L173

CHEMICAL SUBSTANCES DIRECTIVES

Directive 67/548 on the classification, packaging and labelling of dangerous substances [1967] OJ L196 (amended by Directive 79/831)

Directive 73/173 relating to the classification, packaging and labelling of solvents [1973] OJ L189

Directive 73/404 relating to detergents [1973] OJ L347

Directive 73/405 on methods of testing biodegradability of anionic surfactants [1973] OJ L347

Directive 76/769 on restrictions on marketing and use of certain dangerous substances and preparations (polychlorinated terpenyls) [1976] OJ L262

Directive 77/728 on the classification, packaging and labelling of paints, varnishes, printing inks, adhesives and similar products [1978] OJ L303

Directive 78/631 relating to the classification, packaging and labelling of pesticides [1978] OJ L106

Directive 78/610 on the protection of the health of workers exposed to vinyl chloride monomer [1978] OJ L197

Directive 79/117 prohibiting plant protection products containing certain active substances [1979] OJ L33

Directive 79/831 on the classification, packaging and labelling of dangerous substances [1979] OJ L259 (amends Directive 67/548)

Directive 82/242 relating to methods of testing the biodegradability of non-ionic surfactants (amending Directive 73/404) [1982] OJ L109

Directive 83/477 on the protection of workers against the risk of exposure to asbestos [1983] OJ L263

Directive 87/217 on prevention and reduction of environmental pollution by asbestos [1987] OJ L377

Directive 91/414 on the placing of plant protection products on the market [1991] OJ L230

Directive 93/67 laying down the principles for assessment of risks to man and the environment of substances notified in accordance with Council Directive 67/548 [1993] OJ L227/9

Directive 93/75 concerning the minimum requirements for vessels bound for or leaving community ports and carrying dangerous or polluting goods [1993] OJ L247

Directive 94/55 with regard to the transport of dangerous substances by road [1994] OJ L319

Directive 96/29/Euratom on the basic safety standards for the protection of the health of workers and the general public against the dangers of ionizing radiation [1996] OJ L159

Directive 98/8 concerning the placing of biocidal products on the market [1988] OJ L123

Directive 99/45 relating to classification, packaging and labelling of dangerous substances [1999] OJ L200

ENVIRONMENTAL IMPACT ASSESSMENT DIRECTIVES

Directive 85/337 on the assessment of the effects of certain public and private projects on the environment [1985] OJ L175

Directive 97/11 amending Directive 85/337 on the assessment of the effects of certain public and private projects on the environment [1997] OJ L73

ENVIRONMENTAL INFORMATION AND LABELLING DIRECTIVES

Directive 86/594 on airborne noise emitted by household appliances (labelling) [1986] OJ L344

Directive 86/85 on establishing a Community information system for the control and reduction of pollution caused by spillage of hydrocarbons and other harmful substances at sea [1986] OJ L77

Directive 89/618/Euratom on informing the general public about health protection measures to be applied and steps to be taken in the event of a radiological emergency [1989] OJ L357

Directive 90/313 on freedom of access to information on the environment [1990] OJ L158

Directive 92/75 on labelling and standard product information of the consumption of energy and other resources by household appliances [1992] OJ L297

Directive 95/12 implementing Directive 92/75 with regard to energy labelling of household washing machines [1995] OJ L136

Directive 99/94 on availability of consumer information on fuel economy and carbon dioxide emissions in respect of marketing new passenger cars [1999] OJ L12

DIRECTIVES ON GENETICALLY MODIFIED ORGANISMS

Directive 90/219 on the contained use of genetically modified organisms [1990] OJ L117

Directive 90/220 on the deliberate release of genetically modified organisms into the environment [1990] OJ l17

LAND AND AGRICULTURE DIRECTIVES

Directive 76/116 on labelling and packaging of fertilizers [1976] OJ L24

Directive 80/876 on ammonium nitrite fertilizers at high content [1980] OJ L250

Directive 86/278 on the protection of the environment, and in particular soil, when sewage sludge is used in agriculture [1986] OJ L181

MAJOR ACCIDENT DIRECTIVES

Directive 82/501 on the major accident hazards of certain industrial activities [1982] OJ L230

Directive 87/216 on the major accident hazards of certain industrial activities (amending Directive 82/501) [1987] OJ L85

Directive 96/82 on the control of major accident hazards involving dangerous substances [1996] OJ L10

NOISE DIRECTIVES

Directive 70/157 on permissible sound level and the exhaust system of motor vehicles [1970] OJ L42

Directive 79/113 on the determination of noise emission of construction plant and equipment [1979] OJ L33

Directive 80/51 on the limitation of noise emissions from subsonic aircraft [1980] OJ L18

Directive 81/334 on permissible sound level and the exhaust system of motor vehicles [1981] OJ L131

Directive 83/206 on limitation of noise emissions from subsonic aircraft [1983] OJ L117

Directive 84/424 on permissible sound level and exhaust system of motor vehicles [1984] OJ L238

Directive 84/532 on provisions for construction plant and equipment [1984] OJ L300

Directive 84/533 on permissible sound power level of compressors [1984] OJ L300

Directive 84/534 on permissible sound power level of tower cranes [1984] OJ L300

Directive 84/535 on permissible sound power level of welding generators [1984] OJ L300

Directive 84/536 on permissible sound power level of power generators [1984] OJ L300

Directive 84/537 on permissible sound power level of powered hand-held concrete-breakers and picks [1984] OJ L300

Directive 84/538 on permissible sound power level of lawnmowers [1984] OJ L300

Directive 86/188 on protection of workers from the risks related to exposure to noise at work [1986] OJ L137

Directive 86/662 on limitation of noise emitted by hydraulic excavators, rope-operated excavators, dozers, loader and excavator-loaders [1986] OJ L384

Directive 89/629 on limitation of noise from civil subsonic jet aeroplanes [1989] OJ L363

Directive 92/14 on limitation of the operation of aeroplanes covered by Annex 16 to the Convention on International Civil Aviation 2nd Ed. (1998) [1992]

Directive 92/97 amending Directive 70/157 on permissible sound level and the exhaust system of motor vehicles [1992] OJ L371

Directive 98/20 amending Directive 92/14 on limitation of the operation of aeroplanes [1998] OJ L107

Directive 2000/14 relating to the noise emissions in the environment by equipment for use outdoors [2000] OJ L162

WASTE DIRECTIVES

Directive 75/439 on the disposal of waste oil [1975] OJ L194

Directive 75/442 on waste [1975] OJ L194

Directive 76/579/Euratom on radiation safety standards [1976] OJ L187

Directive 78/176 on waste from the titanium dioxide industry [1978] OJ L54

Directive 80/836/Euratom on radiation safety standards [1980] OJ L246

Directive 82/883 on procedures for surveillance and monitoring of environments concerned by waste from the titanium dioxide industry [1982] OJ L378

Directive 91/156 amending Directive 75/442 on waste [1991] OJ L78

Directive 91/157 batteries and accumulators containing certain dangerous substances [1991] OJ L78

Directive 91/689 on hazardous wastes [1991] OJ L377

Directive 92/3/Euratom on the shipment and control of shipments of radioactive waste [1992] OJ L35

Directive 94/62 on packaging and packaging waste [1994] OJ L365

Directive 94/67 on the incineration of hazardous wastes [1994] OJ L365

Directive 96/59 on the dispersal of polychlorinated biphenyls and polychlorinated tetraphenyls (PCB/PCT) [1996] OJ L243

Directive 99/31 on landfill of waste [1999] OJ L182

WATER DIRECTIVES

Directive 75/440 concerning the quality required of surface water intended for the abstraction of drinking water in the Member States [1975] OJ L194

Directive 76/160 concerning the quality of bathing water [1976] OJ L31

Directive 76/464 on pollution caused by certain dangerous substances discharged in the aquatic environment of the communities [1976] OJ L129

Directive 78/659 on the quality of freshwaters needing protection or improvement in order to support fish life [1978] OJ L222

Directive 79/869 on methods of measurement and frequencies of sampling and analysis of surface water intended for abstraction of drinking water [1979] OJ L271

Directive 79/923 on the quality required of shellfish waters [1979] OJ L281

Directive 80/68 on the protection of groundwater against pollution caused by certain dangerous substances [1980] OJ L20

Directive 80/777 on exploitation and marketing of natural mineral waters [1980] OJ L229

Directive 80/778 relating to the quality of water intended for human consumption [1980] OJ L229

Directive 82/176 on limit values and quality objectives for mercury discharges by the chlor-alkali electrolysis industry [1982] OJ L81

Directive 83/513 on limit values and quality objectives for cadmium discharges [1983] OJ L291

Directive 84/156 on limit values and quality objectives for mercury discharges by sectors other than the chlor-alkali industry [1984] OJ L74

Directive 84/491 on limit values and quality objectives for discharges of hexachlorocyclohexane (Lindane) [1984] OJ L274

Directive 86/280 on limit values and quality objectives of certain dangerous substances included in List I of the Annex to Directive 76/464 (carbon tetrachloride, pentachlorophenol and DDT) [1986] OJ L181

WILDLIFE AND COUNTRYSIDE DIRECTIVE

PART ONE

Regulating the Environment through Standard-setting

CHAPTER ONE

Introduction: Regulation, Standards and Environmental Law

INTRODUCTION

Environmental law has developed sufficiently over the past years to suggest that a fresh approach to its study is required.[1] This book is intended to offer a new outlook on environmental law through understanding environmental standards. Regulating the environment in the changing economic climate of the world's economies requires new strategies for managing and protecting scarce resources. Such management is a prerequisite for achieving sustainable development. The development and implementation of environmental standards have emerged as responses to growing concerns about the environment and demands to strengthen pollution controls. Recession in many countries has forced changes in industrial policy and the cost of implementing standards has to be balanced in terms of jobs, employment opportunities and industrial success.

How might environmental law address such concerns and meet high public expectations about improving the environment? In Britain, the historical legacy sets the scene and provides a context for the book. The nineteenth-century inheritance of environmental law provided a wide

---

[1] See McEldowney, J. and McEldowney, S., *The Environment and the Law* (Harlow, Longman, 1996).

range of statutes and case law intended to penalise polluters. Systems of inspection and low-key regulation developed. Prevention strategies gained support on an incremental basis and deterrence was used in an attempt to prevent any recurrence of pollution problems. Building on the legacy of pollution controls, environmental law has come of age over the past two decades with the development of strategic techniques and methods to enable a more proactive approach to the environment. Prevention is generally seen as more cost-effective and reliable than dealing with the effects of pollution. Examples illustrative of this new conceptual framework and approach are to be found in developments such as environmental impact assessment, integrated pollution control and environmental management standards. An integrated approach to regulating the environment may be found in the creation of the Environment Agency under the Environment Act 1995 and the creation of a European Environment Agency. Planning for sustainable development sets the scene for better practice and promoting *standards* for a better environment is critical to the success of sustainable development. This comes at a time when public expectation is that legal controls over the environment will prove effective. There is the added dimension of the Human Rights Act 1998, which is likely to have a profound effect on environmental and planning law and to provide the public with still greater expectation of the right to a pollution-free environment. Information on the environment and the investigative powers of regulatory bodies are subject to human rights considerations (see *R v Hertfordshire County Council, ex parte Green Environmental Industries Ltd* [2000] 1 All ER 773). The idea of a *Charter of Fundamental Rights*, put forward in the European Union in 1999, adds a further dimension to European law within member states. A proposed Bill of Rights for the European Union, if implemented, is likely to encourage a more juridical approach to public institutions and, in the coming decade, litigation centred around human rights issues is likely to increase. There is evidence already that the courts in the United Kingdom are developing a more proactive approach to the interpretation of legal rules and economic instruments. One of the consequences of membership of the European Union is that EC Directives have the potential for 'direct effect' in domestic law. For example, the Court of Appeal recently accepted that the Directive on Environmental Impact Assessment might have 'direct effect' in the United Kingdom (*R v Durham County Council, Sherburn Stone Company and the Secretary of State for the Environment, Transport and Regions, ex parte Huddleston* [2000] JPL 409, CA).

Innovation and change are also much in evidence. Regulation in the energy field, with a single Gas and Electricity Authority, and increased guidance on social and environmental objectives for utilities, including water, are part of the new proposals contained in the Utilities Act 2000.

There is, also, consideration of proposals for an Environmental Court for England and Wales.

The environment offers a valuable case study of regulatory techniques in public and private law. Environmental standards take many forms, for example:

(a) Standards that set targets to limit environmental release of particular compounds and toxins. Examples include air quality standards with specified maximum concentrations for particulate and gaseous pollutants in the atmosphere.
(b) Standards that are source-related. These may include emission standards, process or product standards. Examples of these include water quality standards setting the maximum concentration of specified pollutants in designated controlled waters, standards such as noise levels from a building, or process standards that relate to the process or procedure in the way effluent is treated and controlled.

In all these examples, the strengths and weaknesses of standards may be analysed and discussed. How easily are standards enforced? Are standards clearly defined? Standards appear to offer objective and verifiable criteria. Many standards fall into the category of setting objectives rather than providing a legally enforceable set of rules. They may lack precision. There may be little thought given to how standards may be implemented, or how costly this may be. Inconsistency between standards may lead to confusion. The criteria set by the particular standards may be left so vague that they become largely self-regulatory or even ignored. An over-reliance on standards may lead to complacency. The Royal Commission on Environmental Pollution in its 21st Report warned that standards may lead to over-regulation and that this may be counter-productive. We need to question the validity of many assumptions that lie behind setting standards. The science that underpins the setting of standards may in itself be problematic. Science provides data for the assessment of risk based on the best available scientific knowledge. The prediction of outcomes is made on the basis of a calculation of the varying degrees of uncertainty. The calculation of risk is made all the more difficult because of the speed of change in the area of science and technology. Environmental regulation based on the setting of standards involves a degree of rigidity that may be unable to take account of the rapidly changing needs of society and technological innovation. For example, the recent developments in the Genome Project may lead to a discovery that the genetic make-up of some groups increases susceptibility to environmental toxins. This has important medical, social and economic consequences (especially for the insurance industry) and may have unforeseen implications for setting standards.

REGULATING THE ENVIRONMENT THROUGH STANDARD-SETTING

There are many theories and justifications for regulating the environment and the prevention and eradication of pollution is just one. However, environmental regulation is also a necessary component in the protection of the public interest against private interests, which justify their decisions on market choices, profitability and competition, rather than on the environment. The use of scientific data and the imposition of environmental standards are an essential element in the techniques adopted to regulate the environment.

The focus of this book is on the *implementation* of the standards set by environmental law. Implementing environmental standards is the key element in new policy measures to regulate the environment and this raises a number of important questions:

- What are the relevant standards required by the law that apply to environmental problems?
- How are environmental standards set?
- How might environmental standards be met?
- Who has the obligation to meet environmental standards?
- How are the costs of implementation to be met?

Increasingly important in addressing these questions, particularly in the context of sustainable development and prevailing world economic conditions, are arrangements to quantify the costs of standard-setting for industry and government. There is a need to find effective *strategies* for the implementation of environmental protection and regulating the environment through setting standards permits a variety of legal and economic instruments[2] to be used. In many United Kingdom statutes, environmental controls require the application of measurable standards. Developments in the environmental policy of the European Community have seen the use of different standards, for example, Directive 91/271 on Urban Waste Water Treatment, Directive 76/160 on Bathing Water and Directive 80/778 on Drinking Water. As will become clear from the discussion in the chapters that follow, the future of European Community environmental law is bound up with the creation and application of environmental standards throughout the member states.

---

[2]*This Common Inheritance — The Second Year Report* (Cm 2068, 1992)

The increasing reliance on and use of regulatory instruments that provide environmental standards are recognised in successive government White Papers to be 'at the heart of Britain's system of environmental control'.[3] The range and variety of standards vary. There are standards to be found in the Planning and Policy Guidance for the Planning System (see the Environmental Protection Act 1990) and other types of standards include setting targets for control of pollution or harm in the various media such as water, air and land.

Regulating the environment through the application of environmental standards is not new. What has changed, however, is that the vague and poorly defined environmental standards of the past have been replaced by clearer standards and guidance on how to meet the expectations of today. It is commonplace for environmental standards to provide for the regulation of the environment rather than continuing to rely on existing legal remedies adapted to fit environmental problems. The shift in adopting and using environmental regulation calls for a new approach to understanding environmental law. By concentrating on environmental standards this book will facilitate the understanding of the legal framework that applies to the environment through a variety of economic and scientific instruments. In this way environmental law has created a regulatory system that is both reactive to the specific environmental problem and proactive in preventing environmental harm. The nature of standard-setting permits controls to be made at both the local and central level. One of the fascinating questions for the future is whether the European Community will insist on centralised, uniform standard-setting at the Community level, or permit the principle of subsidiarity to allow each country to set and implement its own standards.[4] The answer to this question hangs in the balance between competing views within the Community.

THE COMMON LAW INHERITANCE AND THE ENVIRONMENT

It is useful to begin by remembering how environmental law developed. Historically, environmental law was built on the proposition that, in common with the treatment of most legal subjects, it could be conveniently defined in terms of a distinct legal discipline. Property and planning lawyers could point to the development of the environment as a feature of

---

[3]*This Common Inheritance* (Cm 1200, 1990).
[4]See Somsen, H. and Sprokkereef, A., 'Making subsidiarity work for the environmental policy of the European Community: the role of science' (1996) 1 *International Journal of Biosciences and the Law*, 37.

land use planning or the built environment. The Housing, Town and Planning etc. Act 1909 created in embryo form the development of a system of town and country planning in Britain (see the Town and Country Planning Act 1947). Public health and housing lawyers could see the environment as an important dimension that added to the focus of their work. Legislation such as the Public Health Act 1875 formed the foundation of the modern law on public health, the Alkali Acts of 1863 and 1968 (see also the Alkali etc. Works Regulation Act 1906), intended to control emissions from part of the heavy chemical industry in nineteenth century Britain, created the first inspectorate, and legislation to control and prevent river pollution may be found in the Rivers (Prevention of Pollution) Act 1876. Together these Acts heralded the beginning of pollution control strategy and laid the foundations of the 'inspectorate' approach to solving environmental problems. Tort lawyers expert in negligence and nuisance liability could see environmental law as a development of the case law approach to pollution control and cases such as *Rylands* v *Fletcher* (1868) LR 3 HL 330 highlighted the private law approach in applying remedies to ensure environmental protection. Reconciling the rights of the private landowner and the need for environmental protection was an important question in the development of the law of nuisance (see *St Helen's Smelting Co.* v *Tipping* (1856) 11 HL Cas 642). The law on trespass similarly was applied to meet environmental problems.

Building up environmental law in this *ad hoc* way was also part of the statutory response to environmental problems. The Public Health Acts of the nineteenth century laid down statutory procedures for their enforcement and the development of statutory nuisance was also a response to the protection of the environment in the area of public health. The development of public nuisance followed a similar pattern of applying existing legal remedies available under the common law to the problems of noise and air pollution.

Remedies such as damages and injunctions provide limited redress to the private citizen seeking legal resolution of environmental problems. Over the past decade in the field of public law there has been a growth in the application of judicial review to the area of the environment. This allows a variety of public law remedies to apply to protect the environment.[5] These remedies are available against public bodies, including regulators and environment enforcement agencies, such as the Environment Agency.

---

[5]See generally McEldowney, J., *Public Law*, 2nd edn (London: Sweet and Maxwell, 1998).

In common with the study of many legal problems, environmental law is defined in the way the subject has developed. This approach is unsatisfactory, however, for several reasons. First, the environment and its protection are not capable of exact legal definition. Many environmental problems are intimately related to economic and social issues,[6] and environmental policies involve a broader definition of law than one that is narrowly focused on legal remedies and their application. Secondly, in recent years environmental law has developed quite successfully its own specialist responses to environmental problems. A wide variety of mechanisms and techniques are applied that are both proactive and reactive. Thirdly, understanding environmental law requires economic, scientific and policy evaluations. This is not only an interdisciplinary task, but it also requires a focus on the question of environmental standards. This is an area where environmental law has most developed its own identity and where science faces one of its greatest challenges. It is also the area where future growth is likely. The evidence supporting the need for a new approach to environmental law will be examined in more detail below.

A NEW APPROACH TO ENVIRONMENTAL LAW THROUGH REGULATORY INSTRUMENTS

It is clear that environmental law in Britain has changed, particularly over the past 25 years. Enough time has passed, and the scale of changes is sufficient, for a reappraisal of Britain's environmental laws to be appropriate. The main textbooks and literature on environmental law reflect very well how environmental law developed in the *ad hoc* way described above, where gaps were filled through legislative and judicial creativity and solutions to environmental problems developed on a case-by-case basis. It is no longer possible to question whether environmental law exists as a subject in its own right. It clearly does, and this has been acknowledged even by the most ardent sceptics. Environmental law today, however, has been changed from a reactive subject providing remedies for environmental pollution to a more proactive subject providing standards to meet and avoid environmental problems. Various preventative measures may be adopted in environmental law designed to reduce or eliminate the risk of environmental damage and such measures and the regulation of processes and activities have become important in the attempt to avoid or mitigate any harm. The part that regulation has in the British system of environmental control is much neglected and it is time to look afresh and

---

[6]See Gouldon, A. and Murphy, J. *Regulatory Realities: The Implementation and Impact of Industrial Environmental Regulation* (London: Earthscan Publications Ltd, 1998).

devote a clear focus on regulating the environment through standards. This will permit a more detailed analysis of the subject than is available in the current literature.

It is possible to distil the main principles that guide environmental law today, while acknowledging the complexity and diversity of the subject. The three principles that are relevant to our analysis are the following:

(a) *The principle of sustainable development.*[7] This principle sets the agenda for the future by endeavouring to ensure that environmental problems are addressed and controlled. This involves an attempt to reconcile the conflicting demands of economic development as against social, environmental and resource protection. It ensures that the benefits of any development outweigh its costs, including environmental costs.

(b) *The principle of 'the polluter pays'.*[8] This principle is currently in vogue. It asserts that the polluter should pay any costs that arise from harm to the environment, or ill-health or injury to individuals caused by the pollution. The law has developed a number of strategies to implement this principle.

(c) *The 'precautionary principle'.*[9] This principle means that the absence of scientific proof for a risk of environmental harm is not a sufficient reason for failing to take preventative action. In recent years it has largely been interpreted in terms of risk assessment and predicting harm. Barnett and O'Hagan[10] relate how science may have several uses: 'We could remark here on the value of scientific knowledge. In general, we have seen that weak knowledge must lead to more stringent standards, on precautionary grounds. The value of science is to allow us where appropriate, to *relax* the standards.'

---

[7]Sustainable development was first defined in terms of social, economic and environmental criteria by The World Commission on Environmental Development (the Brundtland Commission) in *Our Common Future* (the Brundtland Report, 1987).

[8]This principle originated from the UN Conference on the Human Environment held in Stockholm (1972). The principle is embedded in Article 174 (ex 130r(2)) of the Treaty Establishing the European Community 1957 (the Treaty of Rome) (as amended).

[9]First found as 'Vorsorgemassnahmen' in the Bremen Declaration of the First International Conference on the Protection of the North Sea. The principle now has a broader definition and is embedded in Article 174 (ex 130r(2)) of the Treaty of Rome.

[10]Barnett, V. and O'Hagan, A., *Setting Environmental Standards* (London, Chapman and Hall, 1997), at 39.

All three principles are open to differing interpretations. Assessing risk, balancing costs, and predicting harm are inevitably open to widely different assumptions and methodologies of assessment, but even so, it is possible to devise strategies for implementing the three principles through the setting of standards for the environment.

UNDERSTANDING ENVIRONMENTAL STANDARDS

Having explained the rationale for the book, it is now appropriate to give some more details of environmental standards. As a first step it is necessary to provide further elaboration and definition of standard-setting as a technique in regulating the environment. There is a variety of different categories of standards that may be identified. The list below is not exhaustive and the categories are not exclusive:

(a) *Emission standards*. Emission standards set the levels of discharge into different media. For example, under the Environmental Protection Act 1990 limits may be set for the total amount of any particular substance which may be released into the environment. Limits may be established by the Secretary of State. The range and extent of emission standards are immense, involving controls on the discharge of organic and inorganic chemicals and particulates to each medium, and on the disposal of solid waste. They can relate to emissions from sources as diverse as the food industry, the chemical industry, the energy-producing industries, and transport.

(b) *Quality standards*. Such standards set the maximum allowable levels of pollution in the environment. Targets are set which may vary from noise levels for aeroplanes to air quality standards for sulphur dioxide levels. There are many examples of such standards, including water standards for drinking water and standards for bathing water.

(c) *Process standards*. These standards apply to fixed installations such as factories or chimneys. Process standards stipulate the means of production leaving no discretion to the polluter. They are useful as a means of regulating a hazardous activity, thereby preventing accidents. Process standards may be targeted at manufacturers and may require information and analysis of dangerous stages in the manufacturing process.

(d) *Product standards*. This example of standard-setting is familiar in relation to pharmaceuticals, food, packaging and labelling. Scientific information is often given on labels and instructions for safe usage and warnings about hazards may also comprise the standard required for the product. Pesticides and chemicals in everyday use may conform to these requirements set by the product standard.

The range of standards reaches beyond these, and their diversity may be further highlighted by two additional examples. First, there are environmental management standards, such as ISO 9000, providing certification ensuring that companies have an effective environmental management structure and environmental programmes. The requirements set by the Advisory Committee on Releases to the Environment for field trials of GMOs may be considered an example of standard-setting, which is carried out on a case-by-case basis after risk assessment. Secondly, there is a draft international standard related to the green claims made by manufacturers for their products, ISO 14021.[11]

All standards are under continual development. This may be related to improvements in scientific knowledge and data, or the risks of harm being more fully resolved. Changes to standards and the introduction of new standards may also be related to social and economic criteria. The development of new standards may require industry itself to provide additional information on the impacts of products[12] and will often involve policy discussion in the development of the standard.[13]

EUROPEAN COMMUNITY AND INTERNATIONAL LAW

It may reasonably be asked at this stage, what are the sources and influences that have contributed to the application of standards as a means of regulating the environment? Are there particular influences that may be identified as responsible for the growth in standard-setting? Perhaps the most important influence on British environmental law is the development of the environmental policy of the European Community. In its own right European environmental law has created an emerging specialist literature on Community aspects of regulating the environment. An important step was taken by the introduction of the European Environment Agency.[14], which sets regulatory standards for the environment, and is likely to gain in importance over the next decade.

---

[11]See the ENDS Report No. 280 (May 1998), *ISO 14021 Pushed as Basis for Implementing Green Claims Code*, at 31.
[12]See the ENDS Report No. 285 (October 1998), *The chemicals debate gathers pace*, at 23–26.
[13]For example, see DETR, UK Climate Change Programme Consultation Paper (1998).
[14]Established in 1990 (1212/90 EEC, 7 May 1990).

As regards the sources of law for environmental standards, account must be taken of the many recent Directives and laws of the Community that contain standards as the means of regulating the environment. These standards require interpretation within British law. A number of illustrative examples serve to make this point:[15]

- *Setting standards for water.* In addition to the Directives on Bathing Water (76/160) and Drinking Water (80/778) already mentioned above, there are a number of Directives that similarly set standards for Dangerous Substances in Water (76/464), for Groundwater (80/68), Shell Fish Water (79/923), Freshwater Fish (78/659), and Nitrates (91/676).
- *Setting standards for air.* There are the Air Quality Standards Regulations 1989 (SI 1989 No. 317); and for noise, the Noise in the Workplace Directive 86/188.
- *Setting standards for waste.* There are a plethora of different Directives, ranging from the Framework Directive on Waste 75/442 (amended by 91/156) and the Urban Waste Water Treatment Directive 91/271.
- *Setting standards for genetically modified organisms.* See Directives 90/219 and 90/220 (now amended by 94/15).
- *Setting implementation standards for environmental law.* Directive 85/337 on Environmental Impact Assessment, amended in 1997, provides one of the key ways to assess the impact of the array of standards in the environment when applied to specific public and private projects. This is important in terms of major infrastructure developments.

Setting environmental standards also falls within the remit and the influence of the international community. The Convention on Wetlands of International Importance especially as Waterfowl Habitat 1971, known as the Ramsar Convention and the Vienna Convention for the Protection of the Ozone Layer 1985 provide general guidance as to acceptable standards in the environment. An example of the development of labelling techniques and the precautionary principle can be found in the United Nations Biosafety Protocol, which sets standards for the safe transfer and handling of living genetically modified organisms. The Protocol imposes labelling requirements and a system of prior informed consent for the authorisation of the shipment of such materials. The new framework is intended to promote public confidence in and provide information on the contents of GM foods, but the regulatory oversight and sanctions appear to be weak. The recent United Nations Treaty on curbing fossil fuel emissions,

---

[15]A list of relevant Directives is to be found in Bell, S. and McGillivray, D., *Environmental Law* (London: Blackstone Press, 2000).

provides agreed limits on fossil fuel emissions in an attempt to limit climate change and sea-level rise. International agreement reached in Kyoto has proposed that an 8 per cent reduction of greenhouse gas emissions be achieved by 2012, but there are doubts as to whether such a reduction is attainable within the time scale. The international meeting at the Hague in 2000 failed to come to an agreement about mechanisms to reach the goals and standards set by the Kyoto Protocol.

MANAGING CHANGE AND THE ENVIRONMENT

The increasing emphasis on standards and (over recent years) a shift to reliance on economic instruments in environmental law have required the development of different techniques for implementation and enforcement. Invariably this has led to the creation of new institutions with the precise purpose of regulating the environment using the techniques of legally enforceable standards. In Britain the Environment Agency, created under the Environment Act 1995, provides a formal Enforcement Code that encapsulates the new policy for environmental regulation. The four principles contained in the Code are consistency, transparency, targeting and proportionality in the approach to enforcement. Enforcement strategies must conform to the Code of Practice.

Enforcement of standards may also take the form of self-regulation. There are voluntary agreements, such as those contained in the Regulations on Ecolabelling (see Regulations 880/92 and 1836/93), which require the industry to self-assess and implement ecolabelling as a prelude to enforceable rules for implementation. In the UK, however, the Ecolabelling Board was disbanded in late 1999 and the award of ecolabels was subsumed into the DETR. The absence of support from industry is a sign of partial success at standard setting. There are other interesting possibilities for the enforcement of standards through taxation strategies in various forms, such as tax incentives aimed at encouraging good environmental practice. Additional incentives may be found in favouring the adoption of new technology, for example the introduction of catalytic converters for cars. Standards set for the environment may be met by other innovative taxation devices[16] intended to secure compliance through influencing consumer choices and the Blair government[17] has advanced the cause of 'green taxes' as a further commitment to a proactive and preventative approach to the environment. However, political sensitivity towards Government policy on transport and climate

---

[16]See O'Riordan, T. (ed.) *Ecotaxation* (London: Earthscan Publications, 1997).
[17]See the White Paper on Transport Policy (1998).

change was illustrated by the UK fuel crisis in September 2000, which demonstrated that standard-setting operates in a social and political, as well as a scientific and legal context. Cutting vehicle excise duty for large lorries (40 tonnes or over) will make it more difficult for the Government to meet its target of lowering CO_2 emissions by 2010.

There is also the strategy of increasing the costs of non-environmental friendly energy sources in order to subsidise friendly environmental energy sources. The fossil fuel levy used in the calculation of electricity prices is intended to provide an initial period of subsidy for more expensive electricity produced by wind, solar or non-fossil fuel systems and electricity distributors are required to buy a certain percentage of non-fossil fuel. The government has set a target of 10 per cent for all electricity produced in this way by the year 2010.[18]

A further approach is to change the way key energy industries are regulated. For example, in the recent White Paper on Energy, some fundamental changes are proposed in the regulatory structure of the major utilities, with the environment receiving particular attention. The change in culture is intended to set priorities for environmental standards in the regulation of the industries. The Competition Act 1998 prescribes more robust standard-setting powers in relation to the water, gas and electricity industries. Section 54 of the Act strengthens the rules against price-fixing and abuse of a dominant position and demonstrates a cross-boundary approach. The separate regulation of gas and electricity is ineffective in providing a sustainable energy policy and, by analogy, water pollution must be tackled through the management of land and air sources of pollution.

Implementing standards depends on greater public awareness of the environment and greater access to environmental information has been encouraged through the EC Directive on Freedom of Access to Environmental Information (90/313). The Environmental Information Regulations 1992 (SI 1992 No. 3240) in force from 31 December 1999 implement the Directive, which is supported by the European Ombudsman,[19] and is part of a general trend in international law in favour of access to information. This has an important impact on how environmental standards can be monitored and the significance of the availability of environmental information was reinforced as one component in sustainability strategy for business in a recent Consultation Paper.[20]

---

[18] See DETR, *Op. cit.* n. 13 (1998)
[19] [1994] OJ L46/58. There is also a development in international law — the United Nations Convention on access to information, public participation and access to justice in environmental matters 1998.
[20] See DETR, Consultation Paper on Sustainable Business, (1998).

Lastly, reinforcing the approaches identified above is the work of the Nolan Committee on Standards in Public Life.[21] The Nolan recommendations reflect the need for public confidence that the standards of decision-making comply with the Nolan standards of openness, public participation and fairness. In the planning system, which provides an important form of anticipatory regulation of the environment, Lord Nolan demands greater openness, increased public participation and transparency, particularly in areas of planning controversy, such as planning agreements[22] entered into by the local authority and the developer in particular.

It is clear that setting standards for the environment is consistent with the general trend of setting standards in public life. It must be remembered, however, that environmental standards have their own, distinct, specialist quality. In Chapter 2 we discuss the historical basis for environmental standard-setting in Britain. It is apparent that the use of a scientific methodology in the early development of environmental law was significant, and such influences have been largely overlooked. It will be shown that the way scientific data were applied and laws were developed may help to explain the unique British approach to environmental regulation. Significantly, scientific methodology, particularly through the assessment of risk, is influential once more in the future development of standard-setting and in the understanding of environmental law.

---

[21]Now under the Chairmanship of Lord Neill.
[22]See Report of the Planning and Environmental Law Reform Working Group, *Planning Obligations*, chaired by Mr. Justice Keene (London: The Society for Advanced Legal Study, November 1998).

CHAPTER TWO

The History of Environmental Regulation and Standards

INTRODUCTION

The foundations of environmental regulation may be found in the United Kingdom in developments in the eighteenth and nineteenth centuries.[1] During that time environmental law grew out of demands of public health and a limited response to problems of pollution. Solutions to environmental problems developed in a piecemeal fashion and in recent times environmental law has continued to evolve in an organic way, responding to new scientific developments and the introduction of new processes. Scientific knowledge has improved to the point that environmental law has begun to become less reactive and more proactive and in that regard, environmental law and regulation are increasingly dependent on scientific understanding and the continuous development of new techniques for assessing the quality of the environment and risks posed to it.

An additional issue is how the regulation of the environment has contributed to public safety. The science of safety based on trial and error permeates Victorian attitudes to engineering works, including bridge building and construction systems. Safety standards improved following

---

[1]The chapter is reproduced with the kind permission of Oxford University Press and Helen Reece, editor of *Current Legal Issues* (Oxford, Oxford University Press, 1998).

major disasters and calamities as the public demanded better quality in construction and improved safety systems. A fine balance between experiment and innovation was measured against caution and reliability. Victorian entrepreneurial skills exploited new wealth in developing endeavour while reliance on construction and building techniques followed a more conservative path.

In this chapter it is intended to explore the foundations of the relationship between the environment, science and law. An historical approach is adopted with a particular focus on the rise of statistical studies, which informed the development of the social sciences and provided a bridge between mathematical science and law. Interest in political economy in the seventeenth century gave rise to the development in the eighteenth century of mathematical inquiry applied to social problems. Interest in statistical study formed the focus of the rise of the statistical movement and the creation of a number of statistical societies both nationally and provincially in the middle of the nineteenth century. The statistical societies provided a national and international forum based on an interdisciplinary collaboration between science, mathematical probability and law and provided the basic framework for law reform, particularly of the laws on public health[2] and pollution. The scientific method of collecting evidence to prove hypotheses informed the methodology of the Royal Commission and Parliamentary inquiry in an unparalleled period in which law and science provided a forum for common issues to be analysed.

Particular emphasis is given here to the question of how science and law may require differing methodology and levels of proof. Assessing the interrelationship[3] between law and science requires an increasingly specialised knowledge[4] and the intellectual foundations of environmental law rooted in the eighteenth and nineteenth century require a fresh appraisal to understand how law and science may best be integrated to meet the challenges of the new century.

SCIENCE AND LAW: THE ANALYTICAL METHOD

The common law tradition was particularly adept in encompassing scientific methodology. Before examining the role of science and concerns

---

[2]See Chadwick, E., *Report on the Sanitary Condition of the Labouring Population of Great Britain* (with an introduction by M. W. Flinn) (Edinburgh, Edinburgh University Press, 1965).

[3]*This Common Inheritance, UK Annual Report* (Cm 2822, HMSO, 1995).

[4]See Lepenies, W., *Between Literature and Science: The Rise of Sociology Ideas in Context* (Cambridge, Cambridge University Press, 1989); Gigerenzer, G., *et al.*, *The Empire of Change: How Probability Changed Science and Everyday Life Ideas in Context* (Cambridge, Cambridge University Press, 1989).

about the environment, it is useful to locate the discourse of scientific methodology as part of the common law.[5] The development of the common law rested on remedies and generally avoided directly defining rights and wrongs. The judges, responsive to the need to develop legal rules, attempted to interpret the needs and problems of society through flexible solutions applied in individual cases and much of the development of English law depended on the ability of the law to grant a suitable remedy in an individual case. While remedies may have offered solutions to practical problems, often these were constructed in narrowly defined ways and limited by procedure and form. No codified set of statutes or codified doctrine existed.

The English common law[6] was particularly influenced by the practitioners' concerns. This may explain how its survival and the haphazard nature of its development was achieved. The common law was remarkably anti-theoretical in its approach, with notions of policy, justice and legal doctrine determined by procedure and form rather than through reasoned or theoretical principles. From an impartial view the law had to find an appropriate remedy to solve the case.

Attempts to systematise English law came from two directions. One approach, influenced by Blackstone, attempted to add continental ideas about rights to the reasoning implied in the common law. The other approach, dominated by Bentham, aimed to provide a codification of principles. While different directions may be detected in both approaches, there was common ground. The methodology of science and the reasoning of statistical study were influential in the writings of both Blackstone and Bentham and this ensured that scientific methodology was integral to the analytical methodology and the legal reasoning employed in the development of the common law.

Blackstone encouraged the idea that English law was 'a science which distinguished the criterion of right and wrong'.[7] His attempts to reconcile the historical development of the common law with a flexible and rule-bound system gave rise to an analytical method, which proved to be very influential, especially when later adopted by Dicey in his analysis of the English Constitution.[8] The essence of Blackstone's legacy was that

---

[5] See McEldowney, J., *Public Law* (London, Sweet and Maxwell, 1998), chap. 7; Loughlin, M., *Legality and Locality* (Oxford, Oxford University Press, 1996).

[6] See Amos, S., *A Systematic View of the Science of Jurisprudence* (London, University of London Press, 1872).

[7] Blackstone, W., *Commentaries*, vol. I (London, Strahan Cadell and Prince, 1783), at 5–6.

[8] See McEldowney, J., 'Dicey in Historical Perspective — A Review Essay' in McAuslan, P. and McEldowney, J., *Law, Legitimacy and the Constitution* (London, Sweet and Maxwell, 1985).

English law could be formed from a deductive system of reasoning incorporating natural law principles and this required a mathematical approach. It favoured the formality of legal rules and the formal reduction to specific points of the resolution of any dispute.

It is not surprising to find at the end of the eighteenth century that many lawyers had become empiricists at a time when scientific discovery and science in general attracted the attention of the age. Whether this was coincidence or not is difficult to determine. What was remarkable was that lawyers found that through detailed empirical investigation law was treated as practical and relevant rather than theoretical and abstract.[9] The law on pleading was a clear example of the view that the legal system was a functioning set of rules that provided the tools for the practitioner to fashion remedies for the client. Writers considered 'the science of pleading' rooted in the belief that the precision of rules would give rise to the revelation of truth and the system of writs furthered the idea that correct procedure gave rise to an accurate record, thus laying the foundations of law (see *Mirehouse* v *Rennell* (1835) 1 Cl & F 527, at 546).

On a broader analysis, empirical methodology lay at the root of deciding cases and development of case law followed from the efforts to systematise. The idea that English law could be found in decided cases rested on the development of a reliable and comprehensive system of law reports, the doctrines of *stare decisis* and of precedent resting on judicial reasoning being applied by analogy to cases with similar facts. Technical and formal rules applied in an analytical and scientific way rooted the common law to the empiricist tradition and the logic of the judges.

Within this tradition lay considerable self-doubt and disenchantment. The desire for a clearly defined set of rules for judges to apply prompted many English lawyers to examine the value of the civil law as a source of principles and jurisprudence. Generally there was considerable reluctance to reconcile the common law with the civil law system in all its forms.

Bentham's disillusionment with the common law came from his identification of the inadequacy of the procedural rules, the absence of clear principles and the lack of comprehensiveness. His pursuit of universal codification of English law proved a life-time work which ultimately ended in frustration. There is evidence to show that in determining the contents of codes and their application Bentham shared the techniques implied in the scientific method as a means to determine

---

[9]Also influential was the writing of C. Montesquieu (1689–1755) *De l'esprit des lois* (1748).

concepts and ideas. Lobban explains:[10] '*An Introduction [to the Principles of Morals and Legislation]* was perceived by Bentham to be a "metaphysical" work, standing in relation to the substantive law as a treatise of pure mathematics stood to natural philosophy.' Bentham's codification project was ultimately rejected despite many attempts through numerous Royal Commissions and law reform initiatives. Bentham had sought to devise a science of principles derived from the immutable laws of human nature and in his prinicples of utility may be found the science of law reform. Diagnosing a wider range of social reforms, from prisons to the workhouse, from education to the courts and from the substantive criminal law to a codified constitution, Bentham's ambitious aim was that through codification a legislative solution to the problems of society might be found.

As a result, English law resisted the attempt to provide a single jurisprudence of rights and remedies. Blackstone, Bentham, Austin and Dicey allowed lawyers to conceive law through an analytical jurisprudence rooted in an empirical tradition bearing many characteristics of scientific proof. Strict procedural rules determined the precise point of dispute for deliberation by the court and judges attempted to discover through deductive reasoning the resolution of the dispute from the material facts presented by the litigants in each case. So much lay outside the control of any single system of rule. The litigant determined the cases that came to court and the facts each case presented, the judges responded to the challenge in a haphazard way drawing on a wide range of sources and ideas to find solutions and the jury added to the lack of predictability of outcome. The common law built on the reasoning common to 'ordinary men' and the rules of procedure that guided the discourse set the agenda for judges. The absence of a systematized English law and a coherent theoretical underpining of the principles of law underlines the importance of the analytical method used in the common law. This gives rise to the question of how the foundations of science and economic management played such an important role in shaping the character of environmental law in the mid-nineteenth century.

THE FOUNDATIONS OF SCIENCE AND ECONOMIC MANAGEMENT

The publication of the work of William Petty (1623–87) and John Graunt (1620–74)[11] in 1662 marked a new approach to the study of society.[12] Their

---

[10]Lobban, L., *The Common Law and English Jurisprudence 1769–1850* (Oxford, Clarendon Press, 1991), at 155.

[11]*Natural and Political Observations on the Bills of Mortality* (London, 1662).

[12]Cullen, M. J., *The Statistical Movement in Early Victorian Britain* (London, Harvester, 1975), at 1–6.

approach, described as 'the science of political arithmetic', focused on three elements of what soon led to the generation of natural laws that governed the social sciences and through this means the study of economic, social and political problems could develop on a par with the study of the physical sciences. The three elements in Petty and Graunt's study were:

(a) the collection of statistical data;
(b) the application of statistical or empirical research to a particular problem; and
(c) the development of natural laws that might predict the outcome of events from known data.

As we shall see in more detail below, public health, sanitation and pollution fell within the social problems that came to be addressed through statistical study.

Petty and Graunt's began their analysis with an examination of public finances,[13] and through studies of population and wealth drew up a comprehensive understanding of the economy.[14] The significance of Petty and Graunt's work should not be considered in isolation from the work of other scholars, though. French writers, notably Antoine de Montchrestien (1575–1621),[15] attempted to consider the role of the state and the economy as part of a scientific vision of understanding political and economic questions. It was through the interrogation of how economies developed and how society could be measured that studies into techniques to collect appropriate scientific data were initiated. Partly this was related to measurement of the economy as a whole,[16] partly to the development, in the eighteenth century, of schemes of insurance. In 1762, in Britain, the Society of Equitable Assurances for Lives and Survivorships was established and the development of life-tables to make actuarial calculations began.

Medical inquiries into smallpox,[17] later studies on insanity and into the causes of poverty and destitution, were all based on statistical study. Boards of Public Health were formed to fill the gaps left by inadequate poor law provision and identified by local statistical surveys. Notably,

---

[13]Petty, W. and Graunt, J., *Treatise of Taxes and Contributions* (London, 1662).
[14]See Smith, R., *The Fontana History of the Human Science* (London, 1997), at 308–9.
[15]De Montchrestien, A., *Traicté de l'oeconomie politique* (Paris, 1615).
[16]Playfair, W., *The Commercial and Political Atlas of 1787* (London, 1787).
[17]Black, W., *Observations Medical and Political on the Smallpox* (London, 1830).

from 1780 to 1830 several developments formed the foundation of the application of statistical and scientific data to social problems with the national census instituted in 1800. National criminal statistics for England and Wales began to be published by the Home Office in 1810, followed by Scotland in 1812, and regular returns were made from 1832. Significantly, official and private statistical surveys co-existed. Parliamentary select committees added to their task the compilation of a statistical basis for Parliamentary information and soon what had been *ad hoc* and the response to individual inquiry became routine.

Government departments responded to the curiosity encouraged by the provision of statistical information. The Board of Trade established a Statistical Department in 1832 covering the development of trade and manufacturers and other departments of government soon followed with the establishment of statistical divisions, e.g., the Colonial Office, the Home Office, the Inspector-General of Imports and Exports. Private organisations also engaged in the collection of statistical data.[18] Parliament took an important step in the Registration Act 1836, which provided a General Register Office to index, collate and record the returns on births, deaths and marriages and official recognition of statistical information led to debates as to what the data should be used for and how it might be analysed. Military, as well as civilian, use of statistics was apparent as army statistics became regularly collected from 1834.

THE STATISTICAL MOVEMENT IN THE NINETEENTH CENTURY AND THE ENVIRONMENT

Environmentalism and public health

The revolution that transformed England from an agrarian to an industrial society is well documented.[19] The creation of the Poor Law Commission in the 1830s and 1840s established the remit of government into concerns about the poor and their environment. Urbanisation and industrialisation were considered an achievement and evidence of British ingenuity and innovation, the success of which depended on the Victorian work ethic. On a humanitarian view, however, frequently unhealthy and unsafe working practices placed the new industrialism in a bad light. The rise of

---

[18]The best examples given by Cullen, *op. cit.* n. 12, at 23, were the various leading hospitals: Bethlem, Greenwich, St Thomas's, St Bartholomew's and St Luke's.

[19]Frazer, W. M., *A History of English Public Health 1834–1939* (London, University of London Press, 1950), Lewis, R. A., *Edwin Chadwick and the Public Health Movement 1832–1854* (London, Longman, 1952); Flinn, M. W., *Public Health Reform in Britain* (London, Macmillan, 1968).

trade unions highlighted the plight of the poor, the unsatisfactory nature of the employment of children and the unhealthy working conditions of many. The development of new towns and cities placed a strain on existing water and sanitation systems and poor food hygiene in shops and in the home, and poor living conditions, contributed to many epidemics such as influenza, diarrhoeic illness and tuberculosis. The environmental state of Britain is described as follows:

> While the woeful state of the environmental condition of urban Britain must have been pellucidly clear to anyone who had either eyes to observe the squalid living conditions or the filthy urban air or a nose to smell the effluent covering the street of the waste matter dumped immediately outside houses, it was that most feared disease, cholera, which dramatically and cruelly drew the attention of the public and, more importantly, the government to the unsatisfactory state of the external environment and the deleterious effect it could have on human health.[20]

The cholera outbreak in 1831–2 claimed 32,000 lives[21] and marked the beginning of environmental legislation intended to ameliorate the poor sanitary conditions which were identified in the 1842 Parliamentary Report on *The Sanitary Condition of the Labouring Population of Great Britain.*

The major intellectual influence behind the rise in environmentalism was Bentham, underscored by Edwin Chadwick's concerns about public health. Chadwick's case was weakened by the claims he made from statistical information that often failed to be supported by an analysis of the statistics and acrimonious disputes arose between Chadwick and members of the Poor Law Commission. These shortcomings did not lessen the appeal of statistical information, particularly to support the lobbying activities of the public health reformers.

Unquestionably, statistical information gave a new confidence to law reformers. Social problems and their amelioration through law reform touched humanitarian concerns about the welfare of ordinary people and it is clear that the various law reform movements were built on the work of the statistical movement, although quite often engaged in independent agendas. Cullen, in his major study of statistical societies, chronicles one of the major challenges that confronted the use of statistical information at this time. A common belief, in fact unsupported by statistical data and later to be rejected by medical knowledge, was that disease could be

---

[20]McManus, F., *Environmental Health Law* (London, Blackstone Press, 1994), at 3.
[21]*Ibid*, at 4.

eliminated through the application of the miasma theory. The miasma theory advanced the view that the removal of all putrefaction would succeed in the removal of disease. Miasmatics, as they were known, believed that 'the essential prophylactic against cholera was to cleanse the external environment of refuse, excremental and organic matter'[22] and a series of Nuisance Removal Acts and the Public Health Act 1848 were products of the application of the theory. Local authorities were given powers to construct sewers, remove nuisances, license slaughterhouses and lodgings and a central government department, the General Board of Health, received default powers to regulate and enforce local authority powers and duties. Statistical study was therefore a powerful weapon in the hands of those that chose to apply it. Even when the statistical data appeared to be unsupportive of the views advanced, this did not prevent them from being used.

Equally obvious from a study of the legislation in mid-Victorian Britain is that statistical study was the catalyst for a number of major legislative initiatives. These include the Sewage Utilisation Act 1865 and the Sanitary Act 1866, which gave local authorities additional powers to provide and maintain drains and sewers. Special drainage districts were established with regulatory powers for their maintenance and the Public Health Act 1872 provided for the division of the country into sanitary areas with local authority enforcement powers. Consolidation of the law came in the Public Health Act 1875, which provided comprehensive legislation for England and Wales on all aspects of public health.[23]

The law on housing was similarly reformed. Local authorities received powers to demolish unfit housing and erect buildings for the use of working class tenants[24] and this landmark legislation laid the foundations of public housing in the United Kingdom.

Similarly on food standards and safety, environmental health considerations became a major focus of the legislation from 1872. The Adulteration of Food and Drugs Act 1872 and the Sale of Food and Drugs Act 1875 set standards for the manufacture, sale and consumption of food and drink.

A study of the Reports of the Poor Law Commissioners reveals how statistical data were accumulated and used to service different dogmas and platforms of reform. The disparate nature of these studies, ranging from local to national surveys, reveals how the study of disease and its causes linked the science of medicine with the social science of law reform.

---

[22]*Ibid*, at 3.
[23]In Scotland see the Public Health (Scotland) Act 1897.
[24]See the Housing of the Working Classes Acts 1885 and 1890. Also see the Shaftesbury Act 1851 and the Torrens Act 32 & 32 Vict. C. 130.

Statistical study was also applied to crime, and to the causes of crime. Drawing a link between poverty, crime and social degradation was not difficult, as Cullen has pointed out:[25]

Chadwick expanded upon, but in no way originated, the environmentalist argument that sanitary reform would produce a more stable and thrifty working class. Overcrowding was seen as a 'cause of extreme demoralisation and recklessness, and recklessness, again, as a cause of disease' ... Both moralistic and environmentalist conceptions were inherent in the statement that many new convicts arrived 'in a state of disease from intemperance and bad habits' and were 'improved by the effect of cleanliness, dryness, better ventilation, temperance and simple food.'

The statistical movement and the environment

At the centre of the application of science to the social sciences through the study of statistics lay the term 'moral statistics', a term which has now fallen into disuse. Commonly used in the nineteenth century, it applied to education, crime and religion. The House of Commons became the focal point of the debate and collection of statistics that covered a wide-ranging analysis of the causes of poverty, crime and unemployment.

An important element in the growth in statistical study was the formation during the nineteenth century of the numerous statistical societies which were motivated by the study of social problems and their alleviation. The statistical movement, as it became known, marked a unique period in intellectual activity and was both national and international in its activities. It was also multidisciplinary and complementary to the various popular causes of the time and intellectuals from differing disciplines combined to study through statistical data common social, economic and legal problems. In the British Isles the statistical section of the British Association for the Advancement of Science was formed in Cambridge in 1833 and led to the foundation of the London Statistical Society,[26] renamed the Royal Statistical Society in March 1834. The idea was to have provincial societies meeting regularly and comprising scientists and economists and statisticians. The Manchester Statistical Society first met in September 1833 and five years later the Statistical Society of Ulster was established as part of the Belfast Natural History and

---

[25]*Op. cit.* n. 12, at 63.
[26]The Statistical Society of London had set up a census committee which included William Farr and G. R. Porter.

Philosophical Society. The Social Inquiry and Statistical Society of Ireland began life in 1847 as the Dublin Statistical Society[27] and, significantly, it was modelled on the statistical section of the British Association. The Dublin Society[28] had a large number of prominent Irish lawyers among its membership.

The statistical societies facilitated lawyers, historians, philosophers and economists in the study of the major social and economic problems of the nineteenth century.[29] This included the study of political economy and its application to current social problems. The Irish famine was at its height in 1847, and it was a logical step to set up a society devoted to the study of economics in Ireland.[30]

Statistical study was also influential in the development of the law schools and the university teaching of law. 'Historical jurisprudence', a term which is usually associated with Savigny (1779–1861), undoubtedly had a powerful influence on leading lawyers of the period. Dr Clive Dewey explains the importance of its study: '. . . But the bias of the law schools — in Oxford, Cambridge, Dublin and London — was towards historical jurisprudence. The great legal discoveries of the time were made on the frontiers of historical research: and the leading law teachers — Maine, Pollock, Vinogradoff, Bryce, Maitland, Hancock and Richey — were all historical jurists. . . .'

---

[27]Professor R. D. C. Black, *History of the Society, The Statistical and Social Inquiry Society of Ireland, Centenary Volume 1847–1947* (Dublin, Statistical Society, 1947).
[28]This international dimension of the Dublin Society was reflected in the honorary membership offered to John Stuart Mill and Nassau Senior in 1849.
[29]Cullen, M. J., *op. cit.* n. 12.
[30]See Black, *op. cit.* n. 27 for an historical explanation of the Society and its importance. The account which follows takes much of the information provided by Professor Black's study. Also see Shannon, M., *Historical Memoirs* (Dublin, Statistical Society, 1970), which provides an important biographical source for the Society's membership. The importance of law reform is discussed in Black, R. D. C., *Economic Thought and the Irish question 1817–1970* (Cambridge, Cambridge University Press, 1960). McEldowney, J. F., 'William Neilson Hancock 1820–1888', 1985 *Irish Jurist* 378–402. The following list contains the names of the major lawyers of the Society: Joseph Napier (1804–1882) Born Belfast 1804, Irish Attorney–General 1852, Vice Chancellor of Dublin University 1867–1882, Lord Chancellor of Ireland 1858–1859. See: Alex Charles Ewald, *Life of Sir Joseph Napier Ex Lord Chancellor of Ireland, Dublin, 1892). Thomas O'Hagan* (1812–1885) Lord Chancellor of Ireland 1868–1874, See: J. F. McEldowney, 'Lord O'Hagan 1812–1885: A Study of his life and period as Lord Chancellor of Ireland 1868–1874'. (1979) XIV *Irish Jurist* (NS) 360–377. Hugh Law (1818–1883) Lord Chancellor of Ireland 1881–1883, Professor of English Law, Queen's College Galway, 1849–1858. Drafted the Irish Church Act 1869 and Land Act (Ireland) 1870. Solicitor-General 1872–1879. Attorney-General, 1880. Revd. Franc Sadlier (1774–1851) B. A. 1795, Trinity College Provost 1837–1851. Professor of Mathematics and Greek T.C.D. 1805.

The principal doctrine of the historical school emphasises the role of the lawyer. Lawyers formulate technical and precise legal principles and provide the expertise in the drafting of laws. The content of the laws that are drafted should reflect the interests of the community as a whole and in this task the lawyer becomes an important law-maker by diagnosing problems and providing solutions. The ability of the lawyer to diagnose social problems correctly is dependent on how the lawyer understands the way in which laws evolve. In this respect the study of custom is regarded as an essential feature of the process of understanding law and social problems. Legislation became the most direct and effective means to assist in the development of society. According to Maine's (1822–88) famous *dictum*, '... the movement of the progressive societies has hitherto been a movement from status to contract.'

Environmental interests dominated the work of the various statistical societies, notably in the areas of public health, poverty, pollution and sanitation, as noted above. One example was the Dublin-based Social Inquiry and Statistical Society, James Houghton's (1795–1873) paper in 1863, 'Some Remarks on the Unsatisfactory Tenure of Land by our Farmers at Home and a Few Concluding Observations on the Administration of the Poor Law in England and in Ireland'. A year later, J. K. Ingram (1823–1907) read a paper on the 'Comparison between the English and Irish Poor Law with respect to the Conditions of Relief'.

Statistical study sought to combine the development of the industrial society alongside the environmental impact of that development. Railways, street lighting, improved sanitation, hospital improvements, the education of woman, the regulation of Friendly Societies, the care of the mentally handicapped, the production of sugar and sugar beet and the condition of small farmers, all attracted papers and discussion in the work of the societies.

It is undoubtedly the case that the zenith of the statistical societies was in the nineteenth century. Both local and central government found that they depended on the work of the major statistical societies and found common cause in proposing reforms beneficial to the general needs of society. An interesting observation is that the statistical societies were in fact private organisations and bridged the gap between the private and public sector. As the century came to an end the legislative achievements of the statistical movement looked impressive. Almost simultaneously with their new found success, though, the influence of and enthusiasm for statistical societies ebbed away.

An unparalleled combination of circumstances had resulted in the joining of law and science in common causes. Undoubtedly the foundations of environmental law had benefited from the use of statistical data to develop major legislation but the question remains as to the legacy that statistical study has left.

SCIENCE AND LAW; PROBABILITY AND RISK

In the nineteenth century statistical study provided a bridge between law reformer, social scientist and science. Interdisciplinary work was desirable as part of the innovative first steps taken in the development of a new discipline and in the adoption of a clear legislative strategy.

In the present era, the world of science appears less certain when compared to the enthusiasm that accompanied the pioneering search for new data and understanding in the nineteenth century. Statistical study centred around the statistical society fails to attract as many admirers today but the scepticism of the present day is not shared by everyone. Science retains a certain mysticism, profits from its own believers and offers many attractive claims. It is easily identifiable with the physical reality of the natural world and is portrayed as truthful when based on positive and verifiable outcomes. However, there are increasing signs of disillusionment. The reality appears that science is quite unable to deliver such high expectations and values of truth and fact. Science may depend as much on subjective assessment as on objective fact and is as capable of distorting the facts as any other knowledge-based subject. In fact, as the study undertaken by Barnett,[31] shows, there are many hundreds of publications, ranging across pollution in all its forms and found in a diverse number of disciplines, with little scope for analysis formed out of a common theme or classification. This adds to the difficulty of assessment when knowledge is so broadly drawn.

Science and the environment: a discourse on risk

The rise and fall of the statistical movement has not diverted modern advances. Based on statistical probability, modern developments include predictive models. At the heart of the relationship between science and law is the question of risk assessment and predicting outcomes from known or ascertainable data. How to assess and interpret scientific evidence is a fundamental inquiry with courts providing an examination of what has occurred and only rarely evaluating future risks. In contrast, environmental law must attempt to predict outcomes and take steps in anticipation of risks and some current examples serve to reinforce the link

---

[31]Barnett, V. and Turkman, K. F. (eds), *Statistics for the Environment, vol. 3; Pollution Assessment and Control* (Chichester, Wiley, 1997).

between the assessment of science and law. Principles such as 'the polluter pays', techniques such as 'ecolabelling' and the development of environmental impact assessment and integrated pollution control highlight the distinct contribution environmental law is making to the general development of new concepts in law. Environmental lawyers place reliance on scientific data and methodology in measuring, monitoring and understanding anthropogenic impacts on the environment and science is used to help predict outcomes and deal with the impact, often unforeseen, of man's activities on the environment. Scientists increasingly need to understand the impact of legal rules on the environment[32] and developing suitable legal rules and setting standards to serve the needs of the scientist present formidable challenges for the future.

Responding to risk

At international, European and national level, environmental policies are being shaped, albeit belatedly, that begin to take account of the challenges to the environment in the new century and beyond. The UN Earth Summit in 1992 drew attention to the need for international action to tackle global problems such as climate change, biodiversity and forest loss, highlighting the fact that man's environmental impacts do not recognise national boundaries and that action is required at an international level. The end of the twentieth century saw the realisation that environmental protection and conservation rest heavily on the implementation of policies such as clean technology, waste-minimisation and sustainable development, which are themselves underpinned by the development of standards. In January 1994, the United Kingdom government embarked on a national strategy for sustainable development[33] and despite the absence of a set of coherent or consistent standards throughout the European Union, there are signs that environmental policy in the EU is adopting a more preventative approach (see *United Kingdom* v *Commission* (case C–180/96) [1998] ECR I–2265).

---

[32]Tolba, M., et al. *The World Environment 1972–1992* (London, Chapman and Hall, 1992), at 804–5; Haagsma, A., 'The European Community's Environmental Policy: A Case-study in Federalism' (1989) 12 *Fordham International Law Journal* 311; Hester, R. E. and Harrison, R. M. (ed.), *Waste Treatment and Disposal* (London, The Royal Society of Chemistry, 1995); Kerry Turner, R., Pearce, D., Bateman, I., *Environmental Economics* (London, Harvester, 1994); Kiss, A. and Shelton, S. *Manual of European Environmental Law* (Cambridge, Cambridge University Press, 1993); Kramer, L., *European Environmental Law Casebook* (London, Sweet and Maxwell, 1993).
[33]*Sustainable Development: the UK Strategy* (London, HMSO, 1994).

Contemporary examples illustrate the need to examine the value judgments that underlie various assumptions about science and law. Assessing scientific evidence in order to draw conclusions involves two issues of fundamental importance. First, the concept of the burden and standard of proof; and, secondly, in identifying uncertainty and calculating risk there are implications for law and the science that underpins it.

The standards set by the burden of proof involve lawyers and scientists in a dialogue over methodology and emphasis. In the environmental context, Page [34] has drawn an important contrast between two principles. The first concerns what he calls 'limiting false positives', and the second is 'limiting false negatives'. Limiting false positives involves an hypothesis which appears to be true when it is in fact untrue and limiting false negatives occurs when there is insufficient evidence for an hypothesis which is in fact proved to be correct.

Most experimental science appears to focus on the limiting of false positives. This goal is shared by those who see the aims of the criminal justice system as based on the premise that it is undesirable to convict an innocent person even though this may mean allowing a guilty person to go free. The prosecution must meet a high standard of proof which enables this principle to be maintained. However, there is relatively little attention given to the probability of false negatives.

Scientific methodology may also suffer from the limitations set by the way the question is posed. Different formulations of the same question may provide different answers and scientific data may also appear to offer objective, or at any rate verifiable, criteria that may go unquestioned in the way government formulates its policy. This may result in government accepting scientific evidence and drawing its own conclusions without a proper inquiry into the hypothesis advanced by the scientist.

CONCLUSIONS

A crucial part of the future strategy for the environment is sustainable development, defined by the Brundtland Commission in 1987 as intended to meet 'the needs of the present without compromising the ability of future generations to meet their own needs'. The UK Annual Report [35] noted that the common theme in the sustainable development strategy adopted by the government for the environment was 'to establish more

---

[34] Page, T., 'A Generic View of Toxic Chemicals and Similar Risks' (1979) 7 *Ecology Law Quarterly* 207.
[35] *This Common Inheritance* (Cm 2822, HMSO, 1995), at 12.

specific targets and objectives, together with quantified indicators of progress' for different parts of the environment.[36] This remains a key objective among future priorities.

The lesson from the nineteenth century is that setting objectives and adopting strategies for the environment are multi-disciplined tasks. They rely on the collection of data and on providing adequate analysis. The nineteenth-century statistical societies provided the foundations for the study of the environment and the laws needed to remedy social problems. Their combination of law reform and statistical inquiry proved decisive in the development of an effective legislative agenda.

In the present climate, how might science and law best be combined? Monitoring how environmental laws are obeyed is the first step and this is an evolutionary process, whereby learning how procedures and processes work will help foster a better understanding of regulation and law. Ensuring adequate enforcement of environmental law at national and European Community level sets immense challenges for the future of environmental law and it is also essential to set priorities that make environmental enforcement an essential value in society.[37]

Despite the inability of science to deal in absolutes — either in terms of proof or in standards of safety — it has a fundamental and important role to play in understanding environmental problems. This is particularly clear from the perspective of protecting the environment, as well as in diagnosing and attributing causes of pollution. The techniques of predicting outcomes and consequences from existing data and information remain complex (see chapter 4). Risk assessment techniques and mathematical modelling procedures attempt to establish predictive and quantitative assessments of the likely impact of man's activities on the local, regional and global environment. It is from these predictions that future policies and regulations may be developed. Inherent in setting environmental standards should be a flexibility to respond to scientific advances and changes to the knowledge base.

Scientists may have yet another role to perform in environmental monitoring — determining the probable source of a polluting incident. Evaluating who is responsible for environmental damage may involve a degree of scientific detective work, but may not necessarily provide solutions as to how to clean up the environment or prevent harm in the future. The principle that 'the polluter pays' may simply result in clean-up

---

[36]Following concerns about climate change and biodiversity, the UK ratified the Convention on Biological Diversity on 3 June 1994.
[37]See Kramer, L., *European Environmental Law Casebook* (London, Sweet and Maxwell, 1993), at vi–vii.

costs being borne by the end user who is able to pass costs on to the consumer. Thus a notional environmental 'overhead' may be built into pricing mechanisms but this does not provide long-term benefits for the environment. Scientists must also contribute to environmental management by meeting the challenge inherent in the development of economic remediation and restoration techniques.[38]

Environmental management techniques have adapted to accommodate a more problem-focused and policy-driven approach to the environment. Public education and forging interrelations between science and industry, government and law are an intrinsic part of the work of the environmental scientist today. Scientists may be able to determine the extent of 'harm' to the environment and suggest procedures to limit, control or ameliorate the harmful effects. This knowledge is, however, only truly valuable if it is used to inform industry, policy-makers and the public realistically and fully. The creation of new agencies — the Environment Agency and the Scottish Environment Protection Agency under the Environment Act 1995, and the European Environment Agency — reflects public demands for standard-setting and auditing of the environment, demands that must ultimately be met by scientists.

The optimistic tone of much nineteenth century writing on public health and housing welfare underlined the belief that better laws would 'cure' disease and improve society. In setting standards today much of that optimism remains, but there are now competing values and priorities. For example, setting standards to reduce air pollution may mean more expensive fuel, which may not be acceptable to the public. Government policy may be developed on the basis of public opinion, and may fail to give priority to the environment. If public opinion is ignored or misunderstood, however, the danger is that environmental regulation loses its legitimacy. The nineteenth century legacy has provided an example of an incremental approach to solving environmental problems and the hallmarks of the regulatory system today still reflect that. There is a deep dependence on science to provide the necessary evidence to identify environmental problems and propose solutions. This may have an impact on the degree of regulatory control that may be exercised by the legislature or even government departments. The position is well summarised by Chris Hilson:[39]

> Although legislatures are typically responsible for setting the broad framework of a regulatory system, they seldom if ever take on

---

[38]Steele, J., 'Remedies and remediation: Foundational Issues in Environmental Liability' (1995) 58 MLR 615.
[39]Hilson, C., *Regulating Pollution* (Oxford, Hart Publishing, 2000), pp. 12–13.

responsibility for the detailed, day to day operation of that system. Among other reasons they lack the time and the expertise.

There is also a further dimension to understanding environmental problems. All aspects of human activity — including agriculture, industry and population centres — impinge on the environment in which we live. Environmental problems transcend national, European and international legal systems and the global economy and the use of natural and energy resources must be confronted at every level. The implementation of policies for sustainable development must measure the foreseen benefits as well as the detriments of man's activities, and attempt to predict unforeseen effects. Sustainable development must secure the best use of the world's resources measured in long-term as well as short-term strategies and proactive rather than reactive policy-making must be found in economic and scientific instruments that are sanctioned by law.

The foundations of environmental law and its science-based methodology were firmly established by the end of the nineteenth century and at the beginning of the twenty-first century we should re-evaluate how far we have developed our thinking since then. Constructing our understanding of the environment is a complicated task and it is essential to understand the rich intellectual inheritance that was fundamental to the development of environmental law. The curiosity that prompted the study of statistics to discover the problems of the environment in the nineteenth century needs re-kindling and the state of current science and the complacency of the age should not prevent us from asking how reliable scientific evidence is in contributing to the protection of the environment.[40]

---

[40]See Lowry, J. and Edmunds, R., *Environmental Protection and the Common Law* (Oxford, Hart Publishing, 2000).

CHAPTER THREE

Setting Standards: How and Why?

INTRODUCTION

The questions of how and why environmental standards are set are
addressed in this chapter. The methodology of standard-setting provides
an explanation of how science, law and economic instruments are
combined in regulating the environment. Here the procedures and
processes used in setting standards are evaluated, as are the many
different standards and their importance. The significance of the work of
the European Union in its pioneering efforts in standard-setting will also
be examined. The Royal Commission's *21st Report on Setting Environmental
Standards* estimated that 'four fifths of UK environmental legislation has
its origin in European Institutions'[1] and the adoption of the precautionary
principle in the EU provides the basis for preventative action.

In the United Kingdom setting standards became a key part of the
policy set out in the Department of the Environment White Paper in 1990.
The formulation of standards may be found in a wide range of sources and
include guidelines, codes of practice, and criteria for the implementation
of policy on particular facts. The development of standards may come
from private or public bodies and involve formal or informal rules and
techniques vary for the implementation of standards. Legal enforcement
is possible through the courts when standards are mandatory and

---

[1](London, HMSO, 1998), Chapter 1, p. 7.

standards may also be enforceable through contract, statutory frameworks or legally enforceable licences. Some standards are entirely voluntary, depending on self-regulation for their implementation and observance. Standards may be drawn up through codes of practice, for example, the Environment Agency may be given ministerial guidance under ss. 6–8 of the Environment Act 1995 in respect of its functions. This may provide a framework within which the Agency works.

THE RATIONALE OF STANDARDS FOR THE ENVIRONMENT

The Royal Commission defined the term 'standard' in two senses: in the 'narrow sense of a legally enforceable numerical limit'; and in the broad sense, such that 'standards have a wider remit'. The Commission concluded that from a broader perspective[2] standards that go beyond the strictly scientific are important. This includes:

> ... standards which are not mandatory but contained in guidelines, codes of practice or sets of criteria for deciding individual cases: standards not set by governments which carry authority for other reasons, especially the scientific eminence or market power of those who set them, and some standards which are not numerical.

Environmental controls largely depend on some means of measurement. Public trust in science and in the use of controls is based on the perception that any measurement is reliable and objective. In fact the underpinning science may simply provide an assessment of risk rather than any definitive measurement of or answer to the problem of how safe a process or commodity is. Assessment of risks is described in probabilities, not certainties (see Chapter 4). Measurement also provides a means to quantify professional judgment and transparency becomes available through the presentation and statistical analysis of data and measurement, and through thorough peer and independent review of findings to certify experimental, field and analytical procedures. Full transparency offers a sceptical public a guarantee that professionals are working to the highest standards of verifiable care and the value of transparent measurement is particularly important in a society such as Britain, where the legacy remains of considerable secrecy in government and institutions.[3]

The importance of standards in the environmental policy process is highlighted in the Royal Commission Report which took a broad view of

---

[2] *Ibid.*, para 1.15.
[3] See House of Lords Select Committee on Science and Technology, Session 1999-2000, *Science and Society*, HL Paper 38 (23 February 2000).

standards and considered not only numerical and legally binding standards, but also the other areas of standard-setting that include advisory codes of practice, and policy formulation that may influence how decisions are made. Recommendations for improving the methodology and procedures for standard-setting advanced by the Royal Commission are considered below.

THE FORMULATION OF STANDARDS

The range and variety of standards present difficulties when attempting to describe the methodology for setting them. There are a number of distinct procedures that apply to the formulation of standards, which may be listed as follows:

(a) The first stage is to identify the environmental problem; the definition and formulation of harm is required based on scientific data.

(b) An analysis of harm is considered in the context of the overall policy on the environment. The Royal Commission considers that a key element in making a judgment about an environmental standard is that it must fulfil two conditions:[4]

   (i) it is formally stated after some consideration and intended to apply generally to a defined class of cases;

   (ii) because of its relationship to certain sanctions, rewards or values, it can be expected to exert an influence, direct or indirect, on activities that affect the environment.

(c) The setting of the standard requires consideration of the type of standard that is most suitable, and the content of the standard must be fully defined.

(d) The use of a numerical standard requires careful analysis. There is the inevitable assumption that specifying what is safe or hazardous in numerical terms may imply levels of accuracy that are not justified by scientific knowledge.

(e) Setting general standards may provide a better assessment of harm.

(f) Standards may be formulated through the operation of a wide range of techniques, such as codes of practice, guidance, ministerial directions or through the common law application of legal principles to particular problems.

---

[4]Royal Commission, para. 1.15.

There is no simple mechanism for ensuring that standards are uniform or consistent. The United Kingdom policy contained in the 1990 Environment White Paper is based on the assumption that 'the best evidence and analysis available' should inform the setting of environmental standards. This may be an over-optimistic view of what is achievable and science may fail to deliver the technical data to meet public expectations. A key problem is to ensure easy access to and availability of relevant scientific data, which may be produced from a variety of research, monitoring and technical activities. There are some data available from such sources as the *European Inventory of Existing Commercial Chemical Substances*[5] which lists over 100,000 substances used within the European Union but, given that the number of chemicals in use rises substantially with each year, the *Inventory* is in reality out of date since it was compiled up to September 1981. There is a range of scientific databases that may hold useful information, e.g., the Chemical Abstract database which carries information on millions of chemicals. Information on such sources is provided in the Bibliography.

The scientific assessment of standards has developed and improved over the past decade. The Organisation for Economic Cooperation and Development (OECD) provides common methods for testing toxicity and ecotoxicity, the EC and the Environment Agency are currently developing recommendations for tests in ecotoxicology (a basic consideration of toxicity and ecotoxicity tests is provided in Chapter 4) and the International Standards Organisation (ISO) provides a system of common standards and their measurement.

Regulatory techniques

There are in existence a number of ways that standards may be drawn up, as follows:

(a) *BS 7750 Environmental Standard* Originally pioneered by the British Standards Institute, BS 7750 is based on a self-regulatory or voluntary system. UK companies may introduce environmental management systems that implement standards contained in BS 7750. The basis of the standard is that a quality management system is introduced containing aims, objectives and a process of auditing to ensure implementation and compliance. The certification process is very detailed with a system of records, management and periodic external reviews of the environmental management

---

[5](Brussels, 1990).

system. Gradually the principles enshrined in BS 7750 have become recognised as a benchmark of quality.

(b) *International Organisation for Standardisation*   Similar to the objectives set out in BS 7750, the International Organisation for Standardisation (ISO) has developed a standard known as ISO 14000. This provides a benchmark to improve and formulate environmental management. There are criteria for qualification of staff, systems for managing and auditing and certification and a variety of standards built up on the basis of a series centred on ISO 14000. In 1995 work began on ISO 14031 which sets out guidance on the evaluation of environmental performance. This operates around two basic indicators:[6]

(i)   environmental condition indicators, which include air and water quality and indicators of biodiversity;

(ii)   environmental performance indicators, which provide various parameters for evaluation of the environmental performance of organisations. Energy and natural resources are measured as inputs, and outputs cover emissions, waste and products.

In 1996, ISO 14001 was launched, which is intended to be revised on a five-year cycle. ISO 14001 relates to the needs of smaller firms and contains basic principles about management systems developed with ISO 9000. The idea behind the new revisions is to incorporate into a single standard key elements common to the standardisation scheme, namely:

(i)   mandatory reporting of environmental performance;

(ii)   tightening up standards relating to environmental performance;

(iii)   applying common standards towards sustainability.

The ISO 14001 scheme has been very successful with a steady rise in the number of companies applying for certification and achieving registration.[7] There is also an added international dimension due to the popularity of the scheme in many countries in the world, including Asia. In international terms ISO 14001 has achieved a growth of over 30 per cent per year,[8] with Denmark, Sweden and

---

[6]ENDS Report 288, p. 10.
[7]ENDS Report 286, p. 8.
[8]ENDS Report 287, p. 13.

Finland leading the world in the adoption of the standard *per capita* of the population.

(c) *The EC Eco-management and Audit Scheme* The EC Eco-management and Audit Scheme (EMAS) (Regulation 1836/93) is somewhat tougher than ISO 14001. It is a voluntary scheme to encourage businesses to improve environmental standards across a wide range of activities. The scheme came into force on 12 October 1995[9] and it is estimated that only 70 industrial sites have been registered.[10] The scheme is broad in scope and applies mainly to industrial businesses, including operators engaged in producing electricity, water, gas, steam, hot water and even waste management processes. Environmental policies, programmes of action and implementation strategies have to be prepared and brought into effect. The key elements of the scheme are:

(i)   continuous improvements and monitoring;

(ii)   compliance with the relevant regulations and legislation;

(iii) reviews of management systems including waste and energy usage;

(iv)   an assessment of potential impact and analysis of the management of the site and the means of achieving an adequate environmental protection plan;

(v)   the use of external accreditation of the standards through a national body for accreditation (the National Accreditation Control for Certification);

(vi)   The sanction of suspending registration of a site if there is any breach of the regulatory requirements.

EMAS also has a tougher regulatory regime than BS 7750, with the relevant regulatory bodies having powers of inspection and reporting. In a recent case, however, the Environment Agency chose not to invoke procedures to suspend site registration although a successful criminal prosecution was obtained.[11]

There is also a scheme to encourage environmental management systems to be introduced into smaller firms.[12] The future of EMAS is not in doubt and there are plans to expand the scheme beyond the industrial business into businesses such as supermarkets. A disappointment, how-

---

[9]Department of the Environment Circular 2/95.
[10]ENDS Report 301, p. 53.
[11]*Ibid.*
[12]ENDS Report 290, p. 5.

ever, is in the waste industry where there appears to be some scepticism and doubt about the value of the scheme.

Some conclusions may be provided on the importance of setting standards through the adoption of voluntary systems. These types of quality standards have a number of advantages. They provide a proactive means of ensuring compatibility and through flexible revisions standards may be improved. As part of these types of management programmes there is a requirement for continual review of the effectiveness and efficiency of a company's or site's environmental performance. Any identified shortcomings or problems should be addressed through modifications to the management process, thereby improving environmental performance. There is also a reactive element in providing standards with the flexibility to meet new technologies or address new forms of pollution. The introduction of new technologies or products must be planned for in advance in terms of minimising environmental impacts and incorporating them in any existing management programme. Lastly, there is a preventative element in standard-setting. Observance of the standard provides a means to prevent pollution; and once pollution has taken place it is possible to use the breach of the standard as a means to achieve enforcement. There is considerable success in this approach to environmental standard-setting.

Over 30,000 registrations have been reached for ISO 14001 certificates[13] and a revision of the standard is expected to be completed by the end of 2000. In terms of EMAS, there has been some discussion as to the possibility of making the standard compulsory and, although there is some resistance to this, nonetheless environmental management standards may offer a highly effective form of standard-setting for the future.

LEGAL AND ECONOMIC INSTRUMENTS THAT MAY ASSIST IN THE DEVELOPMENT OF ENVIRONMENTAL STANDARDS

There are a number of distinct principles that guide environmental policy and are influential in setting standards. The main tools for policy-making may be found in the following principles.

Sustainable development

Devising standards is only the first step. Translating standards into an appropriate formulation for implementation is essential. At the outset environmental standards are considered to be an important element in the formulation of environmental policy, but that policy incorporates a range

---

[13]ENDS Report 293, p. 11.

of issues other than the purely environmental. These are defined within the context of sustainable development and economic and social considerations must be weighed in terms of resource and environmental protection. In general policy terms the European Union has been influential. The Treaty on European Union created general objectives for community policy and the environment is integral to the future development of the Union. The Amsterdam Treaty in 1997 built on this framework by incorporating the concept of sustainable development and secondary Community legislation[14] has consolidated this concept. It is generally accepted that this may be too vague to provide a concrete foundation; nevertheless, there is a sense of direction in using the language of environmentalists.

It is reasonable to ask what are the legal principles that might inform the development of environmental protection? Article 174(2) (ex 130r) of the Treaty of Rome is called in aid as a means of establishing general legal principles. In general terms there are measures that might protect human health, natural resources and 'the prudent and rational use' of resources to prevent waste and to encourage its safe disposal and the protection of all the natural resources to be found in the environment. On one interpretation, the most that can be said is that such provisions are general in scope and vague in content in terms of implementation. On another, there is a juridical content to the principles enshrined in Article 174 (ex 130r) that are enforceable and binding. Given the sensitive and delicate nature of member states' cooperation on environmental issues, it may be concluded that at best Article 174 (ex 130r) provides the European Union with a broad framework for the environment. Specific protection of the environment may fall to the member states, or be taken up in the general development of standards for the environment within the European Union.

The development of common European standards is the best way forward. In that way the cost of implementing such standards may be treated as part of the establishment of the internal market and additional costs may be transferred across member states. Distortions within the community would thereby be avoided and the result would be that a coherent approach to environmental standards could be adopted. The concern is that if this integrated model is not adopted then standards may become a problem for trade and commerce within the Union. The dangers of failing to develop an integrated approach are as follows:

- Environmental standards are likely to add to the costs of consumer goods, and the more stringent they become the higher the costs

---

[14]Regulation 3062/95: see [1995] OJL327/9, Article 2(4).

- Standards require community support in order to achieve the goal of improving the quality of the environment
- Manufacturers may face differential costs if there is no uniformity of approach to standards in the Union as a whole
- Environmental standards of variable quality and implementation have the potential to distort the economies of member states. They may impose higher costs on countries with poor environmental records and poor environmental protection regimes. Industrial countries may bear heavier burdens than agricultural countries.

The precautionary principle

Since 1993 the precautionary principle has been an integral part of Community law (Article 174(2) (ex 130r), Treaty of Rome). Following on from the Rio Declaration of 1992, the principle incorporates a fact-based analysis that is centred around 'the best scientific information available' to allow preventative action to be taken. The idea of preventative measures is to avoid or anticipate harm and thus it would be reasonable to ban substances where there is a calculated risk of harm. Kramer[15] gives the example of 'products such as asbestos, cadmium and phthalates'. Asbestos has harmful health effects if particles are inhaled; cadmium is a toxic heavy metal which can be biomagnified in a food chain (see Chapter 4) and phthalates are among the endocrine disrupting compounds.[16]

There are a number of characteristics in the adoption of the precautionary principle:

(a) a scientific assessment of risk;
(b) an analysis of the policy implications of taking measures to prevent harm;
(c) an analysis of the potential effectiveness of measures;
(d) a prediction of the state of future scientific knowledge;
(e) a perception that there is a significant risk of harm.

The precautionary principle, while inserted into Article 174 (ex 130r), does not legally require action to be taken. The aim is to guide policy-makers in the direction of assessing and preventing harm in cases where there are extreme hazards or a significant risk of harm. The precautionary principle, therefore, is effectively interpreted in terms of risk assessment. The

---

[15]Kramer, *EC Environmental Law*, 4th edn (London, Sweet and Maxwell, 2000), at p. 17. The Regulation cited is Regulation 793/93.
[16]The Royal Society (2000) *Endocrine disrupting chemicals (EDCs)*, pp. 1–16 provides an excellent introduction to this area of study.

problems of establishing the likelihood of harm, of risk assessment and of scientific uncertainty are considered in greater depth in Chapter 4.

The discretion to adopt the precautionary principle as part of the policy of government has been recognised by the courts. In *R* v *Secretary of State for Trade and Industry, ex parte Duddridge* [1996] Env LR 325, the Court of Appeal refused to require the Secretary of State to adopt the precautionary principle when considering the dangers of exposure to electromagnetic fields generated by power cables. The precautionary principle should be taken into account with regard to EC legislation. The European Court of Justice has the power to consider to what extent the precautionary principle has been adopted (*Bettani* v *Safety Hi-Tech S&L* (case C–3491/95) [1998] ECR I–4355).

The precautionary principle has also been described by Kramer as 'the prevention principle'. This is intended to convey the idea of taking proactive rather than simply reactive steps. This principle recognises that actions may be necessary even when there is substantial scientific uncertainty about effects.

'Polluter pays' principle

The OECD developed in 1972 the idea that the person responsible for pollution should be involved in paying for the consequences of that pollution. The principle was gradually adopted into legislation in the United Kingdom. First it was embedded in the Environmental Protection Act 1990 and then in the Environment Act 1995. The principle became enshrined in the Treaty of Amsterdam 1997 (see Articles 174–176) but had been in existence in the Community before that date.[17]

The principle of polluter pays is particularly relevant in the case of waste disposal. The landfill tax has the duel aims, first, of reducing the amount of solid waste disposed to landfill purely in terms of volume; and, secondly, any resultant reduction of the amount of organic waste will lower the amount of methane (a potent greenhouse gas) produced as a result of anaerobic degradation of the waste in the landfill. The principle may also be found in the rationale that has been adopted in the development of various economic instruments, such as carbon taxes. These have been introduced to contribute to an overall lowering in the burning of fossil fuels and to the reducing of production of carbon dioxide, a key greenhouse gas contributing to global warming.[18]

---

[17]See Kramer, n. 15 *op. cit.*, at 19.
[18]See McEldowney, J. and McEldowney, S., *The Environment and the Law* (Harlow, Longman, 1996) at pp. 259–62 for a summary of the impacts of global warming and the connection to carbon dioxide and methane. See also Elsom, D. M., *Atmospheric Pollution: A Global Problem*, 2nd edn (Oxford, Blackwell, 1992), pp. 145–68 for more detailed explanation.

The difficulty with the principle and its implementation is that the polluter may see the extra costs simply as an addition to the production costs of the product or process. Consequently, these may be added to the overall price of the product and passed on to consumers. There is little evidence that such a principle will inhibit pollution. Unless polluters are heavily taxed or the penalty in terms of costs is loaded with a deterrent sanction, there is little prospect of the polluter pays principle achieving the goal of preventing environmental harm. There is also the problem that too often the clean-up costs of pollution fall on the public purse. This provides a safety net, but paradoxically it may mean that responsibility for pollution is not fully identified. The polluter pays principle assumes that the polluter may be found and detected and in cases of historic pollution and contaminated land this is rarely the case. Even if the history of a contaminated land site is well known, companies may no longer be trading or the contamination may have arisen even though they were abiding by the standards of the day. In addition, the application of taxes such as the landfill tax may result in evasion of payment by not disposing to landfill, with a concomitant increase in the illegal dumping of waste.

Integrated Pollution and Control (IPC) and Integrated Pollution Prevention and Control (IPPC)

A form of coordination of pollution control systems has been provided under Part I of the Environmental Protection Act 1990. The more 'holistic' approach[19] favoured by IPC recognises that environmental problems do not obey geographical boundaries, and that pollution impacts on all the media in an interrelated fashion over the short and long term and may require a pooling of scientific knowledge to control it. One example of this is found in the release of sulphur dioxide and nitrogen oxides to the atmosphere during the burning of fossil fuel in electricity generation. These gases dissolve in water droplets in the atmosphere, which ultimately precipitate as acid rain in aquatic and terrestrial environments, often at considerable distances from the original source. Acid rain has well-known deleterious effects on aquatic ecosystems, appears to impact severely on some terrestrial environments and causes deterioration of buildings in urban environments.[20] IPC applies to a list of substances and processes (approximately 2,000 processes in England and Wales) approved by the Secretary of State.

[19]Alder, J. and Wilkinson, D., *Environmental Law and Ethics* (London, Macmillan, 1999).
[20]Elsom, *op. cit.* n. 18. Chapter 4 provides an excellent explanation of the causes and effects of acid rain.

A further development of IPC is to be found in the introduction of the 1996 EC Directive on Integrated Pollution Prevention and Control (96/61). The legislation necessary to implement the Directive is found in the Pollution Prevention Act 1999. It is estimated that IPPC will apply to 7,000 installations requiring the integrated protection of air, land and water through the application of EU emission limits. Under this scheme quality standards are adopted using the best available technique principle outlined below.

There are other examples of integrated approaches to environmental protection. Environmental management standards have already been mentioned and others include ecolabelling of products, the environmental auditing of installations and common pollution controls over processes (see Directive 85/337/EEC on environmental assessment of certain projects, Directive 82/501/EEC, amended by Directive 87/216/EEC, on the impact of major accident hazards of industrial activities).

IPC and BPEO

The aims and objectives of IPC fall into two categories, as follows:

(a) It is intended 'to prevent, minimise or render harmless releases of prescribed substances — using the best available techniques not entailing excessive cost'.

(b) An objective of IPC is 'to develop an approach to pollution control that considers releases from industrial processes to all media in the context of the effect on the environment as a whole — the 'best practicable environmental option'.

The first category, the 'best available techniques not entailing excessive cost', is commonly known as BATNEEC. The principles that define its objectives and explain its usage have been subject to change; in the early stages the best available technologies were replaced with best available techniques. There is no clear definition of what is 'best' but in practice the word is interpreted to mean what is practical and available. There are, however, economic factors in the evaluation of what is available and costs of applying one particular technique have to be considered over any alternative that is available. The Department of the Environment issued guidance in 1991, and the revised 1993 guidance considers that for new processes the economic condition of an industrial sector may be considered relevant when evaluating what is required. This view was broadly supported by Her Majesty's Inspectorate of Pollution (HMIP), now the new Environment Agency under the Environment Act 1995, which may look at the most up-to-date standards applied to new processes but recognises older standards applied to older processes. At one point it was considered that renovation of an old plant would result in new standards being applied to the plant as a whole. The current view is that excessive cost should not be entailed, and each case will be looked at on its own merits. Specific requirements for various processes are contained in Codes of Practice issued by the Environment Agency.

The second category of objective for IPC is the 'best practicable environmental option', commonly referred to as BPEO. Its origins are found in the Fifth Report of the Royal Commission on Environmental Pollution in 1976[21] and since then the principle has been substantially added to by the Royal Commission in its Tenth and Twelfth Reports.[22] BPEO has been described as 'the option that provides the most benefit or least damage to the environment as a whole, at acceptable cost, in the long term as well as the short term'. There is no statutory definition of BPEO, but the 1990 Act does encapsulate the principle only 'where the process is likely to involve the release of substances into more than one environmental medium'. Limits on the principle appear from the fact that the 1990 Act does not appear to permit fundamental questions to be raised about the policy merits of a process or the need for a process. The Department of the Environment issued revised guidance in 1993. In the 1991 version, consideration of the effects of a local environmental issue and the effects the proposed process would have on the local environment is required.

Fiscal instruments

The instruments available to improve the environment include a number of fiscal measures. Environmental taxes provide the Exchequer with additional sources of revenue and, indirectly, may be calculated to encourage the implementation of targets for the environment. For example, a climate change levy is intended to raise over £400 million in revenue and contribute to reducing the United Kingdom's carbon dioxide emissions. Other examples are:

(a)   landfill tax;
(b)   taxes on company cars;
(c)   fuel duty; and
(d)   tax on aggregates.

---

[21]Royal Commission on Environmental Pollution, 5th Report, *Air Pollution Control: An Integrated Approach* (Cmnd 6371, 1976).
[22]Royal Commission on Environmental Pollution, 10th Report, *Tackling Pollution — Experience and Prospects* (Cmnd 9149. 1984); 12th Report, *Best Practicable Environmental Option* (Cm 310, 1988).

The taxation strategy is centered around improving air quality, dealing with waste emissions and meeting Treaty agreements for climate change. The aim is simply to reduce the production of pollutants through the setting of financial disincentives. Fiscal instruments occasion considerable debate and there are issues around the best mechanism for applying the taxes and their overall structure. In terms of the climate change levy, they may be applied to large industrial producers of greenhouse gases using a variety of strategies, and also may be applied at domestic level on household fuels.

Undoubtedly this is an area that is likely to see many developments in the near future. In part it is being driven forward by advances at the international level and this is particularly true in terms of the techniques to lower the global production of greenhouse gases and limit global warming.

CONCLUSIONS

There are a number of problems that may be identified with the existing approach to and methodology of setting standards. The current system of standard-setting is weak and standards are uneven in their application. Many do not fit a legal typology and suffer from a lack of transparency in their design, execution and implementation. There is also a tension between local implementation and central control. The Royal Commission has voiced concerns that public trust and perception about standards requires confidence-building measures with the public's views ascertained through opinion polls, focus groups and a more open approach to standard-setting. The current mix of economic and legal instruments provides a rich source for setting and implementing standards and the choice of what is the most appropriate mechanism should be determined by the evaluation of what is likely to be most effective. Direct regulation of particular industries is not regarded as a viable option.

The Royal Commission makes a number of robust recommendations[23] for settling a common methodology for setting standards. The aim is to achieve greater consistency in approach and rationality in explanation and analysis. To that list might be added a further dimension such as simplification. The complexity and vast array of standards leads to confusion, contradiction and a bewildering sense of bureaucratic red tape. The greatest danger is that complexity will lead to abuse. The way forward is to find a common methodology and approach, involving a synthesis of European and international developments. There are five areas where there should be a common approach, namely:

---

[23]Royal Commission, para. 8.4.

(a)   the scientific assessment of the problem;
(b)   an analysis of the technological options;
(c)   an assessment of risk and uncertainty;
(d)   an economic appraisal of the standard and its cost benefit;
(e)   an analysis of implementation strategies, including the geographical scope of standards.

It may be argued that the best approach is to undertake a general codification of standards, including a common methodology for the drawing up of standards. Codification has several advantages. First, it provides a common framework that is transparent, accessible and may encourage some rationalisation of the system of standard-setting. Secondly, codification provides an opportunity for bringing standards to the attention of the public and increasing public confidence in scientific analysis and understanding, following the BSE crisis and the concerns about GMOs. Thirdly, codification provides a substantive contribution to the development of environmental law. Environmental regulation should ideally focus on long-term solutions to environmental problems, but the life cycle of any particular government is ill suited to that strategy. Finally, codification fosters harmonisation between member states, facilitating the fusion of ideas between common and civil law systems.

Following this integrated approach it is hoped that environmental policy will be more clearly articulated. In practical terms, implementing an integrated approach will build public confidence in scientific methodology and improve implementation strategies.

CHAPTER FOUR

Science, Risk Assessment and the Concept of Safety

INTRODUCTION

Scientific assessment falls within the broader category of setting boundaries to the technological risks to which the public is exposed. The problem facing many agencies is that setting standards becomes the main way for avoiding civil liability and preventing hazardous substances from injuring the public. There is the additional question of how to offer the public assurance that risks based on sound science have been correctly predicted and analysed.

In this chapter we examine the assessment of scientific data as part of risk assessment, a fundamental tool in the development of standard-setting.

SCIENTIFIC EVIDENCE

The use of science and scientific data in a variety of ways has a fundamental role in determining what is safe. Scientific evidence and material are used in court hearings; the proof of environmental harm may be crucial in the determination of civil or criminal liability. Sections 111 to 113 of the Environment Act 1995 cover the use of evidence in connection with pollution offences. There is an inevitable tension between scientific evaluation and legal proof before a court. Scientific evidence presented in court falls into the category of evidence received from an expert witness. This means that the court may admit such evidence at its discretion. There are many situations in which scientific evidence may be relevant; for example, in actions for trespass, nuisance and negligence where the enjoyment of land may have been impaired because of some harmful or noxious substance. Noise pollution, odours, vibration, smoke or fumes may be the product of modern industrial processes or procedures.

Car accidents and unsafe workplaces may require scientific evidence to advance any claim. As scientific knowledge advances, previously safe practices become doubtful. Consequently, as science often evolves in an uncharted and unpredictable way, standards need to be flexible and adaptable. Scientific uncertainty is often at the heart of good scientific methodology, but this becomes unhelpful when science is asked to address a wide variety of expectations as to what is safe.

The well-known case of *Cambridge Water Co.* v *Eastern Counties Leather plc* [1994] 2 AC 264 is an example of the problems of scientific knowledge and legal principle. Severe contamination by the solvent perchlorethylene, arising from land used by Eastern Counties Leather, an established tannery, appeared in a bore hole used by Cambridge Water for water extraction. Cambridge Water sued Eastern Counties Leather for more than £1 million. The House of Lords found in favour of Eastern Counties Leather because it had not been reasonably foreseen that the tanning process might cause contamination of the bore hole. By the time proceedings were brought, scientific understanding of the impact of solvents had increased considerably and levels of detection for the contamination had improved. Since the case was decided it appears that further scientific research has revealed that there are additional dangers caused by the use of solvents.[1] Solvent vapours may pose a threat to health. This was neither expected nor known. Even at the time of the House of Lords decision the research on the dangers of vapour pollution appeared to have been overlooked because the key issue in the case was the question of water contamination.

Outside the formal proceedings of a court, scientific evidence may be offered in the formulation of evidence at an inquiry.

ENVIRONMENTAL HARM AND SCIENTIFIC DATA

It is clear from the preceding chapters that it is difficult to think of any area of human activity that does not have substantial (and often realised)

---

[1] ENDS Report 293 (June 1999), p. 5.

potential to cause environmental change. Industrial development, alterations in agricultural techniques and practices, urban expansion and population growth, transport and energy consumption have all impacted in a variety of ways on the environment. Some of these impacts are planned, but many are not. Even those activities that are controlled may have unforeseen outcomes and consequences. Environmental change does not necessarily equate to damage or harm, and setting the boundaries of what is acceptable and what is not involves consideration of social, economic and scientific issues. Science contributes to the debate in a number of ways:

(a) as an evaluative and predictive tool;
(b) as a key element in the design of solutions to perceived problems; and
(c) by providing systems for monitoring impacts.

The development and implementation of environmental standards has required the application of science in all these ways. Finding a balance between social and economic concerns and the implications of scientific data is often controversial, particularly if significant uncertainty underlies the scientific data or if the available data are open to different interpretations.

Any adverse consequences of man's activities are usually defined in terms of their effect on human health and their impacts on the environment. Environmental harm does not fit any easy definition; indeed, the determination of damage to human health induced, for example, by contaminant concentrations in different media may in itself be difficult to establish and open to considerable debate. A recent example of the difficulty in establishing the likelihood of harm is the consideration of the possible impacts of endocrine disrupting chemicals (the so-called hormone mimics) on human reproduction, development and cancer risk, and on the natural environment. In a recent report, the Royal Society[2] presented a diametrically different view to that held in a report by the American National Research Council[3] published barely a year before.

The Royal Society Report provides the basis for considering further research in this area. Three points are made. First, that the collection of direct evidence to prove that there is a threat to human health will take some time. Secondly, that a wide variety of cancers may be linked to

---

[2]The Royal Society, *Endocrine disrupting chemicals (EDCs)* (London, June 2000).
[3]National Research Council, *Hormonally Active Agents in the Environment* (Washington DC, National Academy Press, July 1999).

endocrine disruptors. While the evidence is based mainly on speculation, this should not be disregarded. Thirdly, that it 'would be prudent to minimise public exposure to endocrine disruptors, particularly in the case of pregnant women'. Clearly while it is accepted that there is the need for more research in this area, the most important recommendation is that regulations should be adopted before the scientific evidence is conclusive. The approach taken by the Royal Society is to be applauded. Science has not yet established a link between endocrine disruptors and cancer, but while research is ongoing it is correct in principle that a precautionary approach is taken.[4]

Scientific data and statistical analysis of those data contribute to the understanding of the impacts of man's activities, the mechanisms for those impacts and predictions of the ultimate consequences of the effects. As regards the effects of biological, chemical and particulate contaminants released to all three receiving media, the data are often in terms of numerical measures. Noise pollution is also described in quantitative terms. Standards set for emission limits and quality standards are commonly expressed in numerical terms developed as a result of the interpretation of a variety of data often obtained in experimental, field and epidemiological studies. The application of numerically-based limits may not be an appropriate construct for other types of standards, however. Management standards, for example, may encompass some quantitative information but will also involve the use of descriptive material, such as the environmental management structure in a company. Standards, then, may not only be based on science, but may draw on expertise from other areas to improve process efficiency and effectiveness in terms of environmental protection.

SCIENTIFIC TECHNIQUES IN THE ASSESSMENT OF ENVIRONMENTAL HARM

The potential harm that a chemical may cause when released to the environment is assessed in two ways. First, through investigating the possible impacts on human health as a result of exposure to the chemical. This may be in terms of toxicity testing. Secondly, through determining the toxicity of the chemical to selected species from either aquatic or terrestrial ecosystems (ecotoxicology). In addition, attempts can be made to assess more general impacts on natural environments. Ecotoxicology is a relatively new area of study that has developed primarily in response to the need to understand, quantify and predict the fate and adverse affects

---

[4]ENDS Report 305 (June 2000), p. 10.

of contaminants in the environment. Information on human and environmental effects provides data that can be used in risk assessments (see below) and the development of predictive models for harm caused by pollutants.

An adverse effect is defined by the Royal Commission on Environmental Pollution[5] as follows:

> ... the effect of exposure to a substance on an organism is defined as adverse when it represents a change in morphology, physiology, growth, development, or life-span which results in impairment of functional capacity or impairment of capacity to compensate for additional stress, or increase in susceptibility to harmful effects of other environmental influences.

It is worthwhile briefly to examine the scientific assessment of effects on humans and other organisms and consider factors that are important in attempting to predict outcomes from chemical or pollutant exposure. It is not proposed, however, to describe in detail the techniques involved in these assessments.[6] It is intended, though, to highlight some advantages and limitations of these processes, and future directions that may lead to improvements in the determination of potential harm associated with environmental discharge of substances.

Assessing impacts on natural environments: ecotoxicology

Ecotoxicology[7] addresses two interrelated questions. The first is the impact of pollutants in terms of organisms and ecosystems (the community of organisms living in a particular physical environment, e.g., a river ecosystem or a wood ecosystem). The second is the fate and mobility of pollutants within that ecosystem. In reality neither of these questions is easy to address and elucidation requires cooperation between a variety of specialists within disciplines such as biology, biochemistry, chemistry, soil science, etc.

---

[5]Royal Commission on Environmental Pollution, Twenty First Report, *Setting Environmental Standards* (London, HMSO, 1998), p. 14.
[6]The Twenty First Royal Commission Report (see n. 4 above) provides a useful overview of the procedures and definition of terms.
[7]Moriarty, F., *Ecotoxicology: The Study of Pollutants in Ecosystems*, 3rd edn (London, Academic Press, 1999) provides an excellent description and analysis of the science underpinning ecotoxicology. See also Shaw, I.C. and Chadwick, J. *Principles of Environmental Toxicology* (London, Taylor & Francis, 1998) for a more methodologically based discussion.

Ecotoxicology is used in a number of ways relevant to the setting of standards. These include:

(a) to establish how toxic compounds are to a variety of animals and plants. This can be used to help assess the risks posed by new synthetic chemical compounds;

(b) as a measure of the quality of each of the environmental media (air, soil and water). In this way ecotoxicology may contribute to the development of quality indicators and the definition of quality standards;

(c) to determine the concentrations of substances above which harm is likely to occur in the ecosystem. Such threshold levels can be used in setting discharge standards; and

(d) as a tool to test the toxicological effect of receiving ecosystems, e.g., water extracted from freshwater that receives controlled discharges. This type of monitoring can be used to review the effectiveness of standards set for discharges.

(a)   Acute toxicity tests   Environmental contamination by chemicals particularly relevant to setting standards can arise from a number of sources, including deliberate release, e.g., pesticides, or by-products of industrial processes. Traditionally the impact of a pollutant has been determined through the use of toxicity studies. These are primarily laboratory-based tests carried out on selected animals such as *Daphnia*, earthworms and fish and plants (e.g., algae), either as single species or multi-species tests. The toxicity tests are different for terrestrial and aquatic environments and usually apply only to particular ecosystems.

Toxicity testing for the impact of a chemical in aquatic environments will usually involve tests on representatives from plants such as algae (the primary producers), those organisms grazing on the primary producers (the primary consumers, e.g., water fleas: *Daphnia*), and also secondary consumers or predators such as fish. There are standard regulatory tests for all these. Testing on terrestrial systems is more problematic and not well developed. Worms can be used and some tests exist for other invertebrates (e.g., slugs) and some insects (e.g., bees). Birds are the key vertebrates used in toxicity tests. The majority of these tests are short term, up to 14 days, and define acute toxicity rather than chronic toxicity (i.e., long term and proceeding over a large portion of the life-span of test populations). Acute effects on organisms are rapid, often fatal, certainly obvious and normally non-reversible.

Lethal concentrations (LCs) of substances to test organisms are often expressed as LC_{50} or LC_{70}. This indicates the percentage of organisms, 50 per cent or 70 per cent respectively, killed at a given concentration of the chemical under defined conditions. This is normally linked to a specific exposure time, e.g., 48 h-LC_{50}, since this is important in determining the acute toxicity effects. It is also possible to report the data as median effective concentrations (ECs). For example, EC_{50} is the concentration of a substance that results in 50 per cent of the maximum response under defined conditions. Acute toxicity tests are linked to the probable environmental concentrations of compounds as part of the data assessment that goes to environmental impact and safety.

It is perhaps most straightforward to provide an example of the use of these types of toxicity data in regulation. There are some 1,000 new, synthetically produced chemicals marketed each year. These chemicals must undergo a specified hazard assessment prior to commercial sale and use. Specific information is required during product notification under EC Directive 79/831/EEC, of which toxicity assessment is an important part. Since it is assumed that water systems tend to be the final receiving medium for chemicals, either because of their discharge in industrial effluent and sewage or because of run-off from land, aquatic species are normally used in the toxicity tests. The potential impact of the chemical is assessed from the predicted environmental concentration of the compound and the acute toxicity data, in particular the lowest concentration resulting in 50 per cent of the test organisms dying (LC_{50}). A predicted no effect concentration (PNEC) is derived by dividing the lowest LC_{50} or EC_{50} by 1,000 (under EC procedures), an arbitrary factor to account for scientific uncertainty (see below). The PNEC should be higher than the predicted environmental concentration (PEC). Estimates of PEC include consideration of sources, chemistry and extent of use, etc. (see below). In other words, a 1,000-fold difference between the predicted environmental concentration and the lowest LC_{50} is taken to indicate no significant environmental hazard to water ecosystems.

The predicted concentration of chemicals in the environment is, of course, substantially affected by the likely market size for the substance, and the Directive requires different levels of toxicity testing based on market size.[8] Products likely to have large markets require the greatest range of hazard assessments. These go beyond acute toxicity testing and move into the effects of prolonged exposure, the compound's longevity and likely environmental fate, and the likelihood of biomagnification (defined as the increases in pollutant concentration in the tissues of successive organisms along a food chain) occurring.

---

[8]McEldowney, J. and McEldowney, S. *Environment and the Law* (Harlow, Longman, 1996). See pp. 134 and 135 for information on the level of testing required for different predicted market sizes.

Acute toxicity testing has a number of distinct attractions in terms of its use in environmental regulation and in its contribution to determining impacts and setting some numerical standards. The tests are *in vitro*, i.e. in the laboratory, rather than *in vivo*, i.e. in natural ecosystems, and therefore significantly easier to interpret and derive a quantitative measure of harm. They are relatively simple and rapid and essentially highly reproducible, that is, the test conditions can be tightly controlled. Set procedures can be developed for toxicity tests on individual organisms, which can be applied wherever the assessment is undertaken. A considerable amount of knowledge has been accumulated about the sensitivity of the test organisms to toxins and there is, therefore, ease of comparability between data sets. These are all clear advantages of acute toxicity tests in their contribution to standard-setting. The Environment Agency is at present advancing the application of acute toxicity tests in terms of the use of an assembly of tests for estimating the toxic effects of complete effluents rather than individual chemicals, and also the toxicity of waters that receive discharges. This is being developed under the Agency's Direct Toxicity Assessment Programme.[9]

Care should be taken, however, not to rely too much on acute toxicity testing. Such tests have obvious limitations and important uncertainties. The choice of species on which the tests are undertaken is difficult. It is essential to ensure that they are representative of the particular ecosystem. Ideally the selected test organisms should be among the most sensitive to toxins in that ecosystem and should be those at risk of exposure to the highest levels of the chemical. Both these requirements may actually be quite difficult to achieve, and it is questionable if those organisms currently used for regulatory purposes offer sufficiently robust models. For example, many pollutants and chemicals accumulate in sediments, and therefore the exposure of sediment-dwelling organisms or those that are bottom-dwelling may be substantially higher than that of those in a watercourse. As yet there are no acute toxicity tests for organisms associated with sediment. There are also many types of organisms that have not been tested. Small mammals, for example, in general have not had ecotoxicity tests developed for them. Reliance is placed instead on the data gained from human toxicity tests on laboratory mammals, and these have very different life-cycle and physiological characteristics to their wild counterparts. There is no information on many other plant and animal species. This is problematic since there may be considerable variations between species in their sensitivity to chemicals. Environmental condi-

---

[9]Environment Agency, *State of the Environment* (2000). See http:www.environment-agency.gov.uk for a brief description of developments in this area.

tions may substantially alter the impact of chemicals on organisms. For example, the response of plants to the stress arising from low-level ozone pollution varies with temperature and with water availability. Moreover, during the life-cycle of animals their sensitivity to toxins may vary considerably. Juvenile and reproductive stages in an organism's life-cycle may, for example, be most sensitive to a chemical. These types of consideration are being incorporated in toxicity testing strategies being developed at present.

There are, of course, further limitations in terms of extrapolating results from acute toxicity tests in laboratory experiments to natural environments. This is difficult enough when the extrapolation is on the basis of an individual to a population, but may have considerable uncertainty associated with it when the extrapolation is to the response of a community, i.e. the diversity of plants and animals found in any ecosystem. Some attempt to redress this problem is the use of multi-species tests that clearly have advantages over single-species studies. Even so, they are ultimately limited by the laboratory base for the tests and the organisms selected.

(b) Chronic toxicity testing   In hazard assessments, if the chemical is expected to achieve a large market size then the chronic effects of the substance must be investigated. A large market, of course, tends to mean that ecosystems will be frequently (or even continually) exposed to the chemical. Chronic effects on organisms tend to be the result of long-term exposure often to low doses of the chemicals. Chemicals that tend to persist in the environment may also cause chronic responses. As with acute effects, the response to the chemical varies with the organism, and the stage in the life-cycle. Chronic effects also vary with the chemical and the concentration of chemical, and may be cumulative, increasing with a series of doses. There may be some threshold dose before there is an impact on organisms. This, of course, may vary with species. Long-term exposure may result in biomagnification of the pollutant along a food chain. The story of the impact of DDT on predator birds is well known and was primarily due to this type of effect. Chronic effects on plants and animals are normally sub-lethal with reductions in reproductive success or growth and development rates, or they may cause changes in behaviour. These are much longer-term effects, often lasting over a significant portion of the life-cycle of the organisms.

In reality, in most natural ecosystems it is chronic exposure rather than acute exposure to chemicals that dominates. Chronic toxicity tests are probably more revealing and useful in terms of the likely impact of a chemical or pollutant. They have, however, many of the disadvantages associated with acute toxicity testing, and in terms of regulation may require considerable investment of time given the potential length of some of the experiments. The impacts of long-term effects of pollutants on organisms and indeed whole ecosystems (see below) may be obscured by changes in individual organisms, populations or communities as a result of perfectly normal changes that occur with time. For example, the species composition of a community may change, or an individual or a population may age. At different stages in an organism's life-cycle its behaviour may change substantially, e.g., from swimming in the water column to bottom-dwelling and sediment associated life. These time-related changes inevitably influence exposure and response to contaminants. The fate of substances in an ecosystem is also time-dependent, e.g., washing-out from soil into rivers or the rate of degradation of a compound.

Part of toxicity testing may include an analysis of the way in which an organism takes up the substance, e.g., predominantly in its food or through exposed surfaces, etc. Whether a substance is changed, transformed, through the organism's metabolic activity may be assessed. How much of the substance is excreted or eliminated in some way from the body of the organism can also be determined. All these can vary substantially with the substance under examination and with the organism. For example, many of the radioactive compounds formed during nuclear fission (e.g., plutonium) tend to remain in the alimentary tract of animals and ultimately are excreted, whereas many heavy metals (e.g., cadmium) tend to accumulate in tissues and organs within the animals' bodies. These types of influences may vary with the chemical form of the contaminant that is itself influenced by environmental conditions (see below). Such toxikinetic studies can be used to attempt to predict the possible physiological impact of chemicals on organisms. They can also be useful in contributing to the understanding of the fate of substances in natural environments.

(c) Environmental fate of contaminants Laboratory testing and extrapolation to the environment require some basic perception of the probable fate of pollutants in the environment, their mobility and some measure of how 'available' they are to the living component of the ecosystem, i.e. their bioavailability. These factors essentially describe the likely exposure of organisms in an ecosystem and the pathway between the target organism and the source of the chemical or pollutant. The relationship between the likely concentration of a substance in an ecosystem available to organisms and its uptake and accumulation by them is crucial in terms of attempting to establish probable impacts. The mobility and fate of chemicals in the environment is determined by a number of factors. The physical and

chemical characteristics of the compound itself have a major impact on its tendency to remain relatively stationary in a system or to spread to other sites and even other ecosystems. The nature of the pollutant also influences whether it will be degraded. It may be completely broken down, or only partially and transformed to another type of compound during degradation. Degradation may be rapid or may be slow. Any degradation product will have different environmental impacts than the original compound. It is not necessarily all that unusual for a degradation product to be more toxic than the parent substance and be biomagnified differently. In fact it was a breakdown product of DDT that caused the significant environmental impact as a result of the application of this pesticide. In the case of radioactive elements, there is a characteristic decay pathway with one element being transformed to other radioactive elements, the so-called 'decay daughters'. These may be more toxic, more radioactive and behave very differently from the original radioactive compound. The situation is more complex in that the mobility and fate of a compound will be considerably influenced by *in situ* environmental conditions, e.g., soil type, pH, oxygen availability etc., and the biological component of the ecosystem. Environmental conditions can vary over very short distances; the longevity and movement of a chemical may be different at different ends of a field and between the sediment and flowing water in a river. In determining the likely pathways of exposure of organisms in an ecosystem to a chemical, it is possible that contamination may arise from more than one source. For example, possible metal sources on agricultural land include metal in sewage sludge and atmospheric emissions from cars and road run-off.

In natural environments it is rare for organisms and ecosystems to be exposed to only one polluting compound. This adds significantly to the difficulty in predicting impacts. The substances may still cause individual effects, or they may interact in some way and have a combined influence. This may be:

(a)   additive — the effect of the mixture of pollutants is the sum of their individual effects;

(b)   synergistic — the effects are significantly increased due to interactions between the compounds; or

(c)   antagonistic — the compounds again interact, but the overall effect is to reduce toxicity.

It is possible that all these interactions are modulated by environmental conditions, so that two chemicals may interact in different ways in different environmental conditions and ecosystems. Both acute and chronic toxicity tests can be carried out on mixtures of compounds and go some way to addressing this type of problem, but they have limitations. They are not necessarily true representations of natural environments and each ecosystem will be different. The development of the Direct Toxicity Assessment Programme by the Environment Agency is recognition of the importance of interactions between chemicals in effluents and receiving waters in determining levels of toxicity. Care again must be taken in extrapolating to natural environments in light of the comments made above.

Prediction of environmental concentrations, pathways and exposures, then, is exceptionally difficult and associated with a range of uncertainties. In general, mathematical models are used to predict the environmental fate of chemicals. Such models may be partly based on fundamental scientific understanding of the physical and chemical characteristics of the substances, which is used to predict their likely mobility, etc. Data from a range of sources, e.g., existing data on the fate of related compounds in the environment, may be used in the development of models. As with all models, it is essential that the knowledge base for the model is reliable and robust.

(d)   Whole ecosystem effects   Acute and chronic toxicity tests and predicting environmental pathways and exposure to contaminants may not provide a true representation of the damage or harm actually done to the diversity of species within communities and to the ecosystem itself. Ecosystems are dynamic with interactions between species, e.g., host–parasite interactions, prey–predator interactions, and within species, e.g., competition. Energy, trapped initially by photosynthetic organisms from the sun, flows through ecosystems, i.e. from primary producer to decomposer, to primary consumer and predator. The impact of pollutants is more properly described in terms of these processes, but they are highly complex and difficult to determine. We know little enough even about pristine ecosystems — an essential starting point if we are to be able to establish pollutant impacts on community dynamics and energy flow through ecosystems and thereby establish any detrimental effects of a single pollutant or multiple pollutants. Diversity within ecosystems may in itself be difficult to establish. Population and community data in terms of chemical impacts are absent for the majority of ecosystems. Different ecosystems will vary in their susceptibility to any deleterious effects; even the productivity of an ecosystem may alter its response. In fact a chemical may exert its effect in a rather indirect way, making organisms, populations or communities less tolerant to other environmental pressures and stresses. This may be particularly difficult to assess. It is developments in

our understanding of the structure, function and species diversity of both pristine and contaminated ecosystems that are the challenge for the future and will greatly enhance our ability to develop standards that avoid ecological 'harm'.

Assessing impacts on human health

Humans, like other animals and plants, can be exposed to chemicals through a variety of sources, e.g., atmospheric pollution, ingested in food and water, and through exposure of the body's surface. Two different types of scientific analysis are used to study the health impacts of human exposure to substances through any of these routes — toxicity tests and epidemiological studies.[10]

A variety of toxicity tests may be used in studies on human toxicity, from mammalian cells to studies on model laboratory mammals. The Ames test, for example, is a laboratory-based procedure that assesses if a chemical has any mutagenic effect on cells, i.e. causes genetic mutation. Where animal tests are undertaken, usually more than one species is studied since (as noted above) different species respond differently. Effects may be measured in a variety of ways, from carcinogenicity to changes in the function of organs (e.g., kidney damage, breathing disorders). The distribution of the toxicant in the test animals may also be determined. Data from these types of studies are then extrapolated to predict effects on the human population. This is usually achieved through the application of models.

As for ecotoxicological studies, these human toxicity tests are based on pollutant concentration, exposure route (e.g., oral, dermal, inhalation etc.), and effect. Many of the problems associated with ecotoxicological tests also produce uncertainty in human toxicity data. The laboratory-based studies tend to be similar to acute toxicity studies, with short-term exposure to relatively high concentrations of the test substance. As for ecosystem exposure, human exposure to chronic low levels of the substances over prolonged periods is more likely. In addition, exposure to cocktails of chemicals rather than to single substances is the norm. These may interact in a variety of ways, as indicated above, modifying the toxic impacts of compounds in the environment. There are also problems in extrapolating from animal test experiments. Given the very major species differences in response to toxins, how well do the mammals used mimic human responses to contaminants? Part of the protocol laid down for

---

[10]See Royal Commission, *op. cit.*, n.4, at 15–21 for a more detailed description of these tests.

animal tests is that they should be genetically very similar. This essentially reduces some biological variability (see below) in determination of toxicological effects and makes tests more reproducible. There is a problem, though — the human population itself is highly variable, making extrapolation difficult. The mapping of the human genome has raised another issue. It is possible that certain groups of people may be particularly susceptible to environmental toxins because of their genetic make-up.[11] Segments of the human population will anyway respond differently to toxins; susceptibility may be greater in children and older people, and possibly in people with an existing illness, e.g., asthma sufferers are more susceptible to low-level ozone or particulate pollution.

Much more useful in human toxicological assessment are data that relate directly to human responses. Epidemiological studies are particularly pertinent. Again the aim of the studies is to determine dose and effect relationships. They may be carried out on the general population or selected groups of the population, or on occupational groups (these often have higher exposure levels to particular substances). There are a number of uncertainties in this regard too. There is little control over the range of exposure to different compounds encountered by the test group. It is possible that an apparent response to a particular substance is due to some other substance or interactions between substances. The type of study to be undertaken must be carefully stipulated. For instance, if determining the response of a particular group within the population is the aim this should be made clear, e.g., the effect of lead emissions from car exhausts on intelligence in children. Otherwise, the study should not be biased to a particular part of the population; the population used in the study must be representative of the general population. Misreporting of impacts or misclassification of responses may result in an effect being missed.

Lastly, there are other problems in epidemiological studies with regard to measuring the levels of exposure to specific compounds for participants in the study. For example, the adverse health effects of pollutants arising from car exhausts require an estimate of the exposure level of participants. Measurements of pollutant concentrations will vary substantially between a suburban street and a town or city centre, between measurements taken at three feet (perhaps more valid for children) and at five to six feet (adult height), and between inside and outside, etc. Overlay on this the variation in life-styles of any representative section of the population and the problems of establishing exposure levels are obvious. Nevertheless, epidemiological studies are one of the best sources of data for the adverse

---

[11]McEldowney, S. and Warren, L., 'The New Biology: A Challenge to Law' (1998) 4 *Int. J. Biosciences & the Law* 315.

effects of substances on humans. They are, however, limited in one other way. They are possible only after the human population has been exposed to the compound and may not contribute to the setting of new standards other than on the basis of knowledge about related compounds. They are, of course, highly relevant and useful in terms of reviewing possible impacts or monitoring responses when concerns have been raised from other data.

Other types of studies on human responses also contribute to understanding the adverse health impacts of compounds. These include the use of human volunteers where the experiments can be much more controlled than in the case of studies of the general population. The Royal Commission on Environmental Pollution provide an excellent summary of how the range of studies described above may contribute to the development of an air quality standard for benzene.[12] The setting of this standard relied on animal laboratory tests and occupational exposure epidemiological studies.

SCIENTIFIC UNCERTAINTY

There are some important points in terms of scientific method and the limitations of experimental sciences that it is relevant to consider at this juncture. These are crucial to our understanding of the inherent problems in setting numerical standards and for the interpretation of scientific data in terms of the precautionary principle. Essentially these problems can be explained and defined within the confines of scientific uncertainty. Ultimately it is a social question whether the extent of such uncertainty on any given question is acceptable or not, an issue in part addressed through risk assessment.

Scientific information must be provided to lawyers and regulators in an easily understandable and concise form. This is clearly one of the attractions of toxicological testing. It is important to remember, however, that it is often difficult to reconcile this with biological data. Organisms, populations, communities and ecosystems are highly complex and there is an inherent biological variability, which is not uncommonly substantial. This can be difficult to account for in simple data sets. Biological data are inherently variable for this reason, and also because there are inevitable measurement or technical errors associated with any laboratory-based testing or studies undertaken in the field. Analytical equipment operates within a range of reliability and accuracy, and therefore contributes some error to any analysis. Moreover, any analytical equipment has a lower detection limit below which no measurement can be made, even though a

---

[12]Royal Commission, *op. cit.* n. 4, at 21.

compound may still be exerting a biological impact. This may be true of endocrine disrupting chemicals that exert their influence at exceptionally low concentrations. There are operator and observational errors, which again contribute to overall experimental problems. It is also possible that suitable analytical techniques may not always be available to gather appropriate data. The difficulties and errors associated with toxicity testing have already been discussed above. These variabilities and errors are, of course, addressed in the statistical techniques applied to data analysis and within risk assessment and the development of robust predictive models (see below). It would be unwise, however, to neglect this part of scientific uncertainty. Implicit assumptions that the data are accurate should be tempered by an understanding of the problems associated with biological experimentation and data.

The problems of uncertainty are broader than the difficulties linked to acquiring reliable scientific data. Scientific assessment and understanding are inevitably based on the knowledge available at the time. This may be deficient. There is the implicit assumption that all the possible human and environmental ramifications of a release of a chemical, or the commercial use of genetically modified crops or impacts of a new industrial process, etc. are foreseeable. In other words, to assess and test for possible impacts we must ask the right questions. But to do this we have to rely on current understanding. There is no doubt that in many cases scientists and regulators do just this and adequate protection has been provided. Unfortunately it is equally clear that mistakes in this regard can be made, with unforeseen consequences occurring. This has undermined public confidence, both in scientists and in the regulatory process. Recent examples of problems and responses that find their origin in scientific uncertainty and the limits of scientific understanding include the following:

(a) Predictions about the probability of the prion (a small infective protein) disease in cattle (bovine spongiform encephalopathy: BSE) jumping the species barriers between the ruminants and to non-ruminants. The BSE prion appears to have infected humans causing new variant Creutzfeldt-Jakob disease (vCJD), although this was originally viewed as an unlikely event. The uncertainties about the number of individuals infected and the length of incubation are significant and make predictions for the likely extent of the vCJD epidemic in humans problematic.[13] There are

[13]Hodgett, G. R., 'Ethics, Science and the Social Management of Risk: The Bovine Spongiform Encephalopathy Epidemic' (1998) 1 *Int. J. Biosciences and the Law* 359 provides an excellent review of the BSE epidemic in the context of risk.

now concerns about the possibility of BSE occurring in sheep. This may have been partly masked by a prion disease that has always occurred in the UK's sheep flocks, scrapie, which poses no human health risk.

(b) The risks posed by endocrine disrupters to human health and fertility, and to aquatic ecosystems. It is only in the last few years that scientific evidence has started to suggest that several different groups of chemicals (e.g., some pesticides, phthalate plasticizers, anti-fouling paints and dioxins) affect hormone control in animals and humans with the consequences of lowering fertility and reproductive success. Not only has there been a lack of scientific foresight and considerable uncertainty with regard to these chemicals disrupting physiological processes in humans and animals in this way, but also other sources of uncertainty have occurred. For example, it was not predicted that phthalate plasticizers would migrate from packaging into food, thereby entering the human food chain. The evidence is still sketchy, and associated uncertainties and unanswered questions are substantial. Essentially, very low concentrations of these compounds may be able to elicit these effects with levels, for example, substantially lower than those regulated for in acute toxicity tests for pesticides. The impact of endocrine disrupting chemicals is likely to be chronic and long-term. The question arises whether caution should be exercised in respect of these compounds acting as hormone mimics, or whether scientific information is considered too scarce and incomplete to act on.

(c) A review of pesticide approvals. The Advisory Committee on Pesticides (ACP) raised concerns that pesticide approvals had a number of uncertainties associated with them. It was felt that there was insufficient information on pesticides in aquatic environments and drinking water, partly due to a lack of appropriate data and partly to a limitation in existing analytical procedures. These concerns were largely borne out by the 1996 Report prepared by the Working Party on the Incidence of Pesticides in Water (UK).[14] The Working Party had been established in 1991 in response to the ACP's concerns.

(d) The agricultural use of genetically-modified (GM) crops. There are a number of uncertainties and risks associated with the commercial growth of GM crops. The first is that the genes used to modify the crop, e.g., herbicide or insect resistance, are transferred to other

---

[14]Department of the Environment (London, HMSO, 1996) *Pesticides in Water*.

strains and species forming new genetically-modified plants with novel properties and unknown impacts. The second is that the GM crop itself may become invasive and move from managed agricultural ecosystems to natural ecosystems. Again the effects of such an event are difficult to predict. It is possible that either might cause deleterious ecological consequences. There is the possibility that new pest species might result which possess traits making them difficult to control, e.g., herbicide resistance. These are not the only uncertainties associated with GM crops in the environment, though. For example, the incorporation of a herbicide resistance characteristic in crops may increase the use of herbicides by farmers, thereby raising the environmental concentrations of pesticides. This would have obvious environmental ramifications and raises questions about underlying assumptions in terms of pathways and dose of pesticides made in standard-setting for these chemicals (see above). The House of Commons Environmental Audit Committee began an inquiry into the possible impact of GM crops and the regulation of the biotechnology industry in March 1999. There is also uncertainty and debate about the possible health implications of GM food.[15] This has been controversial in recent years, with claim and counterclaim abounding. Uncertainties still remain and the public perception of risk is heightened in this regard at present.

Scientific uncertainty is an important and unavoidable component of experimental science and scientific data. The design of numerically-based and data-based standards should take due cognizance of this and incorporate safety margins to account for uncertainty. It is desirable to have continual reassessment of the scientific evidence and scientific understanding that contribute to numerical standards. This will provide a basis for reappraisal of the standards and their modification if safety is jeopardised. There is currently in the regulatory regime periodic review of existing substances to establish if further testing is required or if new data suggest that a change in regulatory response is required. It is wrong to think of numerical standards as established and immutable; they must be flexible and responsive to changes in scientific knowledge.

Even in the use of numerical standards there is an element of social participation that should not be forgotten. This is evident particularly in

---

[15]Seidler, R. J., Watrud, L. S. and George, S. E., 'Assessing Risks to Ecosystems and Human Health from Genetically Modified Organisms' in P. Calow (ed.), *Handbook of Environmental Risk Assessment and Management* (Oxford, Blackwell Science, 1998), at 110–46 provide an excellent review of the uncertainties and estimating risks.

terms of the concept of safety and what risk is considered tolerable. There is an inherent conflict in the setting of any standards between the reliability of the science, social acceptance and the economic consequences of those standards. Industry also contributes to the development of numerical standards since demanding standards have cost implications, for example through substantial investment in treatment technologies. The microbiological standards set under the Bathing Water Directive are currently under review. There has been considerable debate about the benefits to human health in tightening the standards, particularly in virus limits, and the costs related to increased sewage treatment. In effect, even setting numerical science-based standards is a participatory process with science providing one element, albeit an important element, of the jigsaw. Standards may be set within the confines of BATNEEC (see Chapter 3).

Judgments based on scientific and socio-economic criteria are required for the application of the precautionary principle. Risk assessment is one tool that provides a mechanism for coping with scientific uncertainty in the setting of standards, and also provides a framework within which the balance between social and scientific criteria can be interrogated.

RISK AND ASSESSMENT

It has already been shown above that the likelihood of a chemical causing harm is assessed in terms of the concentration of the chemical and an effect. This can be described in a number of ways and through a number of different tests. These may set specific factors for investigation, from human toxicity studies to acute toxicity and death of target populations, to chronic effects such as reproductive success or the productivity of an ecosystem.

The actual likelihood of harm occurring in the environment depends on a large number of factors, including exposure and dose levels, the fate and mobility of the contaminant, interactions between contaminants, the susceptibility of organisms, environmental conditions, ecosystem productivity, community interactions etc. (see above). The determination and measurement of these are all subject to uncertainties that can rarely be quantified, so that the data are usually analysed and presented in terms of probabilities. The likelihood of a deleterious effect depends on the probability of the target organism or population being exposed to a chemical at levels exceeding some threshold concentration, the critical effect level. The significant concentrations of chemicals, effluents, etc. can be described using other terms such as 'no observed (adverse) effect level' (NO(A)EL). This simply is the largest concentration or amount of a substance that has no adverse effect as determined by laboratory-based experiments or through field studies. The 'lowest observed (adverse) effect level' (LO(A)EL), in contrast, is the lowest amount of a substance that causes no detectable effect. (The determination of PEC and the calculation of PNEC and their role in chemical control legislation have been outlined above.) Risk assessment, put at its simplest, is a statistical technique which involves the comparison of predicted exposure levels with likely effects at those concentrations or quantities of a substance.

There is a difference between risk and uncertainty, explained by Calow:[16]

> Risk assessment recognizes a range of possible outcomes, the relative likelihood of which can be predicted on the basis of the full understanding of the scenarios. Uncertainty assessment recognizes some outcomes as being a possibility but it cannot quantify them; it usually involves computing likelihoods on the basis of presumptions about what might happen and/or by introducing 'noise' to risk assessments in a 'controlled way' such as simulation.

Risk assessment, then, can make some contribution to overcoming the problem of scientific uncertainty in a number of ways, for example, by incorporating in assessments:

(a)   the nature of the risk(s) that might arise in a worst case scenario;
(b)   the magnitude of the risk and the probability of the predicted impacts occurring;
(c)   the reversibility of any impact;
(d)   the reliability of the scientific data and the reasons for and extent of scientific uncertainty.

The prospects of obtaining improved scientific information in the foreseeable future may also be considered.

There are a number of limitations in the application of statistical probabilities to risk assessment. The assessment of risk usually relates to the probability of one person dying per year as a result of exposure to the contaminant. Provided there are sufficient quantitative data, this may be relatively easy to establish. There are clear limits to the use of such a criterion, though. Effects of pollutants and other substances are more normally chronic rather than acute and lethal. Estimating risk in terms of the probability of death may not reflect true impacts in terms of illness.

---

[16]Calow, P., 'Environmental Risk Assessment and Management: the Whats, Whys and Hows?' in P. Calow, *op. cit.* n. 14, at 3.

Such a measure of risk goes no way towards predicting the effect on plants and other animals and has no relevance to ecosystem effects. Risk assessments are poor in expressing risk to natural environments. Another problem in terms of the application of statistics is that risk may be uneven across a population. As noted above for human epidemiological studies, children and older people may be exposed to different levels of risk, etc. For example, young people appear to be at highest risk of developing vCJD, while men over 55 are at highest risk of contracting legionnaires' disease. It is also possible for the risk to be particularly associated with one particular geographical area. A universal measurement of risk does not account for this type of variability. It may be useful, then, to develop a more target-directed risk analysis for those groups showing greatest sensitivity or for those groups likely to be exposed to the highest levels of a substance. The distribution of risks across the population should, then, be described as part of risk assessment.

It can be argued that risk assessment not only is underpinned by science, but also must take due account of the public perception of risk and the economic implications of the scientific identification, measurement and prediction of effects and risks. A range of socio-economic criteria is important in risk assessment and in many ways cannot be separated from its scientific outcome. These criteria include:

(a) The estimated costs of implementing standards based on risk assessment. This has been a clear problem in the implementation of the Wastewater Directive in the UK. The water companies have estimated the cost of complying with the Directive in the order of billions of pounds. The balance between cost and precaution may be found under such instruments as BATNEEC (see Chapter 3).

(b) The technical feasibility of achieving the standards. Difficulties may exist in actually achieving levels advised by risk assessments. For example, it may not be technically possible to reduce (say) the concentration of pesticides in drinking water to accommodate any new regulatory proposals.

(c) The public perception of risk. The public may be prepared to accept different levels of risk for different activities. Events in recent years (such as the BSE crisis and the GMO debate) have tended to undermine public confidence in science and the scientific assessment of risk. In part this can be addressed through full transparency and explanation of the risks associated with a chemical or process, etc. The uncertainties should be explained. A dialogue is needed to re-establish an understanding of and public confidence in the regulatory process. It may be a difficult and demanding task to design methods to communicate the risks to the public accurately and acceptably. The levels of risks and possible effects must be explained clearly, ensuring the problems are understood without over-simplifying the issues.

(d) The tolerability of the risks. Establishing whether a level of risk can be tolerated may vary with the context of the risk. Science can be used to establish the levels of risks through determining probabilities, e.g., predicting the likelihood of one death resulting from a given exposure level in any one year. Setting the limits to tolerability is a social, political and regulatory process. The Royal Commission on Environmental Pollution[17] summarises HSE guidelines for risks related to nuclear power installations based on the probability of one individual dying in any one year, as follows:

> *1 in 1,000* as the 'just tolerable risk' for 'any substantial category [of workers] for any large part of a working life';
>
> *1 in 10,000* as the 'maximum tolerable risk' for members of the public from any single non-nuclear plant;
>
> *1 in 100,000* as the 'maximum tolerable risk' for members of the public from any new nuclear power station;
>
> *1 in 1,000,000* as the level of 'acceptable risk' at which no further improvements in safety need be made.

These levels of 'acceptable risk' are in increasing usage and are being applied to delineate levels of risk considered tolerable for a variety of industrial processes. It is interesting that in essence this is setting benchmarks or (to put it another way) standards of acceptable risks. Development of these types of probabilities also allows the risks associated with different processes and substances to be compared.

Factors other than the risk in terms of an individual dying in any one year may also contribute to decisions on the tolerability of a risk. These include the costs of remedying any damage arising if controls are not sufficiently stringent. The reversibility of any adverse effect may be another consideration. This is particularly the case in terms of 'harm' to ecosystems. For example, one of the difficulties in establishing the tolerability of risks associated with GM crops is that any horizontal gene transfer from the crop plant to wild relatives or invasiveness on the part of

---

[17]*Op. cit.* n. 4, at 53.

the GM plant (see above) may not be easily reversed.[18] Risk to natural environments cannot, of course, be attributed in terms of human deaths and the problems of risk assessments in terms of probabilities for ecosystems has already been mentioned, but reversibility may be key in establishing tolerability.

Over recent years, the setting of standards has increasingly employed the use of risk assessment. In the case where substantial and robust data exist then the level of exposure for a given acceptability of risk can be established. This relies on adequate information being available on issues such as hazards and exposure levels related to effects, i.e. dose–response relationship. Even if data are incomplete, risk assessment can be an essential tool in identifying sources and areas of uncertainty in likely effects. Risk assessments can contribute to safety in a number of other ways, for example, the effectiveness of various options for controlling effects, e.g., through controlling exposure routes. They can be used in the design of any monitoring regime. Indeed, they can form an essential part of monitoring the effectiveness of a standard and determining when standards should be re-set in the light, for example, of new scientific evidence. It is possible to use risk assessment even when data are available largely only in a qualitative form. Calow[19] briefly describes the use of risk assessment in helping to design an environmental management system. Such a process may help a company in achieving an environmental management standard.

ENVIRONMENTAL AUDIT

Developments in the assessment of risk and in forming strategies to integrate environmental policy-making with risk assessment are part of the 'audit culture' that has evolved in the United Kingdom over the past decade. The term refers to the strategies adopted by successive governments to increase the visibility and effectiveness of audit in identifying waste and achieving effective public expenditure.[20] Internal management and control systems as outlined in Chapter 3, involving ISO 14000 and BS 7750, contribute to the management of resources in terms of prioritising environmental concerns. Evaluating the costs and benefits of specific

[18]Seidler, *et al.*, *op. cit.* n. 14 provide an excellent discussion of risks associated with genetically engineered organisms. See also Royal Commission on Environmental Pollution, Fourteenth Report, *Genhaz — a System for the Critical Appraisal of Proposals to Release GMOs into the Environment* (Cm 1557, June 1991).
[19]Calow, *op. cit.* n. 15, at 3–4.
[20]Power, M., *The Audit Society: Rituals of Verification* (Oxford, Oxford University Press, 1997).

environmental policies is essential in establishing some objective criteria to make a reasoned analysis.

In November 1997, the government created a new Environmental Audit Committee of the House of Commons (EAC). The aims of the Committee are to monitor the performance of programmes and the contribution of departments to the protection of the environment and in developing strategies for sustainable development. In addition, a new Cabinet Committee has been formed to develop an integrated approach to environmental matters and a strategy of environmental policy-making across government departments. The coordination of a strategy for sustainable development is also strengthened by the creation of the Environment Protection Group within the Department of the Environment, Transport and the Regions.

The advantages of adopting an audit structure for monitoring the environment are as follows:

(a) targets and indicators may be used and reviewed in a common strategy for determining performance over the short, medium and long terms;

(b) value for money type evaluations may be used providing valuable data and introducing comparability in performances across the public and private sectors;

(c) improvements may be introduced on the basis of an incremental evaluation of performance.

If the model of the National Audit Office — the body responsible under the Comptroller and Auditor General for the audit of the public expenditure of central government departments — is adopted, the environment would gain a valuable means of external scrutiny. There may be some disadvantages, though. Studies into public-sector auditing show that there are concerns that the audit system may favour a static or non-interventionist approach. Too often the audit culture may encourage risk aversion and inertia. Despite these reservations, it is clear that the tools for developing an audit assessment of the environment are already in place. These include the adoption of environmental considerations as part of the Comprehensive Spending Review, the adoption of environmental appraisal in government policies, and the use of targets and reporting on the environment in government departments. Additional strategies on the environment may be found in setting environmental taxes and in government policy on public procurement.[21] It remains to be seen whether such strategies will be adopted over the long term.[22]

ENVIRONMENTAL ASSESSMENT

Lastly, the operation of environmental impact assessment leads to an evaluation of environmental harm. Environmental assessment became an intrinsic part of the planning system. In 1988, the introduction of EC Directive 85/337 on The Assessment of the Effect of Certain Public and Private Projects on the Environment into the town and country planning system integrated environmental assessment into the day-to-day practicalities of large-scale planning. Altogether there are about 20 major provisions implementing the Directive and setting the category of project that requires an assessment. Further amendments to the Directive have taken place through EC Directive 97/11, which came into force on 14 March 1999. The regulatory details of the system of environmental assessment are to be found in the Town and Country Planning (Environmental Impact Assessment) England and Wales Regulations 1999 (SI 1999 No. 293). Major projects such as highways, land drainage, harbour works, electricity and pipeline works fall within the requirements of the Directive.

There are three elements to the process of environmental assessment. First, an environment statement is provided setting out the terms of the planning application and the potential impact on the environment. Environment information provided by the developer is then used to evaluate the planning proposal. It includes queries raised, responses given and third-party consultation, as well as correspondence with any of the statutory authorities. The third element is publicity. Four copies of the statement must be provided to the local planning authority, and in determining planning permission the scope of the development and its potential impact on the environment is assessed.[23]

Extensions of the environmental assessment for water resource programmes are under consideration. It is planned for environmental assessment to be mandatory for major groundwater or artificial recharge schemes in the form of draft regulations currently being considered at the consultation stage.[24]

---

[21]ENDS Report 276, pp. 29–30.
[22]Hollingsworth, K., 'Environmental monitoring of government — the case of an environmental auditor' (2000) 20 LS 241.
[23]See Moore, V., *A Practical Approach to Planning Law*, 7th edn (London, Blackstone Press, 2000), at pp. 231–85.
[24]ENDS Report 288, p. 43.

CASE STUDY: THE BSE CRISIS

The recent Report of the BSE Inquiry, chaired by the Master of the Rolls, Lord Phillips (HMSO, London, 2000) provides an important case study into the use of scientific data. The Report is concerned with the spread of bovine spongiform encephalopathy (BSE) and variant Creutzfeldt-Jakob disease (vCJD) in the United Kingdom. Over 170,000 animals died or had to be destroyed, with many more slaughtered as a precaution against the spread of BSE. The Report provides factual evidence linking the BSE epidemic with intensive farming practices, that included the recycling of animal protein in ruminant feed. The BSE crisis provides a useful case study into the assessment of risk, and questions are also raised about the treatment of known and unknown hazards.

In assessing the measures taken to address the known hazards to animals and the unknown hazards to humans, the Phillips Report concluded that, while the measures were sensible, '... they were not always timely nor adequately implemented and enforced'. The main findings of the Report are as follows:

- The problems that the Government experienced in the co-ordination of the measures that were introduced as a response to the crisis meant that there was inadequate implementation and enforcement.
- It was noted that there were on occasions unnecessary delays when the Government chose to rely on independent scientific expertise when the Government might have reached its own decisions more swiftly and efficiently.
- There were delays in making decisions because of the bureaucratic process.
- The Government were preoccupied with preventing public alarm.
- The campaign of public assurance was a mistake.
- The Government's admission on 20 March 1996 that BSE had probably been transmitted to humans left the public feeling betrayed.

The Phillips Report reveals how assessment of the hazards and source of BSE was undertaken. A key document was the report chaired by Sir Richard Southwood, which concluded that the risk of transmission of BSE to humans appeared to be remote, that 'it was most unlikely that BSE would have any implications for human health'. The Southwood Report was not capable, in scientific terms, of supporting this conclusion.

The lessons of BSE are clear in the assessment and evaluation of risk. In general terms, scientific risk assessment should never be used as a substitute for policy making. Scientific evidence requires careful consideration, especially when there are hazards that may not be capable of precise scientific evaluation. The BSE crisis underlines the need for public openness and transparency. If the public are not fully informed about the risks, public confidence in science and scientists is diminished. Policy makers are then faced with enormous difficulties in providing adequate measures to protect the environment and human health.

CONCLUSIONS

Science and scientific understanding in the context of the environment may be evaluated in a number of ways. First, science is linked to sustainable development. Sustainable development[25] aimed at enhancing the environment, protecting future generations against harm and securing a rise in the living standards of society as a whole rests on measuring change and preventing harm. Economic indicators rely on factual evidence rather than conjecture or subjective opinion. Scientific data set the parameters for informed discussion and analysis. Risk assessment and the evaluation of harm are based on objective indices. The precautionary principle,[26] supported both by European law and in international treaties, requires an analysis of risks. As the Royal Commission concludes, risk assessment is central to the future strategy in developing environmental policy.[27]

Risk assessments prepared in support of decisions on environmental policies or standards should start with information about the nature of the hazard which the policy or standard seeks to address and the extent and quality of the evidence available for assessing the risks it poses. This part of the analysis should indicate whether the hazard is of the relatively well-understood type; if it is unfamiliar, an attempt should be made to identify the most nearly analogous hazards and the aspects which are not understood.

Great care must, however, be taken when science is used in different settings and subject to different levels of proof. In order effectively to set standards and determine risk scientific information is the obvious and necessary starting point. In the application of that science to standard-

[25]The Amsterdam Treaty introduced this concept as part of Community law. The concept may also be found in a variety of Community legislation such as Regulation 306/95. See Kramer, L., *EC Environmental Law* (London, Sweet and Maxwell, 2000), at p. 7.
[26]This is contained in Article 2 (ex B) of the Treaty of European Union and in Article 2 of the EC Treaty as part of the environmental objectives of the European Union: see EC Treaty, Article 174 (ex 130r).
[27]Royal Commission Para 4.50 p. 61.

setting, however, it is essential to have a high degree of confidence in the experimental techniques used to acquire the information and in the rigour of the analysis. A firm perception and appreciation of the uncertainties in the science and methods used to account for experimental and biological variability is also needed. The range of interpretations based on the available evidence and uncertainties should be clear. The scientific method and interpretations that underlie any standard-setting should be transparent and available not only to regulators but also to the public. A public opinion poll undertaken by MORI in 1999 for the DETR established that officials and politicians were seen as the least trustworthy in protecting the public from risks posed by genetically modified organisms. This is a sign of the frailty of public confidence on GMOs which is a source of great public unease.[28] Standard-setting must be an open-ended process. Science and scientific understanding that contributes to individual standards and the processes of standard-setting generally must be open to review. Increasingly the courts demand a more open and accountable formulation of standards, an inevitable consequence of the availability of judicial review.[29]

---

[28]ENDS Report 289 p. 3.
[29]See Chapter 6 for an analysis of the role of the courts. See: *R v HM Inspector of Pollution, ex parte Greenpeace Ltd (No. 2)* [1994] 4 All ER 329.

CHAPTER FIVE

The Regulators and Standard-setting

Regulating the environment through standard-setting is carried out by a number of bodies. In this Chapter the traditional UK approach to regulation is examined in the context of the various United Kingdom regulatory agencies relevant to the environment.[1] The chapter also sets the scene for Chapter 6, where the legal mechanisms for regulating the environment are examined.

THE REGULATORS AND ATTITUDES TO ENVIRONMENTAL REGULATION

Gerd Winter defined environmental law as '... the law regulating the relationship of us to nature, understood both as the world around us *and* as the nature we carry within ourselves'.[2] Winter's analysis places regulation at the heart of environmental law. Yet it remains unclear to what extent the UK is prepared to adopt environmental rights to form the bedrock of protection for the environment. There is also a noticeable tendency, identified in Chapters 1 and 2, to see the UK as having developed a sophisticated means of regulating the environment through a

---

[1] The development of a strategy for the environment in the EU is recognised in Article 2 of the Treaty of Rome which contains for the first time an explicit recognition of 'sustainable development' and the protection of the environment.
[2] Winter, G., 'Perspectives for Environmental Law — Entering the Fourth Phase' (1989) 1 JEL 39.

plethora of agencies and bodies (as outlined below) but subject to rather weak enforcement. Under-resourced agencies, or agencies which lack a coherent sense of priority or which are unable to distinguish between conflicting demands, all lead to a weak regulatory structure. There is a tendency to follow a common law approach to problem-solving and case-by-case decisions are seen as building from experience and learning from mistakes. Seldom, however, does this approach meet the (not unreasonable) demands from the public for a safe and secure environment. As much of environmental protection is also linked to the control of land-use planning, it is not surprising that the regulation of environmental standards is haphazard.

The broad approach to environmental regulation fits the definition advanced by Harlow and Rawlings[3] in attempting to define regulation in the UK in general:

> Regulation is a slippery concept: confusion arises because the term has acquired a variety of meanings. Sometimes it is used loosely to describe any form of behavioural control; effectively the main output function of government. Sometimes it is placed in opposition to markets, being used in economics to describe the activity of the state — including nationalisation, taxation and subsidy — which determines or alters the opposition to markets. More manageably, to adopt Selznick's formulation, regulation refers to sustained and focused control exercised by a public agency over activities that are socially valued.

In terms of regulating environmental standards, the elements of standard-setting and enforcement include the following:

(a) rule formulation through setting standards and ensuring their application. A good example is in the formulation of BS 7550 and ISO 14000;

(b) monitoring and inspection through the operation of regulatory bodies such as the Environment Agency;

(c) enforcement and sanctions through the courts, or compliance agreements such as discharge consents.

In meeting these different objectives, regulation for the environment has had to fit within the general category of regulatory experience in the United Kingdom. This may be characterised as follows:

---

[3]Harlow, C. and Rawlings, R., *Law and Administration*, 2nd edn (London, Butterworths, 1997).

(a)   There is a generalist tradition that pervades public institutions including the courts. Specialist expertise is placed to one side in favour of a generalist approach to problem-solving. In the courts, for example, the magistrates are generally lay persons, as are the jury which are often preferred by defendants in the Crown Court. The lay element is seen as an important characteristic of our system of justice. The judges are expected to see environmental problems in the context of the general work of the courts rather than from any specialist viewpoint that they may possess.

(b)   There is no coherent body of environmental law. Opinions differ as to what should or should not be included, and on how or what environmental law is intended to achieve.

(c)   There are competing views as to the most effective form of regulation, ranging from the interventionist style of direct regulation over specific industries to voluntary forms of self-regulation.

The British approach to regulation was characterised in the 1980s as 'flexibility and informality'.[4] Yet today the range of instruments and their impact on the environment have been drawn from the influences of the European Union which prescribe formal rules, to be rigorously enforced and monitored by regulators. The emphasis on environmental audit and on greater transparency in terms of environmental information suggests that the British approach to environmental regulation has changed. The combination of self-regulation with different forms of direct regulation suggests that a different analysis is now pertinent. Economic analysis of how the environment might be regulated provides a viable alternative.

ECONOMIC REGULATION OF THE ENVIRONMENT

Environmental policy[5] in the United Kingdom may also be informed by the adoption of a range of economic instruments. Sustainable development and Agenda 21 strategies offer the challenge of finding a convenient way to balance competing aspirations — economic growth set against protecting the environment, with a higher priority afforded to preserving the latter over the former.

Regulation may be characterised as offering two different and contrasting styles. There is the command-and-control regulation, described by

---

[4] See Vogel, D., *National Styles of Regulation* (Ithaca, Cornell University Press, 1986).
[5] See Petts, J., 'The regulator-regulated relationship and environmental protection: perceptions in small and medium sized enterprises' (2000) 18 *Environment and Planning* 191. Also see Gunningham, N. and Grabosky, P., *Smart Regulation* (Oxford: Oxford University Press, 1998).

Petts as '. . . a system of direct control over activities and organisation which has a legal basis and is operationalised through a range of structures and procedures'.[6] This is the basis of the most common form of intervention to ensure that environmental protection is achieved as against market forces which may resist such an imposition in terms of cost or freedom of the market. The alternative is to offer to the regulated activity the opportunity to regulate itself. There is evidence that voluntary agreements may seek to adopt this strategy, for example, through EMAS (see Chapter 3), which allows the main participants to reach workable agreements.

In designing regulatory systems it is possible that both forms of regulation may have a place. The United Kingdom has adopted both styles of regulation through a combination of two strategies:

(a)   a proactive enforcement of environmental inspection and monitor-ing systems leading to the application of sound science to remedy environmental problems; and

(b)   a reactive strategy building on the acceptance of quality standards and policing standards such as discharge consents and emission standards. Prosecutions are taken to ensure individual compliance and collective warnings are issued.

The combination of both approaches fairly sums up the British approach to environmental standard-setting. There has been inadequate attention given to a comparative evaluation of what works best and why. Measur-ing the value of the two styles of regulation in terms of the most effective is an important, unanswered question for the future development of environmental policy.

THE MAIN REGULATORY BODIES AND THE ENVIRONMENT

Despite efforts to provide a uniform approach to environmental problems, there is no single unitary system for the regulation of the environment. Various responsibilities for the environment are held by a number of agencies, some governmental and others non-governmental. The environment has been subject to fairly *ad hoc* developments, and at times considerable innovation. An example of the latter is the appointment of the Royal Commission on Environmental Pollution, a body that advises the government on pollution problems. The Reports of the Royal Commission are authoritative and widely respected at both

---

[6]Petts, *op. cit.*, n. 5, 192.

national and international levels with the focus on making suggestions in the area of policy for the protection of the environment. The Royal Commission's Report on Environmental Standards broke new ground by moving away from an over-dependence on science as the basis for developing environmental standards. A full list of its reports may be found in the Bibliography.

The bodies discussed in this chapter are identified as relevant in the development of environmental policies, and therefore have a role in standard-setting or are involved in the implementation of standards. The Royal Commission noted that the interrelationship between environmental policies, science and values is a key to understanding how effective standards might be drawn up and assessed. Given the diffuse nature of the many regulatory bodies, this is difficult to achieve within the existing framework and there is no classification system that neatly provides for the categorisation of regulatory bodies. Each brings its own culture and distinctive approach and they range from appointed to elected bodies. For example, central and local government are both elected, as are the different regional, devolved administrations (see further, below). The Environment Agency (under the Environment Act 1995) is an appointed body with statutory powers.

THE ROLE OF REGIONAL DEVOLUTION

The United Kingdom remains a unitary state in terms of its constitutional arrangements but considerable powers and functions have been devolved to regional assemblies in Northern Ireland and Wales and to the Scottish Parliament. However, the devolution legislation — the Government of Wales Act 1998, the Scotland Act 1998 and the Northern Ireland Act 1998 — retains the United Kingdom government as the body responsible to the European Commission and the European Court of Justice. In effect, while environmental issues are mostly devolved to the new assemblies and Scottish Parliament, the setting of targets and compliance with EU and international obligations rests with the UK government and Parliament.[7] Section 121 of the Government of Wales Act 1998 and s. 4(1)(e) of the Regional Development Agencies Act 1998 provide a statutory framework to ensure sustainable development and this strategy provides the means to monitor the government's environmental performance.

The Greater London Authority Act 1999 provided for the election of a Mayor and Assembly for London in May 2000 and there are a number of key environmental areas that fall within the regulatory powers of the new Mayor. These include:

---

[7]ENDS Report 285, p. 35.

(a) transport, road and parking levies;
(b) air quality and noise management strategies for London;
(c) waste management strategy; and
(d) a three-year state of the environment report, to include bio-diversity, water management, greenhouse gas emissions and land quality.

THE ENVIRONMENT AGENCY

The Environment Act 1995 established an Environment Agency for England and Wales, and for Scotland a separate Scottish Environment Protection Agency (SEPA: see further, below). The 1995 Act makes detailed provision for the transfer of functions and property rights to the new Agencies from the National Rivers Authority and Her Majesty's Inspectorate of Pollution. Part V of the Act provides for a national waste strategy for England and Wales and for Scotland.

The Environment Agency has been given the principal aim, 'to protect and enhance the environment' taken as a whole so as to contribute to sustainable development, subject to other legislation and 'taking into account any likely costs'.[8] There is no equivalent aim set out for the SEPA. In terms of its remit, the Environment Agency may advise on the National Air Quality Strategy and give guidance to local Air Quality Management Plans.

Criticism of the Agency has come from the current inquiry undertaken by the House of Commons Environment Committee,[9] which has focused on the problem of the Agency meeting its own agenda for its policies rather than on the Agency's impact on the environment.

Section 21 of the 1995 Act provides that the functions of river purification authorities and waste disposal authorities in Scotland, as well as pollution control, shall be exercised by the SEPA. The Agency shall also exercise the functions of local authorities in relation to the release of substances into the air and has a variety of powers to ensure clean air. As mentioned above, the 1995 Act makes detailed provision for the transfer of property rights and liabilities to SEPA to enable it to carry out its functions.

THE EUROPEAN ENVIRONMENT AGENCY

Regulation 1210/90 established the European Environment Agency, which came into being in October 1993. The importance of the Agency is

---

[8]See *Guidance to the Environment Agency on its objectives, including the contribution it is to make towards the achievement of sustainable development* (DoE, 1995).
[9]ENDS Report, 300 p. 35, ENDS Report 298, p. 36 and ENDS Report 299, pp. 31–3.

that it provides member states with information and analysis of the data relating to the European environment. This ensures a broad remit for the Agency which in essence forms a foundation for the information base upon which standards are set. It provides a register and evaluation of relevant data on the environment, assesses the compatibility of the data in terms of making a comparative analysis, disseminates information and provides methods of calculating damage to the environment. The Agency also builds valuable networks between member states and particularly important is the development of a network for the implementation and enforcement of EC law.

The Agency has enormous potential, but in common with many EU institutions, its full potential has yet to be realised. The question of adopting common regulatory standards throughout the EU is within the Agency's remit.

CENTRAL GOVERNMENT AND THE ENVIRONMENT

There are a number of government departments and agencies with responsibilities that include the environment.

The Department of the Environment, Transport and the Regions (DETR)

The DETR was formed on 1 April 1998 and is responsible for a wide range of functions that involve standard-setting. These include roads, planning, local transport, housing, construction, regeneration, the countryside, railways, shipping, aviation, and local and regional government. There are eight executive agencies that come within the remit of the DETR. Key areas for the environment include its responsibilities for the development of policy for the environment, as well as maintaining important links with other government departments where environmental issues are raised. Included within the Department's remit are responsibilities for planning matters, including inner cities, environmental protection, conservation and water.

Within the DETR there is a specialised division dealing with environmental impact assessment, and other divisions dealing with conservation and the countryside. There is also an Environment Protection Strategy Group and an Energy, Environment and Waste Directorate. Significantly from the perspective of science and the environment, the work of the DETR includes that of the Chief Scientist. The Science and Technology Policy Unit provides a link between policy and science and similarly, in the field of health and housing there is a Legal, Health and Safety Group dealing with health-related matters and housing policy. Integration of this kind facilitates standard-setting in the area of housing and health. There are also various scientific advisory committees, such as the Advisory Committee on Releases to the Environment (ACRE).

The Ministry of Agriculture, Fisheries and Food (MAFF)

This department is primarily responsible for government policies on agriculture, horticulture and fisheries in England. The Food Standards Agency takes separate responsibility for setting standards in and ensuring food safety, including labelling and the supervision of additives. MAFF also exercises responsibilities for the protection and enhancement of the countryside and marine environment. There is a Centre for Environment Fisheries and Aquaculture Science that helps to protect the marine environment and an Environment Task Force that oversees environmentally sensitive areas, including environmental aspects of the Common Agricultural Policy of the European Union. Again a number of scientific advisory committees contribute, e.g., the Advisory Committee on Novel Foods and Processes (ACNFP).

The Department of Trade and Industry (DTI)

The DTI is responsible for trade policy, but the Department has an Environment Directorate which coordinates the DTI's strategic policy on environmental issues. Environmental management, ECO-audit regulation and BS 7750 standard-setting are all included within its remit. The DTI incorporates the Office of Science and Technology which provides an important input into the technological side of standards.

The Department of Health

This department has responsibilities for the administration of the National Health Service. One of its divisions is the Health Aspects of the Environment and Food, which deals with many general environmental issues such as radiation and chemical pollution of the environment. It also has responsibilities for toxicology and the chemical safety of food and consumer products.

The Environmental Audit Committee of the House of Commons (EAC)

Established in November 1997, the EAC monitors the government's environment policy and implementation of the national strategy for sustainable development. This is an innovation in the systems that audit and hold to account environmental policy. Alongside the Departmental Select Committee that monitors the work of the DETR, the EAC has enormous potential. Modelled on the Public Accounts Committee which has established an international reputation in the field of public finance, the EAC might adopt a proactive approach in the development of performance measurements to test how far different methods of environmental regulation have become effective. The benefits of this approach might be as follows:

(a) providing confidence-building measures in the development of public responses to the environment;
(b) improving Parliamentary accountability and scrutiny of departmental agencies responsible for the development of an environment policy;
(c) improving systems of monitoring and control.

The Gas and Electricity Markets Authority and the Water Regulator

The Utilities Act 2000 introduces a single authority, the Gas and Electricity Markets Authority, rather than a regulator for each of the gas and electricity industry sectors. In the case of water, the existing structure of OFWAT (which provides the main economic regulation of the industry) may be retained, along with the addition of a new Water Advisory Panel. The water quality standards would be maintained by the Environment Agency.

The key parts of the new arrangements are as follows:

- Powers to review energy policy set against the commitment to address climate change
- Powers to take environmental matters more directly into account
- A mixture of economic instruments, licensing, tradeable assets and pricing to promote competition, protect the consumer and enhance sustainable development strategies
- Measures to enhance the social and economic interests of consumers and to adopt strategies to reduce carbon dioxide emissions to the target of 20 per cent
- A new obligation to supply renewable electricity to be imposed on electricity suppliers
- Environmental policy to be more directed to the different technologies and options may be taken through guidance from the Government to the new regulatory authority.

The new form of regulation provides for a combination of policy guidance from ministers on social and environmental objectives with additional powers to the regulators over the industry in setting performance targets, for example.

LOCAL GOVERNMENT AND THE ENVIRONMENT

Local authorities have wide-ranging duties and responsibilities that have an impact on the environment. They are 'competent authorities' for many EC Directives and regulations, which means that local authorities have a range of legal obligations placed upon them by virtue of membership of the European Union. In addition, they have important enforcement powers over many environmental matters, for example, local authorities possess wide powers under s. 222 of the Local Government Act 1972 to bring an action for public nuisance. Under s. 80 of the Environmental Protection Act 1990, where the local authority conclude that noise amounting to a nuisance exists or is likely to recur in their area, they must serve a notice on the person responsible for the noise.

Local authority powers range from public health, food hygiene, building control and planning policy to trading standards and statutory nuisances. At local authority level the planning department makes important planning decisions within the framework of the Town and Country Planning Acts. Local authorities have also a role in transport, waste collection and management and construction projects, including mineral extraction and change of use. There is usually a planning committee with delegated powers from the full council and account is taken of the various environmental assessment statements under the Town and Country (Assessment of Environmental Effects) Regulations 1988.

There is also an environmental health department which, under the jurisdiction of environmental health officers, has various statutory powers relevant to food and health. The control of smoke, noise and air pollution is also monitored by the local authority in partnership with the Environment Agency. Various statutory duties relevant to consumer protection are exercised by trading standards officers and local government thereby fulfils an important policy role on environmental issues. There are various local government associations throughout Scotland, England, Wales and Northern Ireland. Local authorities may enforce standards within their designated areas, for example s. 222 of the Local Government Act 1972 permits a local authority to bring an action in respect of a public nuisance if it considers it expedient for the promotion or the protection of the interests of the inhabitants of their area. Planning and environmental matters fall within the remit of local authority powers.

Miscellaneous bodies

There are a number of bodies that have an important role in the setting of standards as part of the protection of the environment, which are not part of government departments. There are a number of research councils that provide financial support for environmentally-related research, for example, the Economic and Social Research Council (ESRC) and the Natural Environment Research Council (NERC). Previously, the Science and Engineering Research Council (SERC) and the Agriculture and Food Research Council (AFRC) sponsored projects related to the environment before they were reorganised into three new research councils on 1 April 1994. The new councils are the Biotechnology and Biological Sciences Research Council (BBSRC), the Engineering and Physical Science Research Council (EPSRC) and the Particle Physics and Astronomy Research Council (PPARC). In the case of EPSRC, the Rutherford Appleton and Daresbury Laboratories have been brought under a unified management structure. In general, the BBSRC is key among the new research councils in supporting environmentally-associated research.

There are also a number of bodies that undertake research in particular areas of specialism, such as Horticultural Research International (HRI) which is a charity operating under Next Steps Agency status and sponsored by the Ministry of Agriculture. There is a Pesticides Safety Directorate which became an Executive Agency of MAFF from 1 April 1993 whose main aims are to protect the health of human beings, creatures and plants, and to safeguard the environment. Its role is to ensure the safe, efficient and humane control of pests in advising MAFF on pesticides.

The UK Ecolabelling Board was set up on 2 November 1992 as the body responsible for the administration of the EC ecolabelling scheme within the UK. This scheme is intended to promote the use of goods that have a reduced impact on the environment and to provide better information to the consumer on products from an environmental perspective. The remit of the Board is to encourage industry, retailers and the consumer to be conscious of the environmental impact of products.

The Public Health Laboratory Service comprises a network of 52 microbiology laboratories and 22 specialist epidemiological and reference units throughout England and Wales. Its role is to detect patterns, trends and outbreaks of infectious disease. An important function is to provide methods of disease control and strategies of prevention and it may help to detect and provide solutions to environmental dangers that may affect public health.

The Joint Nature Conservation Committee was established by the Environmental Protection Act 1990 for the purpose of understanding conservation in Great Britain as a whole. It is a Committee of the Countryside Council for Wales, English Nature and Scottish Natural Heritage with independent members drawn from Northern Ireland and the Countryside Commission. Its aims are to provide common scientific standards and to undertake the commissioning of research related to conservation in the UK.

The United Kingdom Atomic Energy Authority was established by statute in 1954 as a statutory corporation (see the Atomic Energy Act 1954 as amended by the Atomic Energy Authority Act 1971). Its aims and functions include the production, use, disposal and storage of atomic energy. It also undertakes research associated with the nuclear industry and ensures the manufacture and the transport of radioactive material under strict conditions. One part of the Authority's trading activities is undertaken by British Nuclear Fuels Ltd (BNF) and the design, operation and supply of plant and equipment is handled by this company. There has been a controversial development of extensive reprocessing facilities at BNF's plant at Sellafield in Cumbria where the reprocessing facilities separate re-usable materials from irradiated fuel produced during nuclear fission. The facilities operate on a commercial basis and there is a commercial market in the import of nuclear waste from other countries.

Another aspect of the Authority's work is undertaken by Radiochemical Centre Ltd, set up under the Atomic Energy Act 1971 and renamed in 1981 as Amersham International. It is operated as a commercial enterprise and supplies radiolabelled materials to research hospitals and industry. Recently, plans were made to privatise parts of the Atomic Energy Authority.

Lastly, under the Deregulation and Contracting Out Act 1994, there is a Deregulation Task Force. Its remit is to identify regulatory burdens on industry and make recommendations for their removal. In its first report, the Task Force identified some of the areas in which business is carrying a heavy regulatory burden and controversially asserted that environmental legislation might place further major burdens on industry and business. The Government's White Paper, *Modernising Government* (Cm. 4310, 1999) sets out the scope for the removal, by secondary legislation, of measures that may be a burden on any trade, business or profession. This strategy may be used to good effect in environmental law terms through simplification of the many, complex environmental instruments. Although simplification of environmental regulation is welcome, the Environment Agency is likely to have to grapple with the problems of deregulation at a time when there is increasing pressure for improvements in environmental standards.

INFORMATION ON THE ENVIRONMENT

Various bodies provide information about the environment that may be used in establishing standards or assist in monitoring the environment. A number of environmental registers must be kept by pollution control agencies and local authorities. Further details are given in Chapters 7, 8 and 9 and access to information not covered by a specific register may be found through one of the central government departments mentioned above or the Environment Agency. The main legal requirements are set out in the Environmental Information Regulations 1992 (EC Directive 90/313, OJ No. L 158/56) and, in the United Kingdom, the Environmental Regulations 1992 (SI 1992 No. 3240).

The following list indicates some of the more important registers for information:

(a) *The Environmental Protection Act 1990.* Registers under Part I of the 1990 Act, containing information relating to integrated pollution control, are maintained by the Environment Agency and various local authority air pollution agencies (see the Environmental Protection (Prescribed Processes and Substances) Regulations 1991). Under the supervision of the various Waste Regulatory Authorities there are registers under Part II that relate to waste on land, under Part IV to litter and under Part VI to GMOs. Under s. 143 of the 1990 Act, registers relating to contaminated land must be kept.

(b) *Town and Country Planning Act 1990.* Registers are maintained of planning applications under s. 69 of the Act, and of enforcement and stop notices under s. 188.

(c) *Water Resources Act 1991.* Registers are provided by the Environment Agency. These are:
   (i)   pollution control registers under s. 190; and
   (ii) registers of abstraction and impounding licences under s. 189.

(d) *Water Industry Act 1991.* The water regulator, the Director General of Water Services, maintains a register on information relating to the appointment and regulation of water and sewerage operators (s. 195), and water quality registers under ss. 67–69 and 213 (also see the Water Supply (Water Quality) Regulations 1989). Registers for the purpose of works discharges are maintained under s. 197. Registers relating to deposits at sea and incineration at sea are maintained under the Food and Environment Protection Act 1985.

(e) *The Clean Air Act 1993.* Local authorities in England and Wales have registers containing information on the emission of pollutants and other substances into the air.

(f) *The Environment Act 1995.* Changes introduced by the 1995 Act include provision for the disclosure of information to the Environment Agency and the SEPA (s. 113). Section 51 provides that the new agencies must make available to the relevant minister information on matters within the responsibility of the agencies. This section is widely drafted to include information that is not within the possession of the agency but which it is reasonable to expect the agency to acquire.

Other registers include the following. Under the Control of Pollution (Amendment) Act 1989 and under the Controlled Waste (Registration of Carriers and Seizure of Vehicles) Regulations 1991, the Waste Regulation Authority has a register of waste carriers. The Control of Industrial Air Pollution (Registration of Works) Regulations 1989 (see the Alkali Act 1906 and Health and Safety at Work etc. Act 1974) provide for industrial air pollution registers to be maintained. There are registers under s. 39 of the Radioactive Substances Act 1993 and under the Environment and Safety Information Act 1988. Registers of noise levels are to be maintained by a local authority under s. 64 of the Control of Pollution Act 1974 (also see the Control of Noise (Measurement, etc.) Regulations 1976).

CONCLUSIONS

The British approach to regulating the environment, described in the past as flexible and informal, has given way to formal and structured systems of regulation. The main characteristics of regulating the environment within the UK are as follows:

(a) There is a diffuse structure to environmental regulation. This structure ranges from the elected form of regulation through government ministers, to appointed agencies with specialist expertise and experience.
(b) There is a tension between generalist forms of regulation and specialist regulatory bodies.
(c) The *ad hoc* nature of regulation creates the style of changing regulatory structures to meet new demands, e.g., in the form of a new Gas and Electricity Markets Authority in the Utilities Act 2000 to replace the individual style of regulation for each energy sector.
(d) Regulation in Britain often depends on the personal preferences and attitudes of government ministers and regulators.

Equally important are the different techniques found in applying standards and regulating the environment:

(a) A broad discretion is given to regulatory agencies.
(b) Different types of standards, targets, performance indicators, licences and contractual obligations are used.
(c) The use of command and control systems is combined with degrees of self-regulation and voluntary agreements.
(d) Policy, ethics and legal obligations, especially from the European Union, are often combined in the common formulation of policy that is required to be implemented.

The future direction and effectiveness of regulation remain uncertain. The Deregulation and Contracting Out Act 1994, with subsequent amendments, points in the direction of allowing market forces greater freedom which may not be compatible with protecting the environment for future generations.

CHAPTER SIX

The Enforcement of Environmental Standards

INTRODUCTION

In previous chapters it has been shown that environmental standards come in many different forms and from a variety of different sources. In this chapter the enforcement mechanisms for environmental standards are examined in some detail. The chapter sets out the main ways in which the legal system may be used to address the question of how standards might be enforced. Enforcement must be considered at both domestic and European levels.

Increasingly, environmental law has moved in the direction of adopting a proactive approach to implementing environmental standards, but there is no uniform method. We address a number of techniques. First there is the role of the courts, which may develop on a case-by-case basis principles for the interpretation of statutes and for strengthening the common law. Judicial review strategies are likely to be intensified, especially with pressure group involvement in strategic challenges to decision-making and the Human Rights Act 1998 is likely to have a major impact in developing judicial attitudes in this area. Standards are likely to become more open to scrutiny than in the past. Secondly, there is the role of agencies such as the Environment Agency. Increasing pressure from the public for the use of criminal prosecutions has resulted in the Agency adopting a more proactive approach in the use of the criminal law, nevertheless, the Environment Agency has still come under criticism for not being more tough in the resolution of criminal prosecutions.

The courts have a dual function in the implementation and enforcement of environmental standards. First, they may enforce standards through the civil and criminal law process as part of the regulatory system and secondly, they may develop their own standards of care or for responsible conduct in adjudicating disputes.

Public opinion is not always a reliable guide for future environmental strategies. However, greater Parliamentary interest in environmental policy is evidenced by the creation in November 1997 of the Environmental Audit Committee of the House of Commons. This is a sign that the environment and the implementation of standards is high on the political agenda. Less certain, however, is the question of whether large companies should be required to make mandatory environmental reports.

Lastly, there is the important influence of the European Union in the implementation of environmental Directives. This strategy has resulted in a more robust response by member states to their obligations under EC law. The question of effective enforcement strategies raises issues about the cost of compliance and the allocation of the financial burden and greater transparency is likely to bring to the fore economic choices for society as to the true cost of protecting the environment and how that burden may be shared.

THE ENFORCEMENT OF ENVIRONMENTAL STANDARDS

Environmental standards come in a variety of forms, and develop as a result of different processes of consultation (see Chapter 1). There is no uniformity of approach and little attempt has been made to codify standards or set uniform procedures for their enforcement. Classification of environmental standards is an invidious task and it is inherent in the nature of standards that they defy easy definition. Providing a strict demarcation line between the different variety of standards may be counterproductive and this reflects the analysis offered in the previous chapters which showed the pragmatic and flexible approach to regulation in Britain. Instead of defined categories, it might be more helpful to consider the way in which standards may be given a legal form.

Environmental standards could form part of the rules enforced through civil or criminal procedures. In that form these are standards that are likely to be mandatory and enforceable. Standards that require compliance may be developed though statute, codes of practice or through the courts creating common law rules that help set standards. This chapter is mainly concerned with legal forms of enforcement through the courts or in other ways requiring legal sanctions.

An example of a common law-developed standard comes from the boundaries of liability in negligence or nuisance determined by the courts in decided cases. In this example the courts operate a flexible and responsive approach to standard-setting, building on a case-by-case basis the elements of safety and the prevention of harm with which an individual is expected to conform.

Because of their diversity environmental standards may form a core of general guidance that informs policy. Perhaps the best example is in the area of planning law, where Planning Policy Guidance forms the basis of setting procedures — and thereby standards — for the development and implementation of planning policy. Such policy may be called in aid in the interpretation of decisions and in the way procedures are applied. There is also a variety of benchmarks that fall within the category of consumer protection involving setting standards. For example, GM food labelling, through the application of the Food Labelling Regulations 1999, requires that genetically modified soya and maize must be clearly labelled unless neither protein nor DNA is present in the genetic modification of the product.[1] The basis of the threat posed by GM modified food formed part of the agenda for the G8 meeting held in July 2000 in Tokyo and it was accepted that an international panel of scientists, modelled on the Intergovernmental Panel on Climate Change, should be formed to establish the risks associated with GM food.

Environmental standards may also be formed through internal agreements or practices. Many, if not all, such standards are not legally enforceable in the same way as those discussed above.

Lastly, there is a useful analogy between standards and the general field of administrative quasi-legislation.[2] Quasi-legislation is a term used to describe the variety of regulations in all their forms that extend beyond primary and secondary legislation and judge-made law that are the main source of law. It is seen by many as an example of the increasing power of the state, and is often ignored by lawyers in their ignorance of this form of rule-making. It is recognised today that there is a wide variety of legal instruments and techniques that form the rules that apply to many aspects of administrative law. Licences, contracts and many different types of economic instruments must also be included.

Environmental standards are an overlooked example of how much the administrative state has expanded. The sources of much administrative

---

[1] ENDS Report 290, p. 49.
[2] Megarry, R., 'Administrative Quasi-Legislation' (1944) 60 LQR 125.

quasi-legislation, such as 'codes, circulars, guidance, official notes and memoranda',[3] describe the different forms that may be used to encompass environmental standards.

THE ROLE OF THE COURTS

The United Kingdom does not have a Ministry of Justice in the continental style. Instead, responsibility for the administration of the courts and court services resides with the Lord Chancellor's Department, complemented by a Judicial Studies Board charged with the education and training of judges, part-time judges and justices. The Court Service Agency was established to provide administrative assistance to the High Court, the Crown Court and a number of other courts and tribunals. The Agency has considerable freedom within its own budgetary controls to set its own performance and activities. The Lord Chancellor's Department has a budget of £2,424 million; two-thirds of this is spent on legal aid, with a departmental staff of 11,000 making the Lord Chancellor's office one of the largest Departments of State. In considering how the courts may be useful in terms of enforcing environmental standards, discussion of the structure and organisation of the courts in England and Wales is required in outline.

There is an important distinction between civil and criminal cases and environmental disputes may fit into either or both categories. The structure of the courts has developed historically and has been reformed only gradually. In civil cases the first-instance courts are the High Court and county courts with the more significant cases heard in the High Court. Appeals lie from the High Court to the civil division of the Court of Appeal, and from there to the House of Lords where leave to appeal is required. The less significant cases are heard in the county court with appeal to the Court of Appeal and to the House of Lords. The Woolf Report identified a number of weaknesses in the administration of justice, including slowness, complexity, expense and inaccessibility. More far-reaching was the finding that a cultural change in the management of cases was needed. The Woolf reforms (contained in the Civil Procedure Rules 1998, as amended) apply to both the High Court and county courts and their focus is to locate the management of litigation in the hands of the courts and away from the parties. The aims and objectives of the new reforms are:

(a) to save expense and encourage an efficient system of justice;

(b) to ensure that the parties to litigation are treated fairly and in an equitable way;

---

[3] See Rawlings, R., 'Concordats of the Constitution' (2000) 116 LQR 257.

(c)   to ensure that each case is dealt with as expeditiously as possible;

(d)   to allocate resources in a fair and proportionate way, taking account of the seriousness of the case and the financial implications for the parties; and

(e)   to look at each case on its merits, but taking into consideration the overall resources allocated to other cases.

Since May 1999, the Woolf reforms, together with a computerised system of case management, have been implemented. There are three procedures available to the citizen. Small claims of not more than £500, or personal injury claims of not more than £5,000, may fall within the small claims procedure. This provides a speedy and simple remedy, with clear steps provided for the final hearing and, if the parties agree, there may be a claim without a hearing. The second procedure is known as fast track, which is available when the small claim track is not being used and the financial value of the dispute is no more than £15,000. It is suitable if the trial is likely to last no more than one day, and the number of expert witnesses is limited to one per field of expertise and there are no more than two fields of expertise involved. The third procedure is multi-track where the court may become proactive in the management of the case. Directions as to time and documentation may be given and a case management conference may be held to limit unnecessary delays. The time of the trial and its management are also within the direction powers of the court.

CRIMINAL LAW AND THE ENFORCEMENT OF STANDARDS

Historical background

As has been outlined in previous chapters, regulation of the environment is the product of a wide range of principles and techniques. Historically English administrative law is weak, with little evidence in the eighteenth and nineteenth centuries of a systematic approach. By the middle of the nineteenth century, self-restraint and self-regulation both dominated the legal culture and the arrangements for regulation. Specific activities were identified and regulation made to fit the special interest of each group involved and little scope was given to proper systems of accountability and participation. In the case of the environment, public health and welfare were dominant in an attempt to focus improvements to meet the ills of society[4] and environment protection or pollution control formed a discrete and partial exception to the generally dismal record of adminis-

---

[4]See Hilson, C., *Regulating Pollution* (Oxford, Hart, 2000).

trative law. The early history of the system of pollution control can be dated from the establishment of the Alkali Inspectorate in 1863, described as 'the world's first pollution-control agency'.[5] Even earlier is the record in the thirteenth century of regulation through Edward I proscribing the burning of tar in ships off the coast of England.

Despite the existence of the various inspectorates set up in the nineteenth century, they depended on cooperation and consensus for their effectiveness. Voluntary compliance and codes of practice with fairly modest enforcement were considered preferable to a more proactive approach and set against this background, the use of the criminal law may be analysed.

A new approach to the use of the criminal law in environmental protection?

In the normal way, the prosecution of a criminal case is taken by the Crown Prosecution Service. The standard of proof in a criminal case is beyond reasonable doubt. Sections 34–39 of the Criminal Justice and Public Order Act 1994 modified the accused's right to silence.

Criminal law and the protection of the environment have to be understood within the general context of how the environment must be regulated. Compliance is a key issue in environmental law, as punishment by its nature is *ex post facto* and there is difficulty in showing that criminal sanctions will act as a deterrent when enforcement strategies are weak. Criminal sanctions have been sparingly used in the enforcement of environmental law, one explanation being that the use of criminal sanctions against a polluter does not fit easily within the traditional analysis of environmental regulation that relies on self-restraint and cooperation. In recent years, however, the consensus of regulation through cooperation has been gradually replaced by a new confrontational approach which arises from a number of influences:

(a) the more proactive and prescriptive approach of the EU to preventing environmental harm;
(b) an increasing awareness that self-regulation may not be effective;
(c) public concern for enforceable environmental standards, such as in food and in animal health;
(d) in the United Kingdom, the creation of a unified Environment Agency under the Environment Act 1995, which has provided an opportunity to strengthen the traditional approach to environmental protection.

---

[5]See Vogel, D., *National Styles of Regulation* (London and Ithaca, Cornell Press, 1986) at 31.

A whole range of sanctions is provided to the Environment Agency, including the possibility of the use of criminal sanctions. Most pollution offences are based on strict liability and an offender who is guilty of accidental spillage or pollution is therefore unable to defend the pollution by showing it was accidental. There is little doubt that this provides the prosecution with very wide powers indeed but, surprisingly even with the advent of the Environment Agency, the numbers of prosecutions are low. Howarth[6] has estimated that convictions for water pollution incidents in prosecutions brought by the National Rivers Authority since September 1989, lie between 300 and 500 per annum.

Various studies[7] have outlined possible reasons for the limited role of criminal prosecutions in the protection of the environment. A balance is often struck between aggressive enforcement and the need for consensus building leading to cooperation between agencies and industry. Doubts exist as to how effective the criminal law may be in preventing pollution. There are many jurisdictions in the world where criminal sanctions against environmental law infringements are more common than in the United Kingdom. An interesting debate in Canada over the past two decades provides a useful point of reference for the principles that should inform whether the criminal law should be used against environmental pollution. However, even in Canada the question of the addition of a specific crime against the environment to the Criminal Code has not received unanimous support.

In the United Kingdom, a number of key points may be made, as follows:

(a) A delicate balance needs to be struck between cooperation over the enforcement of environmental law and the use of criminal sanctions which may inhibit the process of cooperation.

(b) In historical terms there is a widely-felt general perception that regulatory offences are not of the same order of moral severity as crimes against the person or property offences. In fact today there are signs that this perception may be changing. Typical of the approach to crimes against the environment are public attitudes to white collar crimes.

(c) There is also a concern that differentials between the small and large offender would become difficult if general prosecution policy insisted on an increase in criminal prosecutions.

---

[6]Howarth, W., 'Self-Monitoring, Self-Policing, Self-Incrimination and Pollution Control' (1997) 60 MLR 200, at 205.

[7]Hawkins, *Environment and Enforcement*, Richardson, Ogus and Burrows, *Policing Pollution* (Oxford, Oxford University Press, 1982); Hutter, *The Reasonable Arm of the Law* (Oxford, Oxford University Press, 1994).

(d) There are questions about how proportionate the regulatory response to environmental harm should be. Quantifying this is difficult when the costs and chances of success of prosecution have to be balanced against other methods of enforcement. These may include more effective instruments such as damages or compensation, preventative powers to stop the polluter reoffending, and advisory powers to provide proactive prevention systems, including self-monitoring[7] of any potential breach.

(e) There is a long-standing tradition in Britain of not prosecuting for regulatory offences.

(f) Details of current attitudes to enforcement may be found in the Environment Agency's document, *Enforcement and Prosecution Policy*, available from the Environment Agency.

In its own right there is a rationale for making use of the criminal law in that it may set standards which the ordinary citizen is expected to live up to.

The substantive criminal law may contribute to setting standards. Criminal prosecutions may arise from various statutory provisions imposing criminal liability, a common example being the offence of obstructing a regulatory agency from carrying out its powers of inspection. Sections 108–110 of the Environment Act 1995 provide the Environment Agency with a range of powers of entry and enforcement powers to carry out the duties under the 1995 Act with s. 110 making it a criminal offence intentionally to obstruct an authorised person in the exercise of his powers or duties. However, there is a growing recognition that it is only through adequate criminal sanctions that the environment will be protected, but this is an area of considerable controversy. The Law Reform Commission of Canada has argued that the criminal law is 'an instrument of last resort for reaffirming values' and thus it must be used with some restraint in order not to undervalue its importance. Nevertheless, the value of the criminal law is that it helps 'to stigmatise behaviour causing disastrous damage with long term loss of natural resources' (Law Reform Commission of Canada, Study Paper, 1985). This represents a fundamental value in society that can be protected through the criminal law imposing penalties.

Many criminal offences that apply to the environment are offences of strict liability (see *Ashcroft* v *Cambro Waste Products* [1981] 3 All ER 699), underlining the value of the criminal law in the enforcement of environmental standards.

---

[8]Howarth, W., 'Self-Monitoring, Self-Policing, Self-Incrimination and Pollution Control' (1997) 60 MLR 200.

CIVIL LAW AND THE ENFORCEMENT OF STANDARDS

A civil action may provide the means for the court to set standards and provide an overview of the rights of the parties. Civil proceedings arise when an individual who has suffered harm or damage brings an action against the individual or institution that caused the damage, or loss or harm with the complaint based on tort or any other legal wrong. In environmental law the tort of nuisance is frequently the cause of action, where the claimant claims that there has been some unlawful interference with his or her rights involving the use or enjoyment of land. Nuisance is broadly defined to include actual physical interference with the land itself and may arise where there is unnecessary noise, or where the air is polluted. There are limitations on what is actionable, however. Mere interference with the use and enjoyment of land is only relevant in deciding if there may be actionable nuisance. It is not conclusive. Some level of noise discomfort may be considered an acceptable part of living in a busy street, or farmyard smells may be regarded as acceptable while living in the country. There is also the requirement that some real damage must be suffered by the claimant.

Liability may exist because of the rule developed in *Rylands* v *Fletcher* (1868) LR 3 HL 330 which established strict liability (noted above) in civil cases. The rule in *Rylands* v *Fletcher* applies only when persons for their own purpose bring on to the land and maintain there anything which is likely to do mischief should it escape. In such circumstances it may be concluded that *prima facie* there is liability for all damage which is the natural consequence of the escape. There is a requirement that the use of the land must be 'non natural', i.e., out of the ordinary and unusual, the implication being that the bringing of something which has a special use on to the land increases the danger to the public. What constitutes the natural use of land is often highly complicated but guidance can be found in the landmark decision of the House of Lords in *Cambridge Water Co. Ltd* v *Eastern Counties Leather plc* [1994] 1 All ER 53. In this case, their Lordships considered the rule in an action by Cambridge Water claiming damages for alleged negligence, nuisance and liability under the rule in *Rylands* v *Fletcher*. The case is a good example of how modern standards have to be viewed in the context of historic pollution. The chemical perchloroethene was widely used in the tanning industry. Eastern Counties Leather was an old and well-established firm, and when the firm began the knowledge of the dangers of the use of the chemical was limited. The chemical's escape and seepage into the groundwater was detected in water samples taken by Cambridge Water in observance of the standards set by Directive 80/778/EEC on Drinking Water, implemented after the water had been

101

already contaminated. The House of Lords concluded that because the spillages occurred in the past, it could not have been foreseen that harm would have been caused to the water supply. There could be no future liability because the damage had already been done to the land, and this had been unforeseen at the time of the spillage.

The House of Lords' decision provides the basis in legal principle for applying new standards to old pollution. Unless the pollution was foreseen when it first occurred, the burden falls on the present-day user of the land to take responsibility for enforcing the new standards rather than seeking to establish past liability for previous harm. The implication is that the use of the land brings with it responsibility for unforeseen harm. As standards are changing to take account of new scientific discoveries, more accurate understanding and measurement, it is important that the courts provide a workable solution that confronts new developments. This is precisely why the *Cambridge Water* case is such a significant decision for the development of the law on environmental standards.

It must also be remembered that there are other grounds for civil action involving the tort of negligence or trespass and civil liability arising from the imposition of strict liability for ultra-hazardous activities. The continued influence from the European Union creates new expectations of where liability may arise.

EU ENVIRONMENTAL LIABILITY

Over the past three years the European Commission consulted widely before publication of a White Paper on environmental liability. The idea behind the creation of a liability regime within the EU follows on from the analysis that there are common principles that apply throughout the EU and that liability rules should provide incentives for compliance with the rules. Implicit in that analysis is that the courts may increasingly become the arbiters of environmental standards, for example by implementing the polluter pays principle, enhancing the role and status of environmental law and regulation, improving the enforcement of the EU regime in terms of protecting the environment, and promoting harmonisation and integration of EU rules on the environment.[9] The essence of the White Paper is that strict liability should apply for damage to people, property and to the environment arising in the area regulated by the EU, namely in respect of the breach of an existing law or regulation covering a product or activity. In designated sites, such as bird and wildlife habitats, damage to the biodiversity of those sites would also come within the protection afforded by civil liability.

---

[9] ENDS Report 299, p. 47.

The White Paper leaves many issues open to discussion, but it is clear that interest groups or pressure groups can claim protection. Remedies include remedies by way of judicial review, injunctions or damages.[10]

The White Paper is subject to further discussion and debate. No compulsory environmental liability insurance is proposed, though this may become an important safeguard for public bodies. Difficulties with the White Paper include how harm might be quantified, and how the burden of proof might be discharged. It is too soon to say how the proposals will be finally interpreted but it is clear that this marks an important step in the direction of establishing a common standard for civil liability for environmental harm in the EU. The link is made between civil liability and incentives to clean up the environment and in that respect the White Paper may lay the basis for a more uniform approach to standard-setting. For example, in respect of contaminated land it is hoped that further harmonisation will achieve standards common to all the member states.

JUDICIAL REVIEW

In discussing liability for environmental harm we have focused on private law. It is also possible to obtain remedies in public law through an application for judicial review which forms a discrete area of law that is complex and highly specialised. Judicial review is available to challenge decisions or action taken by public bodies and it is important that public bodies are identified and distinguished from private bodies. Private law may be defined as regulating the actions of private persons, whether individuals, corporations or unincorporated associations, in their relationship, with one another. Public law applies only to those individuals or bodies that exercise public law powers. This includes the legislature, central and local government and the large number of fringe organisations that exercise governmental (i.e., usually statutory) powers.

The exclusive nature of the application for judicial review arises because judicial review is not available in private law matters and this point is considered in the House of Lords decision in *O'Reilly* v *Mackman* [1982] 3 All ER 1124. The reason for a separate jurisdiction for public law is that the courts wish to distinguish the way activities of government or governmental agencies are reviewed. Over recent years, though, a more flexible approach to the distinction between public and private law has emerged, such as outlined by the House of Lords in *Roy* v *Kensington and Chelsea FPC* [1991] 2 WLR 239. It must be remembered that the courts have a general

---

[10]ENDS Report 301, p. 42.

residual discretion. As explained in *Pepper* v *Hart* [1993] AC 593, the courts must interpret statutory ambiguity and, on the basis of a wide range of information, give effect to the meaning of legislation as intended by Parliament. However, in *R* v *Secretary of State for the Environment, Transport and the Regions, ex parte Spath Holme Ltd* [2001] 1 All ER 195, the House of Lords adopted a cautious approach with reference to Parliamentary debates and the use of Hansard as a basis for imputing legislative intent in order to challenge the legality of administrative action. A distinction has to be made between the meaning of a statutory expression and the scope of a statutory power. In the former, Hansard might assist in clarifying Parliamentary intent where there is a clear expression of what that intent might mean. In the latter, there is greater difficulty in using Hansard where there is lack of clarity in ministerial statements or where there is ambiguity or contradiction. Lord Brown-Wilkinson in *Pepper* v *Hart* etablished the following criteria for making reference to Hansard:

(a)   Legislation must be ambiguous or obscure or lead to an absurdity.

(b)   The material relied on must consist of one or more statements by a minister or other promoter of the Bill together, if necessary, with such other Parliamentary material as might be necessary to understand such statements and their effect.

(c)   The effect of such statements must be clear.

What is the role of judicial review as regards standards in environmental law? The principle is straightforward, namely that the enforcement of much environmental law depends on various statutory bodies whose decisions are amenable to review by the courts. Judicial review gives the citizen the opportunity to challenge the legality of decisions made by public bodies. In the vast number of planning laws that affect the environment this is the final check or balance offered by the courts. Even the decisions of the Secretary of State may be amenable to review.

An application for judicial review is made to the Queen's Bench Division of the High Court, known as the Divisional Court. The application must be made promptly and within three months of the original complaint. The procedures provided under the application for judicial review are found in CPR, Part 54 and s. 31 of the Supreme Court Act 1981. There are two stages. The first stage requires the applicant to make out an arguable case and show that he has sufficient standing (*locus standi*) in the case, i.e., that the aggrieved person has a sufficient interest in raising the case. At the first stage it is usual for there to be no hearing because the application is made on affidavit evidence and the defendant is not normally represented. If there is a hearing it is before a single judge. At the second stage there is a full hearing of the Divisional Court. Standing may be raised as part of the second hearing, but there is also a full argument of the legal issues raised in the case. The remedies available to the litigant using the application for judicial review include all the private law remedies mentioned in the earlier section on civil cases. These include damages and injunctions or declarations. In addition, but exclusively available under the application for judicial review, are the various prerogative remedies. These are *certiorari* used to quash a decision, *prohibition* to prevent some illegality from taking place, and *mandamus* to command the performance of a public duty. There are technical rules as to which remedy is appropriate on the facts of a particular case.

In terms of enforcing environmental standards, judicial review offers considerable scope for challenging public decision-makers. The most obvious way is for pressure groups to make use of the public law remedies but success is not always guaranteed. In *R v Secretary of State for the Environment, ex parte Rose Theatre Trust Co.* [1990] 1 All ER 754, developers, granted planning permission to erect a block of flats, uncovered what was thought to be an Elizabethan theatre, perhaps dating back to the time of Shakespeare's plays. It was an archaeological site of great importance but the Secretary of State declined to schedule the site under the Ancient Monuments and Archaeological Areas Act 1979. The applicants included well-known public figures in the world of the Arts, who formed a company to campaign for the preservation of the site (which they believed was the Rose Theatre where Marlowe's and Shakespeare's plays were performed). The Divisional Court held that the company did not have sufficient standing and declined to grant a writ of *certiorari* against the Secretary of State.

In *R v Pollution Inspectorate,, ex parte Greenpeace Ltd (No. 2)* [1994] 4 All ER 329, the Divisional Court considered Greenpeace's objections regarding the safety of the Thorp nuclear re-processing plant. The interest of Greenpeace was sufficient to satisfy the court that an application for judicial review should be considered. The issue of standing required the court '... to take into account the nature of Greenpeace and the extent of its interest in the issues raised, the remedy Greenpeace seeks to achieve and the nature of the relief sought' (*per* Otton J, at 349).

Both the above cases illustrate the potential scope of judicial review. Perhaps a better example, where the courts set standards for decision-makers, is *R v Secretary of State for the Environment, ex parte World Development Movement Ltd* [1995] 1 All ER 611. The World Development Movement successfully challenged payments from the British government through the overseas aid budget for the building of a dam at Pergau in Malaysia. The Pergau Dam affair, as the case became known, established that the World Development Movement, an international and well-known pressure group, had standing to sue in the courts. Judicial review exposed internal government decision-making to external scrutiny and revealed some fascinating information about the government's decision to grant aid. It emerged that the Permanent Secretary of the Overseas Development Administration, acting as Accounting Officer, had reservations about the economy and efficiency of the grant in aid to Malaysia for the construction of a dam. The Minister overruled the Accounting Officer's reservations following Treasury procedures notified in writing. As Daintith and Page observed:[11]

> Had the Accounting Officer's objection been on grounds of regularity or propriety, it would than have been his obligation to inform the Treasury and communicate the papers to the Comptroller and Auditor-General; but the objection being on the grounds of economy, no further step needed to be taken beyond informing the NAO [National Audit Office] if it happened to undertake a relevant inquiry.

There are various grounds for judicial review which allow standards to be enforced. The main grounds for review are broadly drawn. They are that a public body has acted outside its powers (*ultra vires*) and this may take a number of forms, e.g., acting in the wrong manner, using the wrong procedures or behaving negligently. For example, the use of guidance issued under an Act of Parliament must be consistent with the authority expressed in the Act of Parliament otherwise it is *ultra vires*.

The legal power to make a decision must be correctly delegated to the requisite legal authority. If it is improperly delegated it may be regarded as *ultra vires*. The courts are reluctant to interfere with the merits or policy behind a decision, which are matters for Parliament, and ministers are accountable to Parliament for the policy of the government of the day. The courts are always vigilant as to the exact nature of the legal powers granted by Parliament, and increasingly their role has expanded from 'filling gaps' through the development of the common law to adopting a proactive approach to laying down standards of behaviour on all public bodies (see, for example, *Associated Provincial Picture Houses Ltd* v *Wednesbury Corporation* [1948] 1 KB 223).

In assessing whether a public body has acted reasonably a number of issues arise. Relevant considerations must be taken into account and irrelevant considerations excluded from the decision. The decision-maker

---

[11]Daintith, T. and Page, A., *The Executive in the Constitution* (Oxford, Oxford University Press, 1999), p. 128.

must not act in breach of the rules of natural justice, meaning that the decision should be free from bias or prejudice and that the citizen is entitled to a fair hearing and to be given an opportunity to be heard. The House of Lords discussed the principles of natural justice in *Ridge* v *Baldwin* [1964] AC 40, *CCSU* v *Minister for the Civil Service* [1985] AC 374 and, more recently, *R* v *Bow Street Metropolitan Stipendiary Magistrates and others, ex parte Pinochet (No. 3)* [1992] 2 All ER 97.

HUMAN RIGHTS AND THE ENVIRONMENT

Environmental cases have shaped the development of human rights in the interpretation of the European Convention on Human Rights (see, e.g., *Osman* v *United Kingdom* (1998) *The Times*, 5 November 1998; also consider *Lopez Ostra* v *Spain* (1995) 20 EHRR 277). The Human Rights Act 1998 (in force on 2 October 2000) is likely to have a profound impact on planning and environmental law, a sign that domestic systems of law are increasingly subject to degrees of internationalisation. In that sense European and international standards become the benchmark of how a legal system is expected to provide rights for its citizens.

In effect, the 1998 Act brings directly within the United Kingdom's domestic law the bulk of the European Convention on Human Rights. Section 19 of the 1998 Act provides for the introduction of a form of judicial preview of legislation. The Minister responsible for a Bill must, before its second reading, make a statement of its compatibility with the 1998 Act, or provide an explanation of why the Bill is being proceeded with. There is no formal entrenchment of the procedures of the Act so future legislation may theoretically repeal the statute. However, this is unlikely as the 1998 Act is sure to be supported by the European Court of Human Rights and domestic courts may give appropriate relief where a public body is said to have acted unlawfully under the Act. The impact of the Act is to provide a 'rights-centred' culture throughout judicial approaches to the interpretation of the law and in the way Parliament is expected to treat legislation. The 1998 Act therefore imports into domestic law the standards expected from the observance of a human rights culture. This is likely to be the basis on which success or failure of legislation will be measured. (See *R* v *Secretary of State for the Environment, Transport and the Regions, ex parte Holding and Barnes plc* (13 December 2000).)

The potential impact of the 1998 Act in giving rights to citizens is controversial. Will the Act be useful in dealing with claims between private parties? The answer depends on interpreting the scope of the statute. Section 6(1) provides that 'it is unlawful for a public authority to act in a way which is incompatible with a Convention right'. The scope of what is a public authority is likely to become the subject of litigation and, in addition, there is the question of whether the Act will have 'horizontal effect' or only 'vertical effect'. In the case of the latter, citizens will be protected only against the acts of public authorities; if the former, private citizens will be protected against each other.[12] In common with many of the current discussions on the potential scope of the Act, it remains to be seen what will be the interpretation given to it by the courts. The arguments in favour of giving a broad scope to the definition and overall remit of the 1998 Act rest on the assumption that the Act should be interpreted as giving individual rights to citizens. There is a 'predilection'[13] implicit in the Act in favour of horizontal effect. If this appears persuasive then the 1998 Act will be given horizontal effect. Those who favour vertical effect only may find support from the judiciary on the assumption that the impact of the 1998 Act should be adopted on a case-by-case basis. There is then the possibility that the 1998 Act may fall foul of the Convention itself and in such a situation the final decision about horizontal or vertical effect may be delivered though the jurisprudence of the European Court of Human Rights.[14]

In the area of the environment, an interpretation in favour of horizontal effect is likely to have some additional significance. It is clear that regulatory bodies, such as public authorities with statutory powers, will be subject to the 1998 Act but private bodies may also be affected with important practical consequences. Utility companies, when exercising their statutory powers as public authorities, will certainly fall within the provisions of the 1998 Act, but how far does this extend?

It is clear that if horizontal effect is adopted, the impact of the 1998 Act is likely to permeate almost all aspects of the information and procedures that apply to environmental decision-makers. Particularly sensitive is the privilege against self-incrimination. The scope of this protection, con-tained in Article 6 of the Convention, extends to the right of the citizen to a fair trial in civil and criminal proceedings and the right to a fair trial includes the right to a reasoned decision, the opportunity to present a case, the right to counsel and so on. An independent and impartial tribunal is also a requirement. Rules of evidence and the presumption of innocence

---

[12]See Wade, H. W. R., 'Horizons of Horizontality' (2000) 116 LQR 217. Contrasting views may be found in Hunt, M., 'The "Horizontal Effect" of the Human Rights Act' [1998] PL 423; Buxton, LJ, 'The Human Rights Act and Private Law' (2000) 116 LQR 48.

[13]See Wade, op. cit. n. 12, at 221, who quotes Markesinis, (1999) 115 LQR 47, at 85.

[14]The most helpful analysis about the Convention in general is to be found in Gearty, C., (ed.), *European Civil Liberties and the European Convention on Human Rights* (London, Martinus Nijhoff Publishers, 1997).

all fall within the scope of the Convention and this allows considerable scope for judicial interpretation. Decisions that are a matter of routine under the planning system of the United Kingdom may become subject to review (see *Bryan* v *The United Kingdom* [1996] JPL 386). Enforcement notices, planning inquiries and the granting of various consents under the planning legislation all fall within the scope of human rights law.[15]

Enforcement agencies may find that a distinction between investigative and trial processes is required (see *Saunders* v *UK* (1996) 23 EHHR 313). In *Saunders*, information was required to be given by the defendant in investigations conducted by the Department of Trade and Industry under the Companies Act 1995. If the defendant refused, the refusal was subject to a criminal prosecution. The same information was later used against the defendant in a criminal trial arising out of the earlier investigation. The obtaining of the information in such circumstances was sufficient to deny the defendant a fair trial. In general, requirements to answer questions may be challenged, though unsuccessfully in the recent case *R* v *Hertfordshire County Council, ex parte Green Environmental Industries Ltd* [2000] 1 All ER 773, HL.

The Convention also provides substantive rights. Article 8, for example, sets out private and family rights. The scope of the protection is widely drawn, subject to Article 8(2) where rights may be interfered with '. . . as is in accordance with the law and is necessary in a democratic society in the interests of national security, public safety or the economic well-being of the country, for the prevention of disorder or crime, for the protection of health or morals, or for the protection of the rights and freedoms of others'. This opens up the possibility of considering how the right to enjoyment of one's home is protected (see *Buckley* v *The United Kingdom* [1996] JPL 1018). Article 8 also raises questions about the right to enjoy freedom from noise or disturbance. In *Rayner* v *United Kingdom* (1986) 47 DR 5, the question of aircraft noise was considered by the Commission and whether this fell within the protection afforded by Article 8 of the Convention.

It may be concluded that the way ahead is likely to be uncertain for some time, although there is the expectation that in the early days there will be some judicial self-limitation over how far human rights and the environment will be intertwined. Pressure groups will see the prospect for debating policy issues through the courts and environment protection agencies are likely to be reactive to the changing nature of the discourse on the environment. So much about everyday life is affected by our

---

[15]See Tromans, S., 'Human Rights and the Environment Procedures, Information, Discrimination and Access to Justice' in Neil Faris and Sharon Turner, *Public Law and the Environment* (UKELA Conference, Belfast, 16–19 April 1999), at 27–37.

surroundings, that the right to life itself may depend on strengthening the legal regime for the protection of the environment. Access to environmental information will of necessity become a crucial part of the debate on human rights and the environment (see *R* v *Secretary of State for the Environment, ex parte Slot* [1998] JPL 693; *McGinley and Egan* v *UK* (1999) 27 EHRR 1).

AN ENVIRONMENT COURT?

The creation of an environment court for England and Wales has been the subject of intense debate. Professor Patrick McAuslan[16] in 1991 canvassed the idea based on the need for specialist expertise, covering a wide range of economic, legal and fiscal instruments that form the core to the regulation of the environment. More recently, a Report undertaken for the DETR has examined the idea from a fresh perspective.[17] The impending growth in judicial review, the increasing use of human rights concepts and the fact that the ordinary courts are faced with a vast array of environmental law to interpret and analyse, all are being considered as relevant to the development of an environment court. The arguments against any such move concern the existing orthodoxy accepted in the United Kingdom that the courts have general jurisdiction and that a specialist court would upset the ordinary values of the common law, supported by Dicey's inheritance[18] and opposition to *droit administratif* in 1885. A further problem is that there is little coherence in the formulation, or indeed the definition, of what is environmental law at present, and this may provide problems for the jurisdiction of such a body if it were established.

There are examples (such as in New Zealand and New South Wales) where a form of environment court works well. Various models of the type of environmental jurisdiction are examined in the DETR Report and the main substance of the proposals includes consideration of whether to introduce an environment court with a two-tier structure, as follows:

(a) A staged development of an environment court based around the transfer of the Planning Inspectorate into the court. Such an environment court might operate on the basis of the Woolf principles outlined above, and the jurisidiction of the court might exclude criminal matters, judicial review and a general civil jurisdiction.

---

[16]McAuslan, P., 'The role of courts and other judicial type bodies in environmental management' (1991) JEL 195.
[17]DETR, *Environmental Court Project: Final Report* (June 2000).
[18]McEldowney, J., *Public Law*, 2nd edn. (London, Sweet and Maxwell, 1998).

(b) The new environment court might operate on two tiers. One tier would comprise the work of tribunals or the jurisdiction of planning inspectors. The second tier would be based on its court functions, i.e., a reserve jurisdiction from the High Court with the capacity for a hearing of the main issues.

(c) A number of changes might be made to the jurisdiction of the magistrates' courts, especially in terms of sentencing powers for environmental offences.

The proposal for developing an environment court is relevant to the overall question of the future direction of environmental law. If such a court is introduced then the opportunity to systematise the regulation of environmental law should be taken. It is difficult to envisage one without the other.

CONCLUSIONS

The questions arise as to the effectiveness of legal enforcement of environmental standards and how environmental standards might be implemented. As outlined above, the courts have a dual function. First, they provide the means for the implementation and enforcement of regulatory standards. This allows grievances to be adjudicated and solutions found. Secondly, in the role of conflict resolution, the courts set their own performance standards through slowly evolving the common law on a case-by-case basis. In this second function the courts may set the limits on human behaviour through imposing levels of civil and criminal liability which it is hoped will ensure safety and good practice.

The impact of the jurisprudence of human rights on environmental matters should not be underestimated. There is bound to be a period of some uncertainty during which the courts will have to decide whether the Human Rights Act 1998 has vertical or horizontal effect. A cautious approach is advisable during the early stages of interpreting the impact of the Act. Decision-makers will have to be conscious of the following factors:

- Fairness in procedures and in the collection of evidence is essential.
- Investigations pending civil or criminal proceedings should not inter-fere with the self-incrimination protection afforded to citizens (see *Saunders* v *United Kingdom* (1996) 23 EHRR 313).
- Consultation processes need to be fair, open and adequate.
- Standards should be verifiable and the data must be capable of supporting the appropriate standard.

- Scientific expertise should encourage transparency and openness in making evaluations based on scientific data.
- Litigation may raise issues of rights when in the past adjudication and decision-making focused primarily on problem-solving.
- The courts may adopt a more interventionist stance in upholding environmental standards.

Environmental standards are so widely drawn that it is difficult to seek uniformity and coherence in their application. The future development of standards will require greater uniformity in approach and coherence in terms of explanation and analysis. Standards will have to be capable of interrogation to ensure that they are fully reasoned and supported by the best available scientific evidence. This inevitably leads to the following conclusions:

- Numerically-based standards should be capable of open and transparent analysis supported by sound science based on verifiable results.
- Non numerically-based standards that include economic or fiscal instruments must be clearly supported with analysis and implementation strategies.
- Standards that allow discretion must ensure that the discretion is reasonably exercised.
- International and European standards must be fully integrated into the domestic system of standard-setting.
- There should be a commonly agreed protocol for the drawing up and implementation of standards.

PART TWO

Specified Environmental Standards

CHAPTER SEVEN

Environmental Standards and Water

INTRODUCTION

The application of specific standards to water is considered in this chapter. Techniques to protect freshwater, groundwater and marine environments through standard-setting will be discussed and European and international standards are considered within the overall context of the United Kingdom. Changes in the regulatory structure of the water industry, the adoption of economic instruments in the case of water abstraction, and the creation of a new competition structure for the industry under the Competition Act 1998 are also considered.

Water is a scarce resource that is essential for life. There are a number of different water ecosystems, including freshwater, groundwater and marine. Water is used for many purposes — drinking, agricultural use, food manufacture, industrial processes and power generation and it directly supports industries such as marine fisheries and the shellfish industry, and fish farming. Water systems contribute to transport and a variety of recreational activities, e.g., swimming and sailing. Sewage and industrial waste is commonly discharged both to marine systems and to freshwater and any one water resource may be used at any one time for multiple purposes. For example, a river may be used for water abstraction for agriculture, industry or drinking water, as a receiving body for effluent, for recreational purposes, and will support the natural wetland and terrestrial ecosystems through which it flows. Judgments are made on the suitability of a given water resource for different roles based on standards set through scientific criteria and, given this diversity in water use, its importance as a resource and the significance of water to natural environments, its protection is demanding and is an essential element of sustainable development.

It is crucial that standards applied to water form an integrated management of this precious resource. A major regulatory focus on water is setting standards to prevent pollution of rivers, etc. and applying standards to ensure that the use of water is safe for wildlife and humans. There are water quality standards that apply, for example, to rivers and coastal waters. Standards for monitoring pollution and preventing pollutants entering aquatic environments are a vital part of successful management of water resources. Monitoring and controlling drinking water is based on setting standards.

Standards for water have been developed on an incremental basis and two influences are apparent in this area. First, the law of the European Community has been significant, especially with regard to the protection of drinking water and marine life. The second influence comes from international law where a number of United Nations Conferences and Conventions[1] have contributed to the setting of water standards.

In recent years, the privatisation of the water industry has resulted in increasing pressure for water standards to be enforced in a more transparent way than previously. Scientific standard-setting has encouraged higher standards in the water industry as a whole, and has required and will continue to require substantial investment in processes and process development to ensure that the standards are achieved. The use of criminal prosecutions for polluting freshwater and groundwater ecosystems is not uncommon and pressure on the Environment Agency and water regulators to ensure that high standards are delivered is intense.

In developing standards for water there are additional benefits. Scientific research is encouraged to provide information about the quality of water and to develop effective processes to protect water resources. Over the years increasing scientific knowledge has given rise to concerns that either have been substantiated as problems that should be addressed through standards, or which have been found to have smaller environmental impacts than initially thought. Examples include:

(a) Heat or thermal pollution entering rivers. Electricity generation requires substantial water to cool and maintain generating plants.

---

[1]Montego Bay 1982, oil pollution: see Convention for the Prevention of Pollution of the Sea by Oil, London (1954) amended in 1962.

This process raises the temperature of the cooling water, and some of the heated water is returned to rivers. There was considerable concern during the 1950s and 1960s about the potential environmental harm caused by this thermal pollution. Rivers could be affected physically (e.g., through a change in water density), chemically (e.g., lower oxygen solubility) and biologically (e.g., different growth rates in organisms). In fact it has been found that the impacts of heat pollution from cooling water are not as great as originally feared and are highly localised. Indeed, they may even be used beneficially, e.g., in aquaculture.[2]

(b) A range of chemicals (e.g., organochlorine and organophosphate pesticides) has been assessed in acute toxicity studies (see Chapter 4) for their impact on a variety of invertebrates and fish. The toxicity effects can be large and the establishment of LC_{50}s for a range of species can aid in establishing river quality standards.[3] The problems associated with fertiliser (particularly nitrate) run-off from agricultural land are considerable. The adverse effects of this eutrophication are now well-researched and well-established. They include significant physical and chemical changes in water, with a consequent major reduction in species diversity.[4] The European Union has responded to this problem through the introduction of standards for fertiliser use by farmers in areas where water courses are at high risk, i.e., nitrate-sensitive areas.

(c) A recent challenge in terms of scientific uncertainty (see Chapter 4) is the possible impacts of endocrine disrupting chemicals on aquatic ecosystems and on human health, e.g., through exposure in drinking water. The Royal Society has highlighted the need for further study to elucidate the potential effects of these compounds.[5] As yet there is a dearth of scientific data, but growing suspicions about the possible significance of endocrine disrupting chemicals have led to funding for research in this area from relevant government departments, the Environment Agency and the research councils. As scientific understanding increases it may be necessary to establish drinking water standards, effluent dis-

---

[2]Mason, C. F., *Biology of Freshwater Pollution*, 2nd edn (Harlow Longman, 1995) see at 189–98 for a succinct consideration of thermal pollution.

[3]Haslem, S. M., *River Pollution and Ecological Perspective* (Chichester, Wiley, 1994) provides some useful lists of LC_{50}s for selected freshwater species and various pesticides. See esp. 82–85.

[4]McEldowney, J. and McEldowney, S., *Environment and the Law* (Harlow, Longman, 1996); see at 136–7 for a brief description of the impacts of eutrophication.

[5]The Royal Society, *Endocrine disrupting chemicals (EDCs)* (June 2000), at 1–16.

charge standards and river quality standards for endocrine disrupting chemicals. Many of the compounds that may act as endocrine disrupting agents have standards set for them already because of other effects, but some do not. Pharmaceutical compounds, for example, are not regulated in terms of environmental effects even though they may be discharged to the environment in sewage. Any standards based on effects of chemicals as 'hormone mimics' are likely to be set at low levels since they elicit their effects at extremely low concentrations. This will inevitably place considerable demands on the development of appropriate reduction technologies, with substantial potential economic burdens for the water industry.

THE GENERAL STRATEGY FOR SETTING WATER STANDARDS

Point and diffuse pollution

In the United Kingdom, the water pollution control system under Part II of the Water Resources Act 1991 applies to coastal waters and territorial waters extending three miles from shore. The pollution control system also applies to inland freshwaters, including lakes, ponds, specified reservoirs, rivers and watercourses. The 1991 Act also contains a definition of 'controlled water' and extends to groundwater and the breadth of this definition provides a wide use of powers that also extends to inland waterways.

Pollution control rests on a distinction between 'point' source pollution and 'non-point' source (or diffuse) pollution. Point sources are clearly identifiable sources of discharges into watercourses from a particular location and are typified by a drain or a pipe deliberately constructed to conduct effluent from a particular point into a watercourse. Discharges from point sources can be continuous in character, for example, discharges from a sewage treatment plant, chemical effluents, discharges from food and drink manufacturing, etc. The continuous nature of the discharges does not imply that they are constant in terms of the volume discharged or the composition and concentration of substances in the discharge and indeed they may be highly variable with time. The substances or contaminants from point source discharges, of course, vary with the particular source, e.g., metal mine drainage will have very different composition and effects than effluent from the food industry. Point source discharges often contain a cocktail of chemicals and other substances that may have substantial individual effects on a water ecosystem. Chemicals may interact in several ways in their effects (see Chapter 4), and with the variable composition of effluent the impacts of a discharge to the environment may be difficult to foresee. Some point sources may discharge intermittently and actually be quite difficult to predict in their occurrence, volume and composition and rain is often a key determinant. Such point sources include urban stormwater drains and discharges arising from farmyards. Typically, the concentration of contaminants declines rapidly with distance from a point source but there can be exceptions to this. For example, chemicals arising from a point source can be transported by currents to other sites where they may accumulate because of local environmental conditions.

Non-point sources (e.g., agriculture run-off, urban run-off and leachate from landfill) arise from a wide area and diffuse sources also include the deposition of atmospheric pollutants, e.g., acid rain. Non-point sources of pollutants are often difficult to identify and may have variable composition. Their discharge to watercourses is considerably effected by rain, etc.[6] and they tend to be low-concentration discharges which elicit chronic effects in the receiving body. There are, of course, areas of overlap and a single source might result in both point and non-point source pollution. For example, pesticide applications may be limited to a fairly specific area or may occur over a large area.

Adopting the distinction, in the case of 'point sources' pollution is controlled principally through a regulatory authority giving advance consent for effluent to be discharged into a watercourse subject to specified conditions and controls. In effect, individual standards are set for each effluent discharged. 'Non-point' pollution is primarily intended to be prevented through tight controls precluding releases from taking place and where they do occur, there are legal controls to attempt to minimise the effects. One example of an attempt to control diffuse pollution is through nitrate-sensitive zones and the restricted application of fertilisers. However, both 'point sources' and 'non-point' systems of control are subject to accidental or unintended events. In the case of 'point source' pollution, an attempt is made to build strategic plans into the system of pollution control where, for example, there is unexpected flooding.

Strategies to Protect Aquatic Environments

The development of a strategic plan to tackle pollution has had a chequered history in the European Union. The 1974 Paris Conven-

---

[6]See McEldowney and McEldowney, *op. cit.* n. 4, at 195–6 (Table 10.1) for a summary of point and diffuse sources and their composition.

tion on the Prevention of Marine Pollution from Land-based Sources resulted in a general strategy. A framework was provided under the Dangerous Substances in Water Directive (76/464/EEC) and added to by Directive 96/61 on integrated pollution prevention and control. The aim of Directive 76/464 was to eliminate certain types of pollution and reduce other types. The Directive applies to the entire aquatic environment and standards of enforcement are applied through lists of substances (129 substances are listed). List I, otherwise known as the 'black list', contains substances whose toxicity makes it undesirable to release them into the aquatic environment. They are set out in terms of families and groups of substances, and any individual compound that belongs to them should not be discharged to water; or if they are, the discharge must be reduced to safe levels. (Also see the Trade Effluents (Prescribed Processes and Substances) Regulations 1989 (SI 1989 No. 1156) as amended by SI 1990 No. 1629 and SI 1992 No. 339.) List I substances include:

(a) organohalogen compounds and substances which may form such compounds in the aquatic environment;
(b) organophosphate compounds;
(c) organotin compounds;
(d) substances the carcinogenic activity of which is exhibited in or by the aquatic environment;
(e) mercury and its compounds;
(f) cadmium and its compounds;
(g) persistent mineral oils and hydrocarbons of petroleum;
(h) persistent synthetic substances.

The List I standard is set on toxicity studies of the compounds, their tendency to persist in the environment and their biomagnification potential. These compounds have the general effect of lowering water quality and they may be toxic to water or sediment organisms, thereby causing changes in community structure, function and diversity. Chronic, sub-lethal effects may occur, e.g., reducing reproductive success or resulting in changed fitness.[7]

List II, the 'grey list', includes substances such as a range of metalloids (e.g., arsenic), metals (e.g., nickel), biocides (i.e., substances that taint water in some way) and cyanides. (For an updated list, see the Surface Waters (Dangerous Substances) (Classification) Regulations 1977 (SI 1977 No. 2560) and 1998 (SI 1998 No. 389).) These are regarded as less

---

[7]Mason, *op. cit.* n. 2, chs 6 and 9 provides some discussion of the effects of these types of pollutants.

dangerous than List I substances but are still harmful, and they can only be discharged under appropriate authorisation.

There are clear scientific limitations in establishing the impacts and risk associated with compounds released to the environment (see Chapter 4). The assessment for inclusion in Lists I and II, and for many discharge authorisations, is primarily based on the ecotoxicology, etc. of individual substances with little consideration of the effects of other substances in a mixture. In liquid effluent there is commonly a mixture of substances and any receiving water is likely to contain a variety of compounds, which raises the question of the efficacy of scientific assessments using existing techniques. Inclusion of substances not currently designated under the Directive must be under continual review to take account of increased scientific understanding and perhaps improved assessment techniques and there must be sufficient flexibility within the Directive to incorporate other compounds and substances when scientific evidence indicates that this is necessary (see Chapter 4). A proactive and responsive regulatory system substantially supports protection of the aquatic environment through standard-setting.

Measures to minimise or prevent pollution

There is a considerable regulatory challenge in adopting a system of regulation that is capable of prioritising different levels of contamination. The law is intended to prescribe different qualities of water for different purposes. The characteristics of the British approach to water quality regulation are described by Bell and McGillivray as follows:[8]

> Indeed, the traditional British approach to water quality regulation has been to defend the view that it makes no sense to start by asking 'what dangerous substances should we prevent from entering water?' since many susbtances can have a damaging impact on water quality in sufficient quanties.

Despite the historical development of 'best practicable means', from the time of the Rivers Pollution Prevention Act 1876, there are problems in addressing the way modern agriculture and industry operate. The variety and diversity of discharges provide a difficult enforcement problem, which is particularly acute where the chemical industry is concerned.

---

[8]Bell, S. and McGillivray, D., *Environmental Law*, 5th edn (London, Blackstone Press, 2000), p. 554.

One strategy that can contribute to the protection of aquatic ecosystems is regulation of the level of effluent treatment prior to discharge. This has an implication as to the technology applied in the treatment, and for investment in appropriate technology. The standard is set for the treatment, and in conjunction with this standards will also be applied to the discharge itself, e.g., through a discharge consent (see below). One example of the type of measure that contributes to increased protection for watercourses is the Urban Waste Water Treatment Directive (91/271/EEC: see SI 1994 No. 2841, the Urban Waste Water Treatment (England and Wales) Regulations 1994) under which the level of treatment required for urban waste water and sludge disposal is controlled.

Sewage treatment can be divided into three different levels:

(a) *primary* (or sedimentation) treatment — suspended solids are separated out forming sludge;

(b) *secondary* (or biological) treatment — microorganisms degrade dissolved and colloidal organics;

(c) *Tertiary* treatment — produces a high quality effluent, e.g., reducing numbers of bacteria in the effluent, suspended solids, biological oxygen demand, nitrates and toxic compounds, etc. The technology used for tertiary treatment depends on the objectives set for the treatment.

The level of treatment is related to the population size being served by the sewage treatment works. Treatment level is also partly related to the likely dispersion of any discharge by the receiving water and to the water quality objectives (WQOs) (see below) set for the receiving water. Considerable investment might be required by water companies to improve treatment processes depending on the designation of the receiving water. One of the aims of this Directive is to enable re-use of water, as well as to protect the receiving body. If water is to be abstracted downstream of a sewage discharge, for drinking water, then tertiary treatment of the effluent is required. In the UK some 30 per cent of drinking water is now abstracted downstream from an effluent point source.

Measures to prevent pollution are also found in the Environment Act 1995. Under this Act, the Environment Agency has powers to serve a notice on potential polluters requiring them to carry out works to an appropriate standard to prevent pollution. In addition, powers are given to ensure that any pollution is cleaned up to appropriate standards. It is an offence not to comply with any notice served on this basis (see the Water Resources Act 1991, ss. 161A–161C, inserted by the Environment Act 1995, sch. 2). In the event of failure to comply then the Environment Agency has powers (under s. 161 of the Water Resources Act 1991) to carry out the work to a suitable standard and to recover the costs. These can be seen clearly as precautionary measures.

Preventative measures can also be taken in terms of diffuse pollution, imposing standards for the maximum use of materials that might contribute to such 'non-point source' pollution. Directive 91/676/EEC on the Protection of Waters against Pollution Caused by Nitrate from Agricultural Sources is intended to control diffuse nitrate pollution. The vulnerability of areas to nitrate pollution is determined, the areas are zoned on the basis of this assessment, and restrictions are placed on fertiliser applications to farmland on the basis of the zoning. Nitrate leaching into rivers and lakes, and even coastal waters causes cultural eutrophication, which occurs because of an increased burden of nutrients in the water that causes algal blooms and a substantial reduction in biodiversity.[9] The Directive also sets maximum permissible limits of nitrates in drinking water (see below). There is a Code of Good Agricultuural Practice for the Protection of Water issued under s. 116 of the Water Act 1989 (now s. 97, Water Resources Act 1991), which sets a code for nitrate fertiliser application and applies not only to those farmers in nitrate-sensitive areas, but also to farmers throughout the country as a preventative measure.

Many of the standard-setting techniques employed to protect water come from EC Directives. Over time new Directives are added to the suite of existing ones, which set values and limit the permissible levels of substances. Standards are thereby created in an incremental form, modified over time and implemented gradually. The standards set a minimum, utilise the best knowledge of the time and provide monitoring procedures. The Directives, then, are responsive in the setting of standards, but flexible and regular review is essential. The setting of standards within Directives should be a transparent process, as for all standard-setting, to ensure public confidence in the preventative and protective measures taken in the Directives. They represent part of the techniques that provide for precaution in pollution control with member states free within the constraints agreed with the Commission to set additional regulations improving the quality of discharges.

WATER QUALITY OBJECTIVES AND STANDARDS

The key to determining the limits of point source discharges, set through the legal granting of consents, is to ensure that they do not have a

---

[9]See McEldowney and McEldowney *op. cit.* n. 4, at 136–8, and Mason, *op. cit.* n. 2, ch. 4 for discussion on the effects of eutrophication.

deleterious or adverse effect on the receiving water. This may be achieved through setting water quality objectives (WQOs) for surface waters. WQOs form part of the management system for watercourses and may contribute to the sustainable use of rivers and other water bodies.

WQOs are based partly on the uses or the potential future uses (e.g., if levels of pollution are reduced) of the water resource. Statutory water quality objectives (SWQOs) are set under s. 82 of the Water Resources Act 1991 for watercourses in England and Wales and note should also be made of the Surface Waters (River Ecosystem) (Classification) Regulations 1994 (SI 1994 No. 1057). The Environment Agency, exercising its water pollution control powers, ensures that SWQOs, which classify water on the basis of a number of scientifically derived quantitative standards, are met. These quantitative standards include:[10]

- dissolved oxygen
- total and un-ionized ammonia
- biological oxygen demand (BOD) (a measure of the biologically oxidisable, i.e. biodegradable, material present in an effluent. If this is too high the water is likely to become deoxygenated and unable to sustain many aquatic organisms, e.g., fish);
- the pH (acidity/alkalinity) measure
- copper and zinc.

SWQOs set under the Act have a target class (classification) and a target date for compliance. Some of the standards used in WQOs originate from European Community Directives and the List I (black list) substances. There are six classifications of rivers (e.g., related to river uses), which reflect requirements of EC Directives. These are:

(a) River or Fisheries Ecosystem (EC Directive 75/440/EEC, the Surface Waters (Fisheries Ecosystem)(Classification) Regulations 1994 (SI 1994 No. 1057) and the Surface Waters (Classification) Regulations 1989 (SI 1989 No. 1148)).

(b) Special Ecosystem (which protects rivers with high conservation value).

(c) Abstraction for Potable (Drinking) Water Supply (EC Directive 75/440/EEC and the Surface Waters (Classification) Regulations 1989 (SI 1989 No. 1148)).

---

[10]Everard, M., 'Water Quality Objectives as a management tool for sustainability' (1994) 4 *Freshwater Forum* 179, provides detail on standards set to achieve water quality objectives.

(d) Agricultural Abstractions (EC Directive 75/440/EEC and the Surface Waters (Classification) Regulations 1989 (SI 1989 No. 1148)).

(e) Industrial Abstractions.

(f) Watersports.

Once the classification of use for a watercourse is established and the WQOs are set, any consent conditions for individual discharges are established to ensure that the water resource remains within the designated SWQOs. Discharge standards are, of course, determined by the particular effluent being controlled, but may vary for the same type of effluent according to location. Thus discharges to a receiving water considered to have a large capacity to dissipate or assimilate contaminants are likely to have lower consent standards than if the watercourse is highly sensitive to perturbation.

There is some criticism of this approach on two fronts. First, because of the nature of WQOs the individual standards are set at the highest acceptable values. In other words, WQOs are not sufficiently demanding and may not encourage continuous improvement of water quality. In some ways this is addressed through classifying a river on the basis of an enhanced level of future use. The second criticism comes from the problem of enforcing individual quality standards and there is some tension in this respect between different EU countries. Some set uniform emission standards (UESs), which embody the philosophy that the level of discharge to a water should not be determined by the existing quality of the receiving water, or its ability to disperse and dilute the pollutants or the use to which it is put. Rather, discharges should be reduced to the lowest possible level and be uniform with recycling or recovery of pollutants given priority. In a sense this type of strategy is more in line with the current UK strategy on waste management, which encourages 'waste reduction, reuse and recovery (including recycling) and the safe disposal of remaining wastes'.[11]

FRESHWATER, GROUNDWATER AND SEAWATER PROTECTION UNDER EC DIRECTIVES

There is a range of Directives that are intended to protect water resources and ecosystems through the application of standards, often numerical standards. These either limit discharges of selected substances, or control activities that may contribute to pollutant loads. Directives may also seek to ensure that the water is of sufficient standard for its intended use.

---

[11]See *This Common Inheritance — The Third Report* (London, HMSO, 1995).

Sampling techniques and regulation

The sampling regime to monitor the achievement of the standard is usually set in the Directive, as are the monitoring techniques to be used and the number of samples to be taken. For example:

(a) The number of samples taken at any one time and the frequency of sampling may be based on the population size served and the characteristics of the receiving water. Sampling may be limited to particular times of the year, e.g., under the Bathing Water Directive (76/160/EEC) to a designated bathing season.

(b) How the samples are to be obtained and the analytical methods used may be stipulated.

(c) Compliance with the standard is often in terms of the 95 percentile. Recorded values must be less than the stipulated values for all criteria at least 95 per cent of the time and be in excess of the values no more than 5 per cent of the time. Derogations from the standards are allowed if climatological or geographical factors make them impossible to achieve.

(d) Both mandatory values (I values) and more stringent guideline values (G values) are often set, as is a time for compliance. The G values are expected to be worked towards in the long term.

The Bathing Water Directive is a case in point. The European Commission took action under Article 169 against the United Kingdom for a failure to conform to the quality standards set in the limit values of the Directive (*Commission* v *United Kingdom* (case C–56/90)). In 1985, the date set in the Directive for the implementation of the quality standards, the UK designated only 27 resorts as Bathing Waters, ignoring the vast majority. The European Court of Justice rejected this approach and accepted that there had been a failure to implement the Directive in the appropriate way.

Standardisation in techniques is necessary to ensure consistency and comparability in monitoring and measurement procedures. If different assessment techniques are used, major variations in measurement might result, for example, different types of analytical equipment vary in the error associated with measurements and their lower detection limit. Variation in how a sample is taken (e.g., top metre of water or just above a sediment) and stored might also introduce disparity in results. Thus, within any given Directive setting standards, e.g., for bathing water quality, there are also standards set for the procedures used. The responsive nature of standard-setting should not only be through alterations in Directives or the development of new Directives for particular environmental standards, but should also reflect the developments in analytical techniques and monitoring procedures.

Considerable care must be taken in providing precise and realistic definitions of individual standards. For example, the term 'total pesticides' was used in a number of early Directives and in terms of laboratory analysis this is problematic. Pesticides are not in fact a single class of compounds, but have a range of different molecular compositions and structures. Analytical procedures to determine their concentration vary somewhat with the class of compound and particular pesticide and Gray[12] describes the outcome of this problem: '... so current practice is often to determine the individual concentration of just three principal substances, parathion, BHC (lindane or HCH) and dieldrin, and to report the additive total as "total pesticides"!' The limitations of this practice are evident. The actual pesticides present in a sample may vary with sample source depending on local (or even distant) application of pesticides, and providing the additive total for only three pesticides may well not reflect the true total concentration of pesticides. In the Drinking Water Directive (80/778/EEC) (see below) the standard is set for 'pesticides and related products'. As Gray[13] points out, '... it is often unclear how values for "pesticides and related compounds" are derived in practice, and how accurately this reflects the total concentration of all those compounds covered under this broad definition'.

Local interpretations of broad definitions may, in practice, result in different levels of standards actually being applied between countries. In addition, it may simply not be practical to quantify all the possible 'pesticides and related compounds' that might occur in any one sample. There are simply too many substances currently on the market, and that will be marketed in the future, that fall under this definition and, realistically, the time and cost of analysing every sample for every possible pesticide may be prohibitive. The problem of assessing the ecotoxicological impact of substances such as pesticides has already been discussed in Chapter 4, as have the impacts of substances on human health. There is considerable scientific uncertainty, for instance, about the chronic effects of long-term, low-level exposure to pesticides in (say) drinking water (e.g., some of the pesticides are endocrine disrupting compounds). It has been suggested that current low levels of standards for pesticides in drinking water are not justified by the scientific evidence to date and it is a question of whether a precautionary stance is adopted or not.

---

[12]Gray, N. F., *Drinking Water Quality, Problems and Solutions* (Chichester, Wiley, 1994), at 138.
[13]*Ibid.*

Standards set for Waste Bodies under EC Directives

The significance of the Urban Waste Water Treatment Directive (91/271/EEC) in the protection of freshwater and coastal receiving waters has already been discussed above. In addition to the Dangerous Substances in Water Directive 76/464/EEC, there is a set of Directives which relate to the control of specific substances and quality standards. These include:

- Directives 82/176/EEC and 84/156/EEC for mercury
- Directive 83/513/EEC for cadmium
- Directive 86/280/EEC for PCP and DDT (as amended by Directives 88/347 and 90/415)
- Directive 84/491/EEC for hexachlorcylohexane (as amended by Directives 88/347 and 90/415)
- Directive 88/347/EEC for aldrin, dieldrin, isodrin, hexachlorobenzene, hexachlorobutanide and chloroform (as amended by Directive 90/415)

There is provision for 'daughter Directives' to be made under the main Directive and these substances are provided for under the Surface Waters (Dangerous Substances) (Classification) Regulations 1989 (SI 1989 No. 2286) and the Surface Waters (Classification) Regulations 1989 (SI 1989 No. 1148). Under these Regulations a system is in place for classifying inland, coastal and territorial waters on the basis of concentrations of List I substances (in micrograms per litre of water on an annual mean basis) (see above).

The Fishlife Directive (78/659/EEC) (see also Directive 91/492) provides quality standards for freshwaters, either to protect them or improve them to support fish life. Rivers are divided on the basis of dominant fish species which are designated either salmonid (most waters in the UK) or cyrinid. The Environment Agency under, s. 104 of the Environment Act 1995, operates a fixed penalty system to protect freshwater fish under amendments to s. 37 of the Salmon and Freshwater Fisheries Act 1975.

Directive 91/676/EEC on the Protection of Waters against Pollution Caused by Nitrate from Agricultural Sources contributes to the protection of waterways vulnerable to nitrate pollution arising from fertiliser run-off from agricultural land.

The Shell Fish Directive (79/923/EEC) sets biological and chemical standards for waters supporting the shell fish industry. As with all quality standards, achieving them may require substantial improvement in chemical and sewage effluent treatments prior to discharge and this is ultimately linked to discharge consents in a locality. Standards are also set under miscellaneous powers for fish farming which cover both the quality of the water intake to the fish farm as well as outflows. This is intended to protect the quality of the water resource and protect wild fish stocks.

The Bathing Water Directive (76/160/EEC) sets standards for bathing water which have been incorporated under s. 83 of the Water Resources Act 1991. The Directive provides a range of biological, chemical and physical criteria which must be met if the standards are to be achieved, but reaching the stipulated requirements may be waived in exceptional circumstances, e.g., heavy rain overwhelming treatment facilities. Bathing waters are designated for both freshwater and seawaters by competent authorities of each member state (in the UK the Environment Agency) on the basis of a 'large' number of bathers using the water. Initially, the UK's interpretation of this meant that only 27 beaches were designated but in *Commission* v *UK* (case C–56/90) the UK approach was rejected, and now more than 500 bathing waters are designated. The UK has only recently started designating freshwater sites following a phased-in approach for the Directive (as with many), with a ten-year period allowed to achieve the bathing water quality standards. The microbiological criteria set under the standards have been the most controversial and (in the UK and a number of other countries) the most difficult to meet. Indeed, the UK has still not achieved these standards for some major bathing waters, e.g., some designated in the Blackpool area. The Directive was issued in 1976. In *Commission* v *UK* the UK had argued (unsuccessfully) that time for compliance should be based on when the bathing water was designated and there is thus the potential at present for further action against the UK by the Commission because of lack of compliance. Again, there are major implications in achieving the standards in terms of substantial investment in effluent treatment by the water companies.

A new Bathing Water Directive was originally intended to be implemented by the end of December 1995, but there have been considerable problems involved in establishing a consensus for the new Directive and it is likely, now, to be implemented by the end of 2001. The new Directive may require higher microbiological standards and, most contentiously, a new zero limit for enteric viruses may be introduced. This will be exceptionally difficult to meet, and is controversial both in terms of appropriate techniques for monitoring and the likely limited improvement in protection to bathers.

The Ground Water Directive (80/68/EEC) provides for maximum concentrations of two lists of dangerous substances for groundwater (see reg. 15 of the Waste Management Licensing Regulations (SI 1994 No. 1056)). List I compounds and List II substances are included. Groundwater presents something of a unique problem in terms of quality standards and pollution prevention as it is often polluted from surface sources, soil and water, a considerable time (years) after the original polluting activity or accident has occurred. Historic pollution in groundwater is the norm due to the often slow rate of ingress from surface sources. Even prior knowledge of a pollution incident that might constitute a threat of contaminating groundwater may not facilitate protection and a pollutant spreading through groundwater can be difficult to contain or treat. Standards for groundwater set a considerable challenge and the Commission is currently considering proposals to revise the Directive.

STANDARDS SET FOR INDIVIDUAL SEWAGE AND INDUSTRIAL EFFLUENTS: CONSENT CONDITIONS

Discharge consents

Since the Kinnersley Report in 1990, *Discharge Consent and Compliance Policy: A Blue Print for the Future* (National Rivers Authority, London, 1990), attempts have been made to provide unity in the different procedures and levels of consent and a national strategy for reviewing all consents on the basis of the catchment area.

Authorisations for discharges (discharge consents) are obtained under a procedure set out in sch. 10 of the Water Resources Act 1991. A consent document sets out the standards for the particular discharge into the receiving water and details procedures and conditions. Consents are periodically reviewed by the Environment Agency, and they may be revoked or modified as a consequence of the review. The original consent stipulates the period or periods during which no such changes can be made (usually two years), and no further changes can be made for a specified period up to four years. If changes are necessary within these time periods then compensation is payable to the discharger, unless there are circumstances that are not reasonably foreseeable. The Secretary of State also has powers of revocation and modification through a direction to the Environment Agency in the following circumstances:

(a) there is a need to comply with any Community Directive;
(b) there is a need to protect public health or aquatic ecosystems and biota;
(c) in response to representations or advice to the Secretary of State.

The two-year rule for consent modifications does not apply for (a) and (b) above. Under sch. 22 of the Environment Act 1995, amendments cannot be made until appeals have been heard, except where the Environment

Agency considers the new standard for the effluent is essential to minimise pollution or protect public health.

The facility for discharge consents to be reviewed is essential, since due notice can then be taken of any changes in scientific understanding and risk assessments or any other factors. Non-numeric consents are used when it is impossible to set numeric standards for the discharge and a satisfactory standard for the process of discharge is also required. The Environment Agency can undertake spot sampling to ensure compliance with the particular discharge standard.

This type of standard set for individual sewage or trade effluents may be in the form of quantitative measurements, expressed usually in terms of quantities or concentrations of specified substances. Often compliance is in terms of the 95 percentile limit with an agreed number of samples taken over a year to assess performance. Standards may also be set on the basis that the discharge may not exceed them at any time. The quantitative standards are set on the basis of the characteristics of substances within the effluent (e.g., their acute toxicity, persistence and chronic effects etc., on the receiving water) and on the ability of the receiving water to dilute and disperse them. They may be given with some regard to discharges already occurring to the receiving water to ensure meeting SWQOs. The past history associated with the discharge operator may be considered as part of setting the standard and, in the light of this, the Environment Agency may append such conditions as it 'may think fit' to the discharge consent. These may include where the discharge may occur, volume, origin, composition and rate of discharge; even discharge treatment and procedures for minimisation of the discharge may be incorporated. The facilities for taking samples, keeping records and making returns may also be stipulated.

An element of transparency in standard-setting is found under sch. 10 of the Water Resources Act 1991. The Environment Agency must publish notice of the discharge in a local newspaper, in the area of the intended discharge, for two successive weeks and in addition the notice must be published in the *London Gazette*. This applies, however, only if there is likely to be an 'appreciable effect' on the receiving water. If this is the case, the relevant local authority or water undertaker must also be informed of the details of the proposed discharge. Guidance in a DoE Circular 17/84 on 'appreciable effect' goes to the use of the resource, if there is likely to be a major effect on water flow, e.g., perhaps in the case of a high volume discharge, and changes in water quality. The effects on water quality resulting in harm to the biota or surrounding ecosystems may be scientifically demanding to predict (see Chapter 4). The Ministry for Agriculture, Fisheries and Food and the Secretary of State for the

Environment must be informed of any discharge consents relating to coastal and territorial waters and a local enquiry into an application for a discharge consent may result from the Secretary of State's call-in powers and written representations to the Secretary of State.

Standards for trade (industrial) effluents disposed to sewers

Disposal of waste to sewers can be regarded as a form of discharge control and the private water companies, as sewerage undertakers, operate important environmental controls under the Water Industry Act 1991. Section 94 of the Act provides a statutory duty on the sewage undertakers to supply a sewage system for the discharge and disposal of domestic and industrial liquid waste with standards set for effluent discharged to sewers from trade (industrial) sources through trade effluent consents. The definition of a trade effluent is widely drafted, under s. 141(1) of the Water Industry Act 1991, and incorporates discharges from industry, agricultural sources, shops, launderettes and research institutions. The definition includes 'liquid wholly or partly produced in the course of any trade or industry carried on in trade premises'. Domestic waste is excluded.

Discharge of trade waste without a consent is a strict liability offence, enforcement of which may involve the sewerage undertaker. There are set procedures for applications to discharge a trade effluent to the sewers which are made to the sewerage undertaker, and a statutory framework is contained in ss. 121(4)(a) and 142 of the 1991 Act. There are wide provisions for the applicant for trade effluent consent and the sewerage undertaker to reach agreements and the procedures for application and considerations on which the consent is based are as follows:

(a) The application must be made at least two months before the discharge starts.

(b) The discharger is expected to minimise costs to the sewerage undertaker by using processes that ensure the discharge is less harmful. The sewerage operator is assumed to control discharges to sewers with regard to the techniques available and economical costs.

(c) The nature and composition of the discharge must be stated.

(d) The maximum proposed discharge for any one day must be given, linked to the maximum rate of discharge.

(e) The discharger has the right to appeal to the Director of Water Services on the ground that any reasonable application for consent cannot be refused by the sewerage undertaker.

(f) The sewerage undertaker may issue a notice under s. 124 of the Water Industry Act 1991 which may vary, revoke or add to consent conditions, although not within two years of the original consent. The discharge operator has a right of appeal to the Director General of Water Services against any change.

One of the key concerns in setting these standards is the impact of the discharge on the sewerage treatment process, which is effectively a microbiological process. The characteristics (e.g., composition, volume and flow rate) of the discharge will have a considerable effect on the efficiency and effectiveness of the operation of the sewerage treatment plant and this is partly determined by the operating parameters of the treatment works. In an extreme case — for example, the discharge of a toxic compound to the sewers — secondary treatment may fail and, as a result, the substance, and indeed domestic and trade effluent being treated at that time, might be discharged to the environment virtually untreated with serious consequences for the receiving water.

In common with all standards set for individual effluents, the ultimate aim of trade effluent consents is to protect any water that ultimately receives the discharge.[14] All discharge consents represent standards set on a case-by-case basis and play a crucial part in the protection of aquatic environments.

STANDARD-SETTING FOR DRINKING WATER

The objectives for setting drinking water standards are clearly somewhat different to those for water ecosystems. In terms of the latter, standards are set on the basis of ecotoxicology, water quality objectives, as well as protection of human health. Drinking water standards are based on the risks to human health of any substances in drinking water. Standards are not only set for the drinking water itself, but there is a link to the quality of the water source, e.g., reservoirs and natural water sources, used for abstraction. The importance of the quality of the water resource used for abstraction is seen in the Urban Waste Water Directive (91/271/EEC) and the in the standards set for SWQO. Water suppliers or undertakers are also under a duty to ensure, as far as 'reasonably practicable' that the sources of their water supply do not deteriorate (s. 68 and Chapter III of Part III, Water Industry Act 1991). There are two Directives (75/440/EEC and 79/869/EEC) that set standards for the abstraction of water for human consumption and the quality of the resources supplying drinking water

---

[14]See Water Authorities Association, *Trade Effluent Discharges to the Sewer* (September 1986).

are therefore protected through the application of a number of different standards.

Standards set for water undertakers

Under s. 68 and Chapter III of Part III of the 1991 Act, water undertakers have the key duty to supply 'wholesome' water. It is a criminal offence to supply water that is not wholesome for the following purposes:

(a) domestic (drinking, cooking, or washing) use; and
(b) food production.

Standards for drinking water under the Drinking Water Directive (80/778/EEC) are incorporated into s. 67 of the Water Industry Act 1991 and set out in the Water Supply (Water Quality) Regulations 1989 (SI 1989 No. 1147, as amended by the Water Supply (Water Quality) (Amendment) Regulations (SI 1999 No. 1524). Under these Regulations, water is considered wholesome if:

(a) it meets the standards prescribed in the Regulations for the particular properties, elements, organisms or substances;
(b) the hardness or alkalinity of water which has been softened or desalinated is not below prescribed standards; and
(c) the water does not contain any element, organism or substance, whether alone or in combination, at a concentration or value which would be detrimental to public health.

There are 11 national standards incorporating 66 specific quantitative parameters and non-numeric, i.e. qualitative, standards applied to the quality of drinking water under the Regulations.[15] These are divided into six catagories:

(a) organoleptic, e.g., odour;
(b) physical and chemical, e.g., conductivity;
(c) substances undesirable in excessive amounts, e.g., nitrates;
(d) toxic substances, e.g., pesticides;
(e) microbiological, e.g., faecal coliforms; and
(f) minimum concentration of softened water, e.g., alkalinity.

---

[15]See Gray, *op. cit.* n. 11, at 21–25 for a full list of the standards set under the Drinking Water Directive.

Directive 91/676/EEC on the Protection of Waters against Pollution Caused by Nitrate from Agricultural Sources also sets standards for the nitrate content in drinking water. There are derogations from achieving the standards because of climatic or geographical factors, but these do not extend to the microbiological or toxic standards and public health must not be put at risk. There is a degree of controversy over some of these standards, for example, there is little toxicological or epidemiological data on the impacts of low levels of pesticides in drinking water and there are difficulties in determining total pesticide content.

There is a requirement to monitor the supply of drinking water at the point of use, i.e., from the consumers' taps and, again, there is an element of self-regulation in this monitoring procedure. The water companies are under a statutory requirement to undertake the monitoring, which is open to checks by the local authority and the Drinking Water Inspectorate. The water company designates a number of water supply zones in its area, with a population base of no more than 50,000 people, which are the basis for monitoring and a single water source serves each of the water supply zones. A specified number of samples are taken each year in each designated zone, based on:

(a) the population served;
(b) the particular parameter, e.g., 10 samples per year are standard for nitrate whereas 12 samples per year are standard for faecal coliforms;
(c) the water source, e.g., surface waters require higher sampling frequency.

The sampling points are carefully selected as being representative of the particular supply zone. For some parameters they can be taken from fixed points, for others (e.g., for microbiological analysis) they must be randomly selected. The Drinking Water Inspectorate ensures that the selection of sampling sites is appropriate. Thus standards are not only set to ensure that drinking water is fit for human consumption, but also to ensure that monitoring procedures are adequate and appropriate. The water companies must inform local authorities in their area of the results from monitoring the water quality standards. The local authority may also take samples as it sees fit. There is a duty on the local authority to inform the water company of the results of its sampling. If the local authority is dissatisfied with the finding from monitoring through any of the parameters exceeding the standards, and this is not satisfactorily explained, then the Secretary of State may be informed. The Secretary of State has enforcement powers under s. 18 of the Water Industry Act 1991 which can be exercised if there is reasonable cause to believe that a water company has contravened any enforceable statutory duty. This includes both lapses in monitoring and infringement of the Regulations. Enforcement powers are not normally used if the breaches are trivial, or if the public water supplier gives adequate undertakings for improvement over an acceptable time-scale. (Section 19 of the Act provides for these exceptions from prosecution.)

Any prosecution for the offence of not supplying water fit for human consumption is taken under s. 70 of the Water Industry Act 1991 and there are fairly straightforward procedures for enforcement. First there is the issue of a 'notice of intention to enforce'. The public water supplier is given time to respond, which response is usually in the form of:

(a) a programme of work.
(b) the suggestion of new measures to comply with the drinking water standards.

Provisional or final orders to ensure compliance are then made by the Secretary of State after taking into consideration standards set in the Drinking Water Directive. If the company is deemed not to have complied then the Drinking Water Inspectorate initiates enforcement action on behalf of the Secretary of State. Enforcement action is taken if:

(a) water quality is breached, or when the breach is likely to recur;
(b) an enforceable regulation (e.g., sampling under reg. 3 of the Water Quality Regulations) is breached;
(c) an existing undertaking or (under reg. 4) time-limited relaxations expire before the necessary improvements are made.

The standards for drinking water quality, then, are ensured through a mixture of self-regulation, supervision and the potential for strong enforcement action. There is a degree of transparency in the achieving of the standards with the maintenance of a public register of monitoring results, which must be made available on demand. The water companies must include information on water supply in their annual reports and local authorities must also provide annual reports containing information on water quality.

Standards set for private water suppliers

The supply of water for human consumption by private water suppliers, e.g., through bottled water, has increased markedly in recent years and statutory water suppliers may supply water in their private capacity. Private water supplies are defined as any supplies of water provided by the statutorily appointed water undertaker (s. 93 of the Water Industry Act 1991) and the Private Water Supplies Regulations 1991 (SI 1991 No. 2790) consolidate similar standards for water quality as are set for public water suppliers. Local authorities monitor water quality standards on the basis of two categories:

(a) Category 1 water is used for domestic purposes;
(b) Category 2 water is for food production, or in premises used for staff canteens, educational, hospital and other residential use or camp sites, or in other places providing short-term accommodation on a commercial basis.

The Regulations stipulate how local authorities must classify private suppliers in their areas. The standards for the water are specified, as are the sampling procedures and the frequency of monitoring that should be undertaken by the local authority. The local authority has the right to make arrangements for sample taking and its analysis, with some exceptions and maximum charges that a local authority can levy for the monitoring process are set. The Drinking Water Inspectorate supports and monitors the local authority in carrying out these duties.

Under the Water Industry Act 1991 local authorities must be kept informed of the standard of water supply in their areas. There is an enforcement procedure through the local authorities serving a notice, on the occupier of the land containing the water source, that specifies the work required to bring the supplies up to appropriate standards for 'wholesome water' and a time-scale for the work. There is a period of at least 28 days for objections to be made to the notice. The local authority must provide the Secretary of State with the notice for confirmation and a public local inquiry or a hearing may be held at the discretion of the Secretary of State. The Drinking Water Inspectorate ensures compliance by the local authority with the Regulations.

Proposals for implementing Directive 98/83 on the quality of water for human consumption were published in April 2000.[16] The proposals include tougher rules about reporting to the public and strengthened procedures for monitoring, with derogations to allow remedial work to be undertaken. Reductions in lead levels are also required by the Directive, and an increase in water bills of an average 4 per cent is expected.

Bottled water, indeed all water sold in containers, actually includes a variety of types, such as spring, table or mineral. Mineral water comes

---

[16]ENDS Report 303, p. 45.

from licensed sources which are exempt from the Drinking Water Directive (80/778/EEC), but instead standards are set under the Natural Mineral Waters Directive (80/777/EEC) which are reproduced in the Natural Mineral Waters Regulations 1985 (SI 1985 No. 71). Standards apply to the source of the mineral water and to the bottled water. The source (e.g., ground water) must be of high quality and have no organoleptic problems and the mineral water must be recognised by the national authority. An application for natural mineral water status must be made in writing providing a local authority with information on a range of parameters. These include information on the source of supply and evidence of its high quality, i.e. no pollutants present, and the water's chemical, physical and microbiological quality. If the mineral water is recognised then details are published in the *Official Journal of the European Community*. There are no restrictions on the mineral (e.g., nitrate, chloride, etc.) content of mineral water, and interestingly this often exceeds the standards set under the Drinking Water Directive. In fact there is a prohibition on treatment included in the Natural Mineral Waters Directive, although microbiological standards are enforced and some treatment may be allowed on this basis (e.g., filtering), provided this does not change the characteristics of the water. All mineral waters must be bottled at source. Other bottled waters must comply with the Drinking Water Directive (80/778/EEC) and local authorities enforce the standards for bottled water under the Drinking Water Containers Regulations 1994 (SI 1994 No. 743). Local authorities also have powers, as food authorities, under the Food Safety Act 1990.

SETTING STANDARDS FOR THE PROTECTION AND CONSERVATION OF MARINE ENVIRONMENTS

The sea is a key resource for transport, fisheries and tourism and is an important and diverse ecosystem which requires cooperation between nation states to ensure its protection. As a consequence, many of the standards for seawater are agreed at international level under the auspices of a number of international organisations, and a variety of international treaties contribute to the protection of the marine environment. Standards are a technique increasingly used for environmental protection on the international stage.

The UK sets its territorial waters under s. 1(1) of the Territorial Seas Act 1987 at 12 nautical miles; a number of straits used for international navigation, defined as 'relevant territorial waters', are included. There is an exception to this in terms of an exclusive fishing zone of 200 nautical miles (see below).

Control of pollution

Standards for the discharge of effluent have been discussed above, and there are specific statutory provisions under the Water Resources Act 1991 for marine environments. The Dangerous Substances Directive (76/464/EEC) applies to the sea and standards for hazardous substances are also set under international agreements and are open to renegotiation. For example, at the 1990 North Sea Conference the list of hazardous substances was extended by 50 per cent from 1985 levels in terms of disposal at sea, to be achieved by 1995. This element of review is important not only because of the ability to react to significant changes in scientific understanding, but also with regard to the large numbers of new compounds marketed each year.

There are statutory provisions on dangerous substances under the Dangerous Substances in Harbour Areas Regulations 1987 (SI 1987 No. 37), which provide standards for the control of dangerous substances in the harbour area, including regulation of:

(a) transport;
(b) handling;
(c) storage;
(d) labelling; and
(e) entry and access.

The harbour master must be given a period of notice before a ship carrying a hazardous substance is berthed, and a flag must be displayed by the ship. The harbour authorities must provide an emergency plan.

Oil pollution is controlled under a mixture of national and international agreements. The International Convention on Oil Pollution Preparedness, Response and Cooperation 1990 sets standards of response for oil pollution arising from ships and offshore installations and lays down reporting procedures, measures to be adopted and response strategies to oil pollution. In effect this amounts to an environmental management standard for such pollution.

The discharge of oil into UK waters by any ship, and by UK-registered ships in non-territorial waters, is a criminal offence under ss. 1 and 2 of the Prevention of Oil Pollution Act 1971. This Act makes specific provisions for harbours under ss. 10 and 11 and lays down emergency powers for accidents involving the discharge of oil (ss. 12–15). Enforcement powers and delegated powers to make regulations are granted to the Secretary of State under s. 17 of the Act. The Merchant Shipping (Prevention of Pollution) Order 1983 (SI 1983 No. 1106) and the Merchant Shipping

(Prevention of Oil Pollution)(Amendment) Regulations 1993 (SI 1993 No. 1680) further strengthen protection.

There has been for many years considerable controversy about the dumping of waste at sea. The impact of dumping on the marine environment is exceptionally difficult to assess, both in terms of immediate, perhaps acute, effects and in terms of cumulative, perhaps chronic, effects. It has been argued that the deep sea should effectively disperse and dilute contaminants and that its vulnerability should be low because of a low density of organisms. However, this has not been fully evaluated and the associated scientific uncertainty is great. In this regard there is now a tendency to exercise caution and dumping of waste at sea has been phased out. In the UK since 1992, the disposal to the sea of liquid industrial waste, power station fly ash, redundant munitions and sewage sludge has been stopped. The North Sea appears to be a particularly vulnerable ecosystem as it is a relatively shallow sea receiving discharges from eight highly industrialised nations. The International Convention for the Prevention of Pollution from Ships (MARPOL), which was originally signed in 1973 and amended by Protocol in 1978, coming into force in 1983, is intended to set standards to control marine pollution. MARPOL, implemented under the Merchant Shipping (Prevention of Oil Pollution) Regulations 1996 in the United Kingdom, designates the North Sea as a special area. A new annex to MARPOL was agreed in London in September 1997. Other international treaties contribute to the control of sea dumping and include the Oslo Convention for the Prevention of Marine Pollution by Dumping from Ships and Aircraft (Cm 4984, 1972) and the London Convention for the Prevention of Marine Pollution by Dumping Wastes and Other Matters (Cm 5169, 1972). These set standards at an international level for sea dumping.

In the UK there is a system of licences for depositing substances from vessels, vehicles, aircraft or marine structures under ss. 5 and 6 of the Food and Environment Protection Act 1985, as amended by the Environmental Protection Act 1990. A licence is required for the scuttling of a vessel and for incinerating a marine structure. Licences are also required for incinerating waste on a vessel which may be granted by the Ministry of Agriculture, Fisheries and Food (MAFF). The regulations controlling the application procedure are extensive. The licence conditions relate to:

(a)   the specific conditions that are attached (the specific standards to be applied);
(b)   maintaining a public register (providing a degree of transparency in licensing);
(c)   allowing periodic inspections.

Changes may be made to the licensing arrangements, and s. 10 of the 1985 Act allows MAFF to undertake operations to protect human life, the marine environment or the legitimate use of the sea.

Marine resource conservation through standards

The Common Fisheries Policy (CFP), through the application of quotas and the exclusion of ships from conservation zones, protects fisheries resources. This has often proved exceptionally controversial and the subject of much litigation. In 1983, a legally enforceable agreement was concluded consisting of a number of elements:

(a) Member state fishermen have an entitlement to fish within the 200 nautical mile limit of their own shores. The European Community established this limit in 1977. (See the Fishery Limits Act 1976, which establishes an exclusive fishing zone of 200 nautical miles.) This limit sets the fishing zone for a member state's fishermen or fishermen from other countries that traditionally fished these areas.

(b) Fishing of Atlantic and North Sea fish stocks is carefully controlled through the setting of quotas for allowable catches. These are divided on the basis of Total Allowable Catch (TAC) for individual fishing nations. TACs are fixed annually based on a number of elements including scientific surveys of the fish stocks under Regulation 4194/88 (OJ 1987 L375/1). If necessary, fishing by particular member states may be halted for prescribed periods if quotas are exceeded.

(c) Regulation 379/81 (OJ 1981 L379/1), amended by Regulation 3468/88 1998 (OJ L305/1), sets a number of important standards for fishing and operates a guide price system. Classification, market, packaging and labelling standards are also set under this Regulation.

(d) The EU can enter into international negotiations on conservation of fish stocks (e.g., the Standing Conference on Stradling Stocks and Highly Migratory Species) and access to waters.

(e) The Common Structural Policy (Regulation 101/76 (OJ 1976 L20/19)) contributes provisions for the modernisation of the industry, redeployment of resources and market development.

In terms of setting standards for the fish industry and for fish management within the EU the importance of CFP is clear. In the UK, the Sea Fish (Conservation) Act 1992, strengthened by provisions in s. 103 and s. 5A of the Environment Act 1995, provides powers to restrict sea fishing.

Standards are set for the types of fishing nets used in seawater, and the carriage of certain nets is restricted or prohibited.

Protection is also extended to freshwater fish and salmon under s. 104 of the Environment Act 1995 and amendments made to s. 37 of the Salmon and Freshwater Fisheries Act 1975. The Environment Agency has powers to operate a fixed penalty system for offences under detailed procedures in the amended s. 37 of the 1975 Act. There are unified grant-in-aid powers, derived from MAFF, and powers for the approval of fish passes held by the Environment Agency under the Environment Act 1995.

There has been a substantial change in UK legislation in terms of the marine environment, in that fisheries can be regulated for environmental purposes and not only for fisheries management. Powers have been granted under the Sea Fisheries Regulation Act 1966 (amended by s. 102 of the Environment Act 1995) to the Environment Agency, sea fisheries committees (which include experts on marine environments) and ministers to this end. This should be put in the context of conservation measures within the UK. The development of marine conservation is largely modelled on terrestrial conservation law (see Chapter 10), but in reality it has a number of unique problems associated with it. There are Marine Nature Reserves (MNRs), which can be designated for land or water from the high-tide line to three miles from the base-line, on a comparable basis to National Nature Reserves. Designation is under the Territorial Sea Act 1987 and s. 36 of the Wild Life and Countryside Act 1981 and is made by the Secretary of State for the Environment, Transport and Regions after representations from interested parties and possibly a public enquiry. MNRs are managed by the Nature Conservancy Council, which can make by-laws under s. 37 of the 1981 Act. There are powers to restrict the killing, taking and disturbance of wildlife, and for the restriction or prohibition of vessels and people in the MNR. This last power is limited since it does not extend to where there is a right of passage or access to tidal water. A number of coastal and marine habitats found in the UK fall under the Habitats Directive (92/43/EEC) and the Bird Directive (79/409/EEC).[17]

International treaties and agreements extend to marine environments in a variety of ways and have considerable significance given the nature of marine ecosystems and the diversity of uses on a global scale. Protection against marine pollution and conservation of the marine environment are key. The United Nations' International Maritime Organisation (IMO) acts to

---

[17]A discussion of marine coastal conservation in the UK is provided by Warren, L. M., 'Law and Policy for Marine Protected Areas' in C. P. Rodgers (ed.) *Nature Conservation and Countryside Law* (Cardiff, University of Wales Press, 1994), at 65–88.

extend cooperation between governments with regard to shipping and marine pollution, which constitutes part of the United Nations Environment Programme, with ten regional areas selected and plans for their protection adopted or being developed. The Barcelona Convention (1978) applying to the Mediterranean built on principles of combating pollution and protection for the Baltic agreed in the 1974 Helsinki Convention for the Protection of the Marine Environment of the Baltic Sea. The pollution protection provided to the marine environment by this type of treaty is to be extended to other seas. The 1993 Agreement on the Conservation of Small Cetaceans of the Baltic and North Seas not only protects dolphins and porpoises, but has also established a research fund. The fund is intended to support research into techniques to prevent these mammals being caught in fish nets, a first step in establishing an international standard.

ECONOMIC INSTRUMENTS AND STANDARDS FOR WATER

Following a consultation paper,[18] the DETR has undertaken a major research study into the advantages and disadvantages of using economic instruments to control water pollution. This covers both *point sources*, at individual outflow pipes, and *diffuse sources*, such as run-off of fertilisers from agricultural land. A variety of different approaches may be taken to implement a strategy for applying economic instruments to the water industry. Tradeable permits would enable, within overall pollution levels, discharges to sell and exchange low abatement costs and high abatement costs. One advantage is that the government could ensure that pollution levels are set and monitored. It is unclear, however, if there are sufficient discharges to create a viable market.[19] There are also taxation strategies, whereby the maximum level of pollution is determined and additional improvements may afford tax incentives. However, it is unclear if the tax savings would justify the additional costs incurred. Following the research undertaken by the DETR, there is considerable interest in the use of economic instruments. As part of an economic instruments strategy, the government published in April 1999 a new regime for abstracting water, adopting some of the economic instruments mentioned in the research.[20] This has been followed by a Consultation Paper for brokering licence trading, published in March 2000.[21] Matters included within the remit of the Consultation Paper are as follows:

---

[18]See *Economic Instruments for Water Pollution* (DETR, November 1997).
[19]*Institute for Fiscal Studies: The IFS Green Budget*, Commentary 67, pp.89-91.
[20]ENDS Report 291, pp. 45-46.
[21]ENDS Report 304, pp. 47-48.

(a)   incentive charges on the basis of the volume of the water abstrac-
       ted, aimed at reducing abstraction levels;
(b)   tradeable licences to achieve optimal results in terms of water
       distribution and sustainable development;
(c)   managing trading through bid price but not auctions of licences.

It is intended that the Environment Agency be given proactive powers to
adopt economic instruments to increase efficiency in the use of water. The
aim is to encourage abstractors of water to adopt different strategies such as
recycling, storage and conservation of water supply. On this basis surplus
water will be identified and form a tradeable asset. Greater transparency in
the information available will be required in order to advance the idea of
trading in water resources. The new Water Bill is intended to implement
the main elements of the new regime. It remains to be seen how effective
economic instruments will be in offering inducements to limit abstraction
and abate pollution as part of the regulation of the industry as whole.

Water privatisation and regulation

The privatisation of the water industry, in common with the other utilities
such as electricity, gas and telecommunications, resulted in a restructuring
of the industry. The Director of Water Services was established by the Water
Act 1989, as amended by s. 1 of the Water Industry Act 1991. The result was
to bring a new form of economic regulation to the water industry. Pricing,
financing and obligations related to investment and environmental
obligations are all part of the remit of the regulator. However, the bulk of
the environmental obligations, in terms of the water quality standards set
out above, rest with the Environment Agency in England and Wales.

The water industry does not presently have a national infrastructure
network analogous to the electricity grid and there are significant
differences in terms of the performance of different water companies on
leakages and water repairs.[22] The target for leakages in 1998–99 is an 8 per
cent reduction on the previous year, an example of standards set by the
regulator, with many water companies currently failing to meet this
standard. Similarly, there is disparity between the price structures of
water companies and the approaches to meeting new EC standards for
drinking water and bathing water.[23]

---

[22]Lege, D., 'Water Ofwat: Report on Leakage and Water Efficiency' (2000) Util. Law
Rev. (Jan–Feb 2000), pp. 17–18.
[23]Report on the 1999 Periodic Review — Final Determinations and Future Water
and Sewerage Charges 2000-05. See (2000) Util. Law Rev. (Jan–Feb 2000), pp. 19-21.

There is considerable tension between balancing the investment needed to improve water quality, fair pricing for the industry and the protection of the consumer, the viability of the industry and the protection of the environment.[24] A competitive industry that seeks to achieve a balance between the competing objectives of each constraint requires a variety of regulatory techniques to achieve that goal. The present criticisms are that competition in the water industry should be increased and that the role of the single regulator needs to be improved, with the regulator currently having too much involvement in 'running the industry', as opposed to providing independent regulation.[25] The Utilites Act 2000 provides a number of solutions:

(a) The Secretary of State has powers to establish a Water Advisory Panel to advise the regulator of the industry (OFWAT).

(b) An additional primary duty is added to the role of the regulator, namely to protect the interests of the consumer.

(c) Water standards and service performance improvements within the industry are to be improved.

(d) A new Consumer Council for Water is set up to protect the consumer and to investigate and report on a wide range of issues including public health and the environment.

(e) Additional requirements are imposed in order to furnish the Consumer Council for Water with relevant information.

(f) A complaints procedure and, where necessary, the power to levy fines has been setup (this power rests on the Director of OFWAT, the Secretary of State, and the Welsh Assembly).

(g) New powers are created under the Competition Act 1998 (in force from 1 March 2000) to maintain fair and effective markets. The Act prohibits restrictive agreements in the industry and abuse by a water company of its market position. A concurrent jurisdiction applies for this element of regulation based on the s. 54 and sch. 10 of the Competition Act 1998, allowing the regulator to act through investigative powers, in conjunction with the Director General of Fair Trading.

(h) Common carriage arrangements are created for the industry as a whole. Guidance from the Drinking Water Inspectorate, issued in March 2000, provides a regulatory structure for the 'effective legal

---

[24]In Scotland, the water industry is owned by the Scottish executive responsible for the regulation of the environment, public health and efficiency of the industry. See House of Commons Library, Research Paper 00/7, p.48.

[25]Robinson, C., 'A Competitive Water Industry?' *Utilities Journal* (July 1999), pp. 38–9.

framework' to set up a common carriage network. The guidance includes matters relating to abstraction rights.[26]

It remains to be seen whether the single regulatory structure, uniquely maintained for the water industry, will be effective. Doubts remain as to the effectiveness of an advisory body as opposed to a panel. The new system of regulation is highly complex and it might be difficult to reconcile competing aims for increased competition in the industry with environmental and consumer interests.

CONCLUSIONS

Regulating the water industry is about to enter a new era. The Utilities Act 2000 and the provisions of the Competition Act 1998 combine to provide a system of regulation that must find a transparent way to balance the competing demands of a competitive and market driven industry with high quality water standards, environmental targets and consumer protection. Two different styles of regulation may be detected in the regulation of the water industry. The first sees water as a natural monopoly, with efficiency improvements sought through setting targets and pricing strategies. Centralised control rest with a pro-active regulator who may effectively help to run the industry and environmental and economic regulation are intertwined, with prioritisation often an *ad hoc* response to public concern and political agendas.[27] The second style of regulation is to place more emphasis on the market and competition. The dynamics of a competitive structure in pricing may begin when there are common carriage rights throughout the country. Massive capital investment, encouraged by the need to uprate the water and sewerage system, inevitably draws in the question of financing and pricing. Prioritising market strategies leads to less emphasis on consumer protection of the direct regulatory kind in favour of more consumer choice.

Choosing between the two regulatory styles, the new Utilities Act 2000 borrows from each. The water regulator is expected not simply to 'facilitate' competition as in the past, but 'to promote competition'. Consumer interests and protection are more directly addressed than in the past and effective financing is regarded as a primary duty. This may inhibit price controls if the aim is to ensure that water companies are financially viable. In a complex and technical system of regulation the

---

[26]ENDS Report 301, p. 40.
[27]Prosser, T., *Law and the Regulators* (Oxford, Oxford University Press, 1997), pp. 119–148.

government may set broader social and environmental duties than in the past and it will be interesting to see how differences may be reconciled and how effective the new regulatory structure may become.

This chapter has illustrated the wide variety of techniques adopted in the regulation of water and in the setting of water quality standards, summarised below:

(a)   legal instruments through EC Directives for the setting of water standards;

(b)   economic instruments that set targets, for example, targets for leakages and water discharges;

(c)   legal powers to ensure price regulatory oversight, with consumer interests protected by law;

(d)   improved strategies for regulation and competition as part of the overall regulation of the water industry.

Standard-setting applies across a wide range of areas, from drinking water to bathing water and from sewage to waste disposal. In order for standard-setting to operate efficiently, a number of distinct elements need to be in place, as follows:

(a)   a tightly regulated industry where the regulator has sufficient power to enforce standards and monitor and control activities;

(b)   standards for the water industry, including *ex ante* forms of control;

(c)   costs in setting and applying standards may be passed onto the consumer through price regulation and control;

(d)   environmental objectives require prioritisation and harmonisation with competing demands on the industry.

In general, it is clear that the quality of drinking water and bathing water and the environmental quality of freshwaters have improved over the past two decades. Regulation has been proactive and reactive in terms of adjusting to the competing demands on the water industry as a whole. As Armstrong, Cowan and Vickers conclude:[28]

The new regulatory regime is in some respects superior to the one that existed until 1989. Price regulation and the setting and monitoring of environmental and quality targets are more open than under the previous regime. It is possible that the privatization of the investment

---

[28]Armstrong, M., Cowan, S. and Vickers, J., *Regulatory Reform* (London, MIT Press, 1998), pp. 353–4.

program has brought forward the dates of the achievement of the overall environmental and quality goals, since the government might not have financed the program in full if the water and sewerage companies had remained in public ownership, especially given the deterioration of the public finances during the recession of the early 1990s.

CHAPTER EIGHT

Environmental Standards and Land

Contaminated land and the disposal of waste products[1] set regulatory challenges for environmental protection. An overview of land use planning is provided here which sets the scene for consideration of the main standards applicable to land. The chapter is divided into two further sections: contaminated land and solid waste disposal. It covers examples of some specific problem areas, such as pollution at landfill sites and there is some consideration given to the problems of genetically modified organisms (GMOs), a controversial subject that has attracted much public and media attention at the interface between law, policy and science.

AN OVERVIEW

Since 1947, land use planning in the United Kingdom has set the parameters of how land is regulated in the general sense of allocating land for particular uses. Regulation has been effected through the Town and Country Planning Act 1947, the National Parks and Access to the Countryside Act 1949 and the Historic Buildings and Ancient Monuments Act 1953 and there are almost 100 additional legislative enactments relevant to land use control.[2] The DETR and other bodies are attempting

---

[1]See Lawrence, D., *Waste Regulation Law* (London, Butterworths, 1999).
[2]See the Society for Advanced Legal Studies, Planning and Environmental Reform Working Group, *The Simplification of Planning Legislation* (July 2000).

to provide some simplification of the planning system, an example of a regulatory system that has developed incrementally. There is a miscellany of consents, such as tree preservation orders, the protection of hedgerows or the notification of proposed works in a site of special scientific interest (SSSI). Planning permission is required for building or changing the use of the land.

In fact English planning law is remarkably flexible. It is noticeable that despite trends in favour of the centralisation of planning, the planning system remains locally based with local authorities enjoying substantial planning responsibilities (this is in the context of the United Kingdom having a remarkably high population density). There is, however, a noticeable shift in powers from local to central government, which sets the boundaries of development control. Primarily central government operates through the Department of the Environment, Transport and the Regions (DETR) which continuously monitors planning policy and decisions. Planning policy guidance is used as an instrument that sets the parameters of planning policy to be implemented at the local level.

Incremental growth has led to a complex and confusing system of controls. There is a wide variety of factors that contribute to effective regulation and compliance and Hutter has noted four[3] elements adopted by Kagan[4] in 1994: '... regulatory legal design; the agency's social, and economic task enforcement; its political environment; and its internal leadership.' All four elements may be found in the way the planning system operates. There is the creation of development plans through legal mechanisms and the adjudication of individual planning applications based around planning decisions by the local planning authority. A number of agencies have a multiplicity of roles in the planning process mostly focused on local decision-making, the political environment of which may shift according to the elected policies of the government of the day. Lastly, planning groups, including pressure groups, have a role in the decision-making process of major projects.

An overview of the essential elements of the planning system provides an explanation of how distinct elements of land use planning contribute to the regulation of the environment as a whole. Planning functions are shared between the two different tiers of local authorities, that is counties and districts. Counties (county planning authorities) are involved in the preparation of structure plans, the control of developments concerning mineral and aggregate workings and processing, waste disposal sites and

---

[3] See Hutter, B. M., *Compliance: Regulation and Environment* (Oxford, Clarendon Press, 1997), at 237.
[4] See Kagan, R. A., 'Regulatory Enforcement' in D. H. Rosenbloom and R. D. Schwartz (eds), *Handbook of Regulation and Administrative Law* (New York, Marcel Dekker, 1994).

developments that involve National Park boundaries. Districts (district planning authorities) are responsible for all other local plans and for development control decisions excluding county matters. The split between county and district applies for non-metropolitan areas. However, there has been considerable reorganisation of local government since the Local Government Act 1992, which created unitary authorities responsible for all matters that had been previously split between county and district.

In Wales, the Welsh Assembly, created by the Wales Act 1998, has assumed powers to make delegated legislation and call-in powers. A Planning Decision Committee, formed in January 2000, hears cases that previously came within the ambit of the Secretary of State for Wales. In Scotland, the Scottish Parliament under the Scotland Act 1998 has assumed responsibility for town and country planning. In London, single-tier boroughs have planning responsibilities and amendments to Part II of the Town and Country Planning Act 1990 established a specialist strategic plan for Greater London. An elected mayor and Assembly for London was created by the Greater London Authority Act 1999. Finally, there are two areas where planning arrangements are treated differently. The National Parks fall under s. 63 of the Environment Act 1995, which created special autonomous planning authorities from 1 April 1997. The Norfolk and Suffolk Broads Act 1988 created Broads Authorities covering planning arrangements for the Broads.

The key instrument for the future guidance of planning is the use since 1947 of development plans, which fall into two categories:

(a)   the structure plans containing strategic issues and policies that require the approval of the Secretary of State; and
(b)   local plans formulated within the general framework of the structure plan (see s. 70(2) of the Town and Country Planning Act (TCPA) 1990 and a new s. 54A of the Town and Country Planning Act 1990, under s. 26 of the Planning and Compensation Act 1991).

The planning system is not intended to be an arbitrary one. The adoption of statutory development plans by the local authority allows it to develop criteria to judge individual proposals to build on land or make a change of use. The public is thereby given some guidance as to what plans are likely to meet with local authority approval, and this may act as an incentive for well-considered developments. The courts provide an overview and scrutiny of the system.

In addition to local plans there are two types of specialist plans provided for under the TCPA 1990. County planning authorities are required to produce mineral local plans (see s. 37, as amended). (The only exception to this is National Parks, where the mineral plan is prepared specially or mineral policies may be included in specific cases within a local plan.) Mineral plans drawn up by the local authority must have regard to the directions of the Secretary of State and must contain detailed maps and policies for the extraction and working of minerals. Included within the mineral plan must be policies that take account of the environment. The second type of specialist plan is the waste local plan. Local plans must contain policies relating to the disposal of waste or refuse and must usually cover a five-year cycle. In formulating such plans, account must be taken of the plans drawn up by waste regulation authorities under s. 50 of the Environmental Protection Act 1990. The waste local plan is also expected to take account of land use. The DETR issues guidance on how to draw up such plans,[5] discussed in more detail below.

CONTAMINATED LAND

Contaminated land poses some specific regulatory problems. First, there is lack of precision in the meaning given to the term. Contaminated land is broadly defined either in terms of identifying sources of pollution or as a means of assessing how clean-up strategies might be adopted. Secondly, the breadth of scientific knowledge today is such that contamination forms a very broad spectrum. It ranges from the need to prevent any immediate harm to human life to a calculation of whether, over the period of a lifetime, harm is capable of being measured or prevented. Thirdly, there is the problem of historic waste and the calculation of the impact on human health and the environment in general.

Improvements in regulating contaminated land have come about through the influence of the European Union and also by the creation of the Environment Agency. The Agency, in consultation with local authorities, has a legal obligation under s. 78U of the Environmental Protection Act 1990 to provide a report on the general state of contaminated land.

Contaminated land provides a good example of standard-setting, where the use of standards is linked to a risk assessment of the future use of the land. One approach is to regard land as suitable for any general purpose; another approach might favour improving the land only up to the level of use required. The current trend favours land being improved up to the level where it may be used for any purpose. This might, however, be costly, difficult to achieve and unnecesary.

As already noted above, contaminated land represents an important challenge to the regulatory structure and systems for land use planning.

---

[5]ENDS Report 234, pp. 21–25.

In considering whether or not to grant planning permission, s. 70(2) of the TCPA 1990 requires the local planning authority to have regard to the provisions of the development plan that are material to the planning application. Contaminated land falls within the category of 'material considerations' to be taken into account when considering a planning application. Wide discretion is given to the planning authority, and there is a requirement that the circumstances of each case must be carefully considered and representations taken into account in the final decision (see *Stringer* v *Minister of Housing and Local Government* [1971] 1 All ER 65, *Tesco Stores Ltd* v *Secretary of State for the Environment* [1995] 2 All ER 636). Almost any consideration that relates to the use and development of land is capable of forming a material consideration for the purposes of planning law.

The publication of *Contaminated Land* (Cm 1161) led to the introduction of a new system of regulation in 1990. This consisted of the creation of a public register, under s. 143 of the Environmental Protection Act 1990, containing details of contaminated land, with a duty on local authorities to keep the register up-to-date. The impact of the designation of contaminated land through the creation of an official public register was problematic. The register was never fully operational because registration inevitably led to problems of planning blight. A new approach was taken with a more extensive and detailed (some would say complex) regulatory structure. Contaminated land is now regulated by s. 57 of the Environment Act 1995, which inserted a new Part IIA into the Environmental Protection Act 1990. This change in the law had the effect of repealing s. 143 of the 1990 Act with effect from 1 April 2000. Contaminated land is defined as land which appears to the relevant local authority to be causing, or to have a significant possibility of causing, significant harm. Harm is defined under Part IIA of the Environmental Protection Act 1990 (amended by the Environment Act 1995 and s. 78A(2)) as: 'harm to the health of living organisms or other interference with the ecological systems of which they form part and in the case of man, includes harm to his property'. As indicated in Chapter 4, 'harm' may be difficult to access accurately. On heavily contaminated sites it may be all too obvious, for example through a major reduction of diversity and density in populations, but even this may not be evident, though, since many of the sites have substantial recent history as industrial and commercial areas, with the inevitable impact on the flora and fauna through infrastructure development. Some sites may have lower levels of contaminants, which elicit chronic and long-term effects which are difficult to establish. Chemical analysis of surface and deep soils at a site to help determine levels of contamination is expensive and demanding, for example, contaminated sites often contain a variety of pollutants, which differ in their distribution across a site and with depth. Taking appropriate samples and analysing for the correct compounds is a difficult exercise and predicting risks to human health and to other living organisms from the amounts and types of chemicals present is equally demanding (see Chapter 4). There are seldom records of the history of sites, which have often had multiple industrial uses and, as a result, any assessment of the probable nature of contaminants from the industries, etc. at a site is likely to be problematic. Local authorities may find designation of contaminated sites a considerable challenge and may require guidance.

Section 57 of the 1995 Act envisages a new regime for statutory guidance and regulations for the identification of contaminated land sites. Accompanying the listing of sites are rules for investigation and remediating those contaminated sites that are identified. Under the new regulatory scheme the registers are more transparent, containing full details of the site, the nature of contamination and the steps needed to remediate the site. Compensation rules are also included in the new regulatory structure and there are procedures for appeals and determination of the matter through a series of detailed grounds[6] (see the Contaminated Land (England) Regulations 2000 (SI 2000 No. 227), the Environment Act 1995 (Commencement No. 16 and Saving Provision) Order 2000 (SI 2000 No. 340)).

There are some problems with the scheme. Local authorities may not be able to meet all the costs of remediation, and the complexity of the regulatory scheme with the inclusion of appeal powers may make for further problems and delays. Local authorities may opt for a voluntary system of agreement that would be less subject to costly appeals. Additional staff and administration costs are involved in the new scheme and this has caused further periods of delay and uncertainty. There is also an important role for leading commercial companies which are asked to draw up plans for the remediation of sites. Remediation techniques, to be effective, will have to balance cost and the degree of harm and will substantially have to rely on risk assessments, which are highly demanding for terrestrial systems (Chapter 4). More difficult is the fact that contaminated land controls may overlap with other areas such as IPC integrated pollution control (and waste licensing). The problem of historic pollution of groundwater, which also falls under the new regime, may overlap with the waste licensing regime. The Environment Agency envisages that guidance on this issue of overlap will fall within the Agency's powers.

Identifying special sites, and licensing contractors to carry out remediation schemes, will provide much additional work. A similar scheme is

---

[6]ENDS Report 301, p. 36 and ENDS Report 302, pp. 36–8.

envisaged for Scotland under the direction of the Scottish Executive.[7] It is estimated[8] by research carried out by W. S. Atkins, a leading engineering consultancy, that contaminated land in Britain is, in terms of size and cost, a major environmental problem:

> ... the area affected is 360,000 hectares — and the costs of assessing and cleaning it up may be around £15 billion. Sectors calculated to have created the largest liabilities are petrol stations, engineering, fossil fuel production, waste management and sewage works.

Particularly important is the finding that a key area of contamination is land held by the water industry, specifically sewage works. The system of remediation is complex and expensive. Remedial treatment may take several forms and involves the removal or treatment of the contaminated land and eventual restoration and reclamation of the land. There are standards applicable to the process of remediation, which includes the following recognised techniques[9]:

(a) the removal of the contaminating substances from the site for subsequent disposal elsewhere under appropriate containment conditions;
(b) on-site retention and isolation of the material, e.g., by encapsulation systems or the use of appropriate barriers, etc.;
(c) dilution of the contaminating substances with clean material;
(d) the elimination or immobilisation of contaminants through biological, chemical and/or physical treatments.

The powers to carry out remedial action are considerable. Sections 78A to 78Q of the Environment Protection Act 1990, as amended, contain details of the procedure, powers of inspection and enforcement powers, such as requiring 'reasonable' remediation measures but with regard to the 'likely costs of measures' and the 'the seriousness' of the harm. The extent to which sites should be remediated is a matter of debate; it is possible to envisage occasions when land may be brought to a standard above its original level.

The contaminated land regime is also integral to the planning process and there are a number of relevant Planning Policy Guidances (PPGs).

---

[7] ENDS Report 304, p. 44.
[8] ENDS Report 305, pp. 4–5.
[9] For further details, see McEldowney, J. and McEldowney, S., *Environment and the Law* (Harlow, Longman, 1996) at 173.

PPG 12 provides that a policy should be adopted on the re-use of derelict or under-used land in preference to development of greenfield sites, an approach which is favoured by the present government. There is also PPG 23 which adopts into structure plans policies on the location of industries that have high pollutant potential. In considering planning permission, it is possible to impose a condition that the developer must first clean up the contamination before work begins, but this power, contained in a planning condition, appears to duplicate the use of the remediation notice scheme noted above. The planning condition is subject to s. 215 of the TCPA 1990 which requires an occupier of land to take steps to remedy any contamination within 28 days. This is subject to appeal under s. 217 where a narrow interpretation is placed on the use of s. 215, namely that there is no breach of planning control where the harm complained of is an ordinary operation of the land. This leaves an untidy system of regulation; ideally, planning controls should be looked at as distinct from the remediation scheme.

The example of contaminated land illustrates the complexity of fitting regulatory structures into existing systems of control. There is also the curious mixture of statutory provision, guidance and consultation that are prerequisites of the British approach to regulation. Implicit in the new regulatory structure for contaminated land is the preference for voluntary agreements and a key incentive in this direction is that anyone who has received a remediation notice will not be able to make use of the landfill tax relief applicable to landfill materials removed from contaminated sites.[10]

WASTE MANAGEMENT AND STANDARDS

The production of waste by an urbanised industrial society occurs at a prodigious rate. In Britain alone something in the order of 450 million tonnes of waste is disposed of each year. Most of this comes from industrial and commercial sources, although a not insignificant constituent is domestic waste. Mining and quarrying produces the greatest amount of waste (approximately 108 million tonnes a year), followed by agricultural waste (80 million tonnes annually). A variety of processes form industrial waste, which is reflected in the variable nature of the regulations. In fact the most diverse waste is household waste.[11] In some ways the generic term 'waste' is misleading since waste incorporates a

---

[10]ENDS Report 297, p. 45.
[11]See Hester, R. E. and Harrison, R. M. (eds) *Waste Treatment and Disposal* (Cambridge, The Royal Society of Chemistry, 1995) for a discussion of waste and waste treatment.

wide range of different materials and substances with a variety of characteristics and attendant risks. Safe transport, disposal and monitoring of waste all contribute to environmental protection and preventing any adverse health effects arising from the waste, and all form an important part of government policy. The setting of environmental standards can contribute to achieving safe disposal.

WASTE STRATEGIES

Government waste management strategy incorporates the encouragement of 'waste reduction, re-use and recovery (including recycling) and the safe disposal of remaining wastes.'[12] A major contribution to the implementation of policies for waste minimisation, re-use and recovery is environmental management standards (see Chapter 3). In establishing an environmental management standard, assessment of the environmental effects of processes, including the generation of waste, is linked to continued improvements in performance.

A key element in the formulation of waste strategy has come from the EU Framework Directive 75/442. This sets the general parameters for the disposal of waste to avoid danger to human health and nuisances to the environment. A further Directive (91/156/EEC) identifies 16 specific types of waste (and in the future this will require the identification of further types of waste to be added to the list). In one sense this is an example where the EU has developed on an incremental basis greater clarification and certainty[13] but in another sense it shows the chaotic problem of legislating for member states where implementation and agreement is difficult because of the division of responsibility between the EU and member states. As Kramer points out:[14]

A consistent Community waste management policy has also not been developed because it is not clear to what extent waste management strategies, policies and measure are to be established at Community or at national level. Member States generally prefer to keep responsibility for management options, including questions on investments into cleaner technologies, clean-up and others, at national level.

---

[12]DoE, *Sustainable Waste Management: A Waste Strategy for England and Wales* (January 1995).
[13]See Van Calster, G., 'The Legal Framework for the Regulation of Waste in the European Community' in Han Somsen (ed.), *The Yearbook of European Environmental Law*, vol. 1 (Oxford: Oxford University Press, 2000), at 161–224.
[14]Kramer, L. (ed.), *EC Environmental Law*, 4th edn. (London, Sweet and Maxwell, 2000), at 239.

The European Waste Catalogue (Council Decision 94/3/EC) provides for a categorisation process by sector for the regulation of waste. In the UK, see Part II of the Environmental Protection Act 1990 and the Waste Management Licensing Regulations 1994 (SI 1994 No. 1056).

In May 2000 , after prolonged consultation and delay, *Waste Strategy 2000 for England and Wales* (Cm 4693) was published. In outline, the strategy document builds on the management plans already noted above. The main intention is to implement the Waste Framework Directive and to adopt specific targets for the period 2000–2010. Broadly defined, the targets are designed to decrease the current percentage of industrial and commercial waste going to landfill by 2005 to 85 per cent of the amount at 1998 levels. Currently, it is estimated that only 10 per cent of domestic waste is recycled. The strategy documents proposes that 40 per cent of domestic waste should be recycled by 2005. It is hoped by 2010 to recover 45 per cent of municipal waste and to recover 30 per cent of all household waste. It is hoped that the combination of incentives and penalties will encourage the targets set out above to be met. The range of economic instruments in use in this area is considered below. The parameters for the waste strategy are:

- a policy on recycling and recovery and re-use
- the adoption of a categorisation strategy for waste, identifying the various forms of waste and the details of waste sites and their management
- the principle of the polluter pays
- regular reporting and monitoring of the main targets and achievements for waste management
- the waste strategy regime to fit within the framework of the EU system of waste management
- the adoption of the best practicable environmental option
- key targets for waste management.

The Pollution Prevention and Control Act 1999 sets the scene for the development of the IPPC regime in conformity with Directive 96/61/EC on integrated pollution prevention and control.

The extensive reserve powers given to the Secretary of State to make regulations will change the existing waste licensing scheme and will have an impact on the existing waste management system. Lawrence explains the extensive nature of the waste management business:[15] '... 600 disposal or recovery facilities of capacities in excess of ten tonnes per day; eight municipal waste incinerators and 130 waste treatment plants. About 1,000 landfills are also covered by the Directive [the Landfill Directive 99/31]'.

---

[15]Lawrence, D., *Waste Regulation Law* (London, Butterworths, 1999), at 31.

Part of a waste minimisation strategy can be found in setting standards for packaging waste through the EU Packaging and Packaging Waste Directive (94/62, replaced 85/339 on 6 June 1996). This is incorporated in regulations under ss. 93–5 of the Environment Act 1995, which include the Producer Responsibility Obligations (Packaging Waste) Regulations 1997 (SI 1997 No. 648), which set targets for the use of re-usable and recyclable packaging and which came into force on 6 March 1997. These Regulations are beginning to make a significant contribution in limiting packaging. Businesses covered by the Regulations are expected to join a registered scheme for compliance with them and additional regulations are provided for individual businesses. The Packaging (Essential Requirements) Regulations 1998 (SI 1998 No. 1165) set essential requirements for all packaging after 31 December 1994. Generally these Regulations have resulted in companies across a variety of commercial sectors reviewing and amending the amount of packaging material used in product transport and presentation, and considering the possibilities for re-use of packaging. They have successfully moved an environmental agenda into retailing, a sector of commerce generally reticent about incorporating environmental strategies into business plans.

Although the reduction of the amount of waste produced is the preferred option, the government has techniques to support the re-use, recycling or recovery of material. Under s. 93 of the Environment Act 1995, the Secretary of State may make regulations in respect of products or materials. Producer responsibility obligations can require the re-use, recycling or recovery of material or products but such obligations can be imposed only in the context of both the environmental gain and the economic costs and benefits of any obligations. Procedures for making such orders and an appeals structure are set out in s. 93 and s. 94 of the 1995 Act, and s. 95 creates an offence of breaching producer responsibility. Nevertheless, there is an inherent limitation in recycling material. Paradoxically this comes not only from technical constraints, but also from material and product standards themselves. Recycling can be technically problematic in a number of ways and may actually result in more environmental harm, e.g., through energy consumption or the use of chemicals subsequently discharged in effluent, than if the material was simply disposed of as waste. Care is needed in balancing risk assessments on health and environmental impacts of waste disposal and risk assessments on the impacts of recycling. In addition, recycled material may contain impurities and, therefore, be below the manufacturers' standards set for raw material.[16]

---

[16]See Gascoigne, J. L. and Ogilvie, S. M, 'Recycling waste materials — opportunities and barriers' in Hester and Harrison *op. cit.* n. 11, at 91–115.

The Environmental Protection Act 1990, s. 75, and the Controlled Waste Regulations 1992 (SI 1992 No. 588) provide a broad definition for 'waste', i.e.:

(a)   any substance which constitutes a scrap material or an effluent or unwanted surplus substance from the application of any process;

(b)   any substance or article which requires to be disposed of as being broken, worn out, contaminated or otherwise spoiled;

(c)   any thing which is discarded or otherwise dealt with as if it were waste shall be presumed to be waste unless the contrary is proved.

Further amendment to the 1990 Act was required to implement Directive 91/156/EEC. Schedule 22, para. 88 of the Environment Act 1995 broadly defines 'any substance or object in the categories set out in schedule 2B to the Act [the 1990 Act] which the holder discards or intends or is required to discard . . .'.

Waste is divided up into a number of categories, which has important implications for the standards set for their transport and disposal:

(a)   *Waste that is not controlled* — this includes waste from mining and quarrying, as well as agricultural waste. It is, perhaps, surprising that agricultural waste is excluded from the 1990 Act and, therefore, from the licensing requirements under the Act.

(b)   *Controlled waste* — there are three types of controlled waste, including industrial, commercial and household waste (Controlled Waste Regulations 1992 (SI 1992 No. 588)). The division into these types of waste is significant only in so far as it determines if they must be collected by a waste collection authority (WCA) and the maximum charges that can be levied. There is a strict licensing regime for controlled waste (see below), and it is an offence unlawfully to deposit or handle controlled waste under s. 33(1) of the 1990 Act. There are various defences and exemptions in the Controlled Waste Regulations 1992. Licensing sets standards not only for the regulated disposal sites, but also for the entire process of waste management.

(c)   *Special waste* — this is defined under the Special Waste Regulations 1996 (SI 1996 No. 972), replacing the Control of Pollution (Special Waste) Regulations 1980 (SI 1980 No. 1709). A special waste is defined as falling within the EU's Hazardous Waste List which contains a variety of hazardous substances that are dangerous to life or have a low 'flash point', or which are a medicine only available on prescription (see s. 130 of the Medicines Act 1968). Most special waste arises from industry, but a number of products used domestically, e.g pesticides and battery acids, are also included.

The Environment Agency is now (under the Environment Act 1995) the national authority for the regulation of waste. Its remit includes overseeing licensing and the regulation of special waste and its law enforcement responsibilities are linked to other duties and supervision powers. The Environment Agency is also a licensing body and exercises regulatory controls over waste carriers. There are a number of other bodies that come under the Environment Agency's system of regulation, including waste collection authorities (WCAs), namely the relevant district council or, in London, the equivalent borough councils. The WCAs are responsible for arranging the collection of household domestic waste and for planning recycling and other strategies for commercial and household waste. The waste disposal authorities (WDAs) are defined as the relevant county councils in England. This includes the non-metropolitan areas or the unitary authorities. In other cases, it is generally the district council or London Borough Council which will exercise this function. WDAs oversee the performance and functioning of privatised waste disposal companies and operate some of the sites for waste recycling. The Special Waste Regulations 1996 provide for a Code of Practice and the regulation and restriction of the movement of waste. Site records, copies of notes and registers are used as part of the plethora of regulatory mechanisms that assist in the regulation of this complex area of law (DETR Circulars 6/96 and 14/96). There are further proposals for reform. A Consultative Paper[17] published in January 2000 also invites consultants to draw up a policy for waste management to incorporate waste reduction, good regulatory practice and the adoption of the waste hierarchy. The waste hierarchy consists of waste reduction, re-use and recovery (including recycling) and the safe disposal of remaining wastes. The strategy incorporates managing disposal, recycling and the recovery of waste materials. The aim being to cover the full 'life cycle' of waste products. This is consistent with the trend away from waste disposal in landfill sites to the management of a waste strategy organised around set targets. Also to be considered is the relationship between waste regulation and the Landfill Directive 99/31/EEC which bans the mix of hazardous and non-hazardous waste at the same site.

There are three further important categories of waste:

---

[17]ENDS Report 300, p. 40.

(a) radioactive waste (Radioactive Substances Act 1993);

(b) explosives (Explosives Act 1875); and

(c) mineral wastes (which fall under planning legislation, see above).

Planning law and waste

Waste disposal is a matter for planning law (see above) and requires planning permission. The Secretary of State must approve waste policies and mineral extraction policies prepared by local authorities for their areas under s. 38 of the TCPA 1990, amended by sch. 4 of the Planning and Compensation Act 1991. In England, the normal arrangement is that waste disposal falls under planning law at a local level. These policies must comply with the structure plans. If an existing disposal site is extended or changes in some other way, it may be deemed to have undergone a material change of use. Detailed policy guidance on waste disposal is contained in PPG 23, including the obligations set out in the Waste Management Licensing Regulations 1994 (SI 1994 No. 1056), sch. 4, Part I. Certain sites will be required to have an environmental impact assessment. There are plans to update PPG 23 through a new PPG 10 published in October 1999, which addresses planning issues associated with the responsibilities of the planning authorities and the Environment Agency. New sites for waste disposal require planning permission with the necessary conditions and safety arrangements, such as venting or gas removal, set as an intrinsic part of the planning controls.

There are specific controls on minerals. Under sch. 16 of the Local Government Act 1972, there is a mineral planning authority designated at county level which is responsible for all planning controls and the management of mineral workings. The Town and Country Planning (Compensation for Restrictions on Mineral Working and Mineral Waste Depositing) Regulations 1997 (SI 1997 No. 1111) apply in circumstances where the deemed mineral planning authority has to modify, revoke or make a discontinuance order in respect of mineral workings.

Standards for waste disposal

The process of waste management is controlled through the use of licences, which set standards for the carriage and deposit of controlled waste, and for the management of a waste site. Application for a licence is to the Environment Agency as the Waste Regulation Authority (WRA) under the Environment Act 1995. (This incorporates the Waste Management Licensing Regulations 1994, ensuring compliance with Directive 91/156.)

A waste management licence sets standards for the licensee and the person in charge of the licensed activity, as follows:

(a) The licensee must be a 'fit and proper person'.
(b) The licensee must have a certificate of competence from the Waste Management Industry Training and Advisory Board (Environment Act 1995).
(c) A technically competent person (under s. 74 of the Environmental Protection Act 1990) must be in charge of the licensed activity.

Under s. 35(1) of the Environmental Protection Act 1990, anyone is prohibited 'from depositing controlled waste or knowingly causing or permitting a deposit in or under land unless a waste management licence is in force and the deposit or the waste is in accordance with the licence.'

A site licence may be granted:

(a) to the occupier of the land;
(b) only in respect of land which has planning permission for the activity, or where there is a certificate of lawfulness (s. 191, Town and Country Planning Act 1990);
(c) after discussions have been held with the WRA and the Health and Safety executive have made submissions (if deemed necessary);
(d) in the case of the land being a site of special scientific interest (SSSI), following consultation with English Nature or the Country Council for Wales.

A mobile plant licence may be granted if appropriate, in which case a number of the above requirements no longer apply. The WRA can reject an application for a licence only on the grounds of:

(a) protection of the environment from pollution;
(b) risk of harm to human health; and
(c) where the land does not have planning permission, serious detriment to the amenities of the locality.

The application may also be refused if it is not made correctly and the applicant is not regarded as a 'fit and proper person'. Scientific assessment and modelling provide a basis for assessing risks in terms of environmental and health impacts, which has associated uncertainties. Appeal against refusal can be made within six months to the Secretary of State.

A licence may have a number of conditions attached to it by the WRA if deemed 'to be appropriate' (s. 35(3), Environment Protection Act 1990). The conditions must be reasonable, not too broadly drawn, be specific to the nature of the application, and cannot substitute for a refusal or be used for an ulterior purpose. The conditions may relate:

(a) to the licensed activities;
(b) to the precautions to be taken to avoid harm to the environment or human health, etc.;
(c) to the works to be carried out in exercise of the licensed activity;
(d) to conditions for other types of waste, i.e. not controlled waste; and
(e) powers may be given to the licence holder to carry out work not previously authorised.

A waste disposal site once filled still has associated health and environmental risks, often for a long time after the site has been closed. These risks may include gas (e.g., methane) generation during the anaerobic degradation of the organic fractions of the waste, and leachate containing heavy metals and toxic chemicals arising from the waste site. In part this is addressed through planning permissions for new sites incorporating requirements for venting, etc. (see above). In addition, s. 35(3) of the 1990 Act provides powers to impose obligations on the licence holder beyond the period of the licence activities. The terms of the licence then may stipulate a set of conditions for the safe disposal of waste, setting a standard on a case-by-case basis.

Monitoring is an important element of the waste management regime, and contributes to ensuring safety and compliance with licence requirements in a comparable way to monitoring liquid effluent discharges (see Chapter 7). It is not possible, however, to set common techniques for sample taking and analysis of waste in the way that a number of Directives and regulations have for liquid effluent and water quality monitoring. Each disposal site varies substantially in a number of ways, including:

(a) the characteristics of the waste it contains;
(b) the engineering design of the site;
(c) the local topography, soil characteristics and hydrology of the site; and
(d) its geographical location.

The monitoring techniques and regime for disposal sites will, then, have to be assessed and modified on a case-by-case basis. The Environment

Agency has recently issued for consultation a guidance document on monitoring landfill leachate, surface water and groundwater for land-fills.[18] This links monitoring to a risk based review on the basis of a monitoring plan. The monitoring plan must be specific to each site and should take into account the characteristics of the site and the waste it contains. The plan is to extend over the life of the landfill and specify site monitoring through selection of monitoring methods 'fit for the purpose', including sample points and their design, and monitoring frequency. A list of 'principal' and 'minor' chemicals for monitoring is provided in the guidance document and the choice of 'minor' chemicals is variable with site. The Environment Agency envisages the establishment of a base-line set of data for local groundwater before a site opens. The monitoring plan should set 'assessment limits' for the monitored chemicals over which remedial and control actions will be triggered to ensure that 'compliance limits' set in the licence are not breached. The Environment Agency should be notified if limits are exceeded and there is a clear element of self-regulation in this context.

The WRA (Environment Agency) has a duty to monitor waste disposal under s. 42(1) of the 1990 Act. This duty is strict and goes to a number of elements:

(a) the operation of the licence and licence conditions to ensure compliance;
(b) the activities in carrying out work under the licence to ensure that no environmental harm, risk to human health or detrimental impact on the amenities of the area occurs.

There is a duty to inform the Environment Agency if water pollution arises because of the licence activities.

The WRA has a number of powers to ensure compliance and safety: a notice may be served on the licence holder to ensure compliance; a licence may be suspended; and there are powers partly or completely to revoke a licence. In these events the site conditions are normally still enforced. The WRA also has powers to enforce emergency work if any harm or risk has been identified arising from activities at the site. Under the 1990 Act, a licence may be modified, transferred or surrendered and appeal can be made to the Secretary of State against the licence conditions or modifica-tion to the licence. In the case of non-compliance or breaches by the licence

---

[18]Environment Agency, *Guidance on monitoring of leachate, groundwater and surface water*. See ENDS Report 301, February 2000, *Agency consults on water monitoring guide for landfills*, at 37–38.

holder, there are penalties in criminal law under the Environmental Protection Act 1990. Statutory defences are found under s. 33(7).

The WRA has additional duties under Part II of the 1990 Act which go to the whole waste management system. It must prepare a plan for the treatment and disposal of controlled waste for local areas based on predictions of the amount and types of controlled waste likely to be produced. Incorporated in this plan must be a cost–benefit analysis of disposal routes. There are statutory requirements for consultation and information that must be observed before approval by the Secretary of State. Consultation must be undertaken with any representative of persons likely to be engaged in disposal or treatment of controlled waste and the Waste Collection Authority (WCA) in the area. Waste collection is tightly controlled. As mentioned above, each WRA is responsible for the licensing of waste carriers, i.e., the district council or London borough council. Under s. 45 of the Environmental Protection Act 1990, the WCA has a duty to collect domestic waste and, if requested, to collect or arrange for collection of any commercial waste from premises in its area. An exception to the duty on the WCA to collect household waste arises if the waste is at a site that is deemed too 'isolated or inaccessible' and would incur unreasonable collection costs. Under the Controlled Waste Regulations 1992 (SI 1992 No. 588), the WCA may charge for collection in some instances (e.g., garden waste), although normally collection is free. Charges may be made for commercial waste provided these are reasonable. The ultimate disposal of the waste must occur only in sites determined by the Waste Disposal Authority (WDA, see below), which is the same body as the WRA. Section 30 and sch. 2 of the 1990 Act provide for organisational separation of the functions and regulatory responsibilities of the WRA and the WDA.

Carriers other than the WCA must register with the WRA and have obligations under the Control of Pollution (Amendment) Act 1989 and supplementary regulations. There are exemptions from registration for WRAs, WCAs, WDAs, local authorities, persons who satisfy requirements of any EU member state, and others. Registration can be revoked or refused if the applicant is not a desirable carrier and there is the right of appeal to the Secretary of State. Enforcement is either by an authorised officer of the WRA, or by the police. There are powers to stop and check a vehicle for unlawful transportation of controlled waste, and a vehicle may be disposed of if the offence is proven.

The WDA has two regulatory responsibilities:

(a) the arrangement of the safe disposal of controlled waste at suitable sites and to coordinate the selection of appropriate sites with the WCA; and

(b) the provision of sites for the disposal of residential domestic waste.

Under s. 32 and sch. 2 of the Environmental Protection Act 1990, local authorities can set up local authority waste disposal companies.

In addition to the duties and responsibilities of the WRA, the WCA and other carriers, and the WDA (i.e. anyone involved in waste disposal) described above, there is a further important feature of the legislation in this area. The Royal Commission on Environmental Pollution[19] recommended that there should be a duty of care imposed on those involved in the disposal of waste. The Commission further recommended that criminal liability should result from any breach of this duty of care. Under s. 34 of the Environmental Protection Act 1990, it is required that persons dealing with controlled waste take all reasonable measures:

(a) to prevent any unauthorised or harmful deposit, treatment or disposal of waste; and

(b) to prevent any escape of waste or products from their control or that of any other person.

This does not apply to disposal of household waste by residents. There is a statutory defence available to a disposal operator in the case of escape of waste if it employed the best practice available at the time. There can be no retrospective application of standards as scientific and technical knowledge advances. The duty of care includes rules for the documentation and details for the proper transfer of waste (Environmental Protection (Duty of Care) Regulations 1991 (SI 1991 No. 2839)). The Secretary of State issues a statutory code under s. 34(7) of the 1990 Act. Penalties for breaching the duty of care, which is a criminal offence, are found under s. 34(6) of the 1990 Act.

There is a degree of transparency in the waste management process, which should evoke some public confidence in it. WRAs are required to maintain a public register (s. 64, 1990 Act) detailing:

(a) current or recent licences;

(b) applicants and matters that are relevant to the application;

(c) any convictions; and

(d) any action taken by the WRA under its legal powers.

Section 66 of the Environmental Protection Act 1990 contains a 'confidentiality' clause under which application can be made for the non-disclosure

---

[19]See Royal Commission on Environmental Pollution, 11th Report, *Managing Waste: The Duty of Care* (Cm. 9675, December 1985).

of information on the public register if that information would be deemed to 'prejudice to an unreasonable degree the commercial interests' of the individual. Appeal may be made to the Secretary of State.

Special waste, radioactive waste and mineral waste

Special waste must be carefully managed and segregated from other wastes. In general the waste management regime and regulatory requirements, i.e. standards, set for special waste are more stringent than for other types of controlled waste. For example, there is the need to record the location of special waste in a disposal site and there is closer supervision of the carriage of special waste. There is also the requirement for an environmental impact assessment for special waste disposal facilities (SI 1988 No.1199). The Hazardous Waste Directive (91/689/EEC) and the Waste Directive (91/156/EEC) may be extended to include other wastes in this category through a system of listing hazardous substances. Obligations also arise from the 1989 Basle Convention on the Control of Transboundary Movement of Hazardous Wastes and their Disposal.

The safe disposal of radioactive waste is a contentious issue and the future holds little prospect for solving the problems of how to store the products of the nuclear energy industry worldwide. The Sellafield reprocessing plant is the main site for deposit in the UK. This has proved controversial, and for the past decade the future of Sellafield has been a mattter of public debate. The nuclear industry in 1957 created one of the first modern safety programmes through the establishment of the Radioactive Waste Safety Standards Programme and it is very likely that the UK will support for the foreseeable future a nuclear energy programme with a proactive research policy. The nature of radioactive waste is defined in s. 2 of the Radioactive Substances Act 1993. The Environment Act 1995 made some amendments to the 1993 Act under sch. 22, paras 200–230. Nuclear installations come under the provisions of the Nuclear Installations Regulations 1971 (SI 1971 No. 381).

There has been low public confidence in the nuclear industry in recent years, partly as a result of a number of high-profile accidents, e.g., to the Chernobyl nuclear reactor. Radioactive waste does not only arise from the nuclear power generation and reprocessing of spent fuel rods, however, but also from hospitals and research facilities. Risk assessments for the safe disposal of radioactive waste are usually in terms of health risks to the general public and to occupational workers and the International Commission on Radiological Protection (ICRP) has estimated risks associated with exposure to radiation and recommended safe levels of exposure. These are put in terms of radiation dose per year (sieverts, Sv) and related, for instance, to the induction of cancer. The assessment of risk associated with radiation dose is complex, and in recent years the levels of dose considered safe have been revised downwards. A portion of the safety assessments is based on estimated exposure doses and their effects on human health arising from the Hiroshima nuclear explosion in 1945, but the estimates of doses received across the city are problematic and recently have been lowered, again underlining the need for regulatory standards to be flexible and responsive to changes in scientific understanding. In terms of the environmental effects of radioactive materials there is considerable complexity and uncertainty. Many radioactive elements are not only radioactive but also toxic, their mobility and fate in the environment may be difficult to predict and their impact on the living component of ecosystems is largely unknown. Also the very nature of radioactive decay means that one element changes to another in a strict sequence during the decay process with each of these daughter elements having different chemical and physical characteristics and different radioactivity. In addition, each element has a different rate of decay (half-life) and the inevitable mixture of radioactive elements arising from a single element is highly complex. When one radioactive element is present in waste, risk assessments must include consideration of all the elements formed in the so-called decay sequence.

The Radiological Protection Board recognises the dose limitation system recommended by the ICRP. All aspects of the radioactive material management are tightly controlled, including the material's use, storage and disposal. This falls under the Radioactive Substances Act 1993 (which is a consolidation of the Radioactive Substances Act 1970, heavily amended by the Environmental Protection Act 1990). The Environment Agency supervises registration of premises (Environment Act 1995). Licences are granted under the Nuclear Installations Act 1965. Carriage of radioactive materials is tightly regulated under the Radioactive Material (Road Transport) Act 1991. The Secretary of State exercises control under the Radioactive Substances Act 1993, as amended by the Environment Act 1995.

There are systems for the remediation of radioactively contaminated land similar to the system in place and described above for contaminated land in general. The Environment Agency has a prime responsibility and the regulations come under s. 78YFC of the Environmental Protection Act 1990, ss. 78E(1) and 78L(1). There is also a discrete set of regulations for the movement of nuclear waste under the Transfrontier Shipment of Radioactive Waste Regulations 1993 (SI 1993 No. 3031).

Specific types of waste generated during mining and quarrying fall under the Environmental Protection Act 1990. The location, size and restoration of mineral waste tips are controlled under the Town and Country Planning legislation. The Mines and Quarries (Tips) Act 1969, together with the Waste Management Licensing Regulations 1994 (SI 1994 No. 1056), require that spoil heaps are safe and stable. The regulations include standards for landscaping waste deposits and for good practice. Under the Coal Industry Act 1994 there are specific obligations to ensure that planning permission is obtained in respect of colliery waste. Six months' notice is required prior to closure of a mine and pollution prevention measures must be taken at this stage (Environment Act 1995, ss. 58–60). Owners and operators since 1999 no longer have statutory protections in case of discharges from mines.

WASTE AND ECONOMIC INSTRUMENTS

One of the important examples of the use of economic instruments in environmental law is the landfill tax for waste. In its origins the tax appears to be a justifiable way to discourage bad environmental practices, while using the revenue from the tax to fund reductions in employers' national insurance contributions. The tax is administered by HM Customs and Excise and indexed at a standard rate of £10 per tonne of waste and at a low rate for inactive waste only of £2 per tonne (current system for 1999–2000). The indexed increase will be at £11 per tonne. Current receipts from the tax are approximately £0.5 billion.[20] In addition, in 1995 government policy favoured the introduction of environmental trusts to engage in the clean-up of landfill sites. The Finance Act 1996 implemented this policy, and the Landfill Tax (Qualifying Material) Order 1996 (SI 1996 No. 1528) and the Landfill Tax (Contaminated Land) Order 1996 (SI 1996 No. 1529) set the parameters of what qualifies as waste. A further innovation is the adoption of tax credits for any environmental body engaged in land reclamation and associated activities, as set out in the Landfill Tax Regulations 1996 (SI 1996 No. 1527).

There are tough penalties for the evasion of landfill tax and the Waste Management (Miscellaneous Provisions) Regulations 1997 (SI 1997 No. 351) contain the main powers for investigation and penalties for evasion. However, it remains to be seen whether the landfill tax will succeed in its aim. There is concern that unregulated dumping may occur and evasion of the tax may become an acute problem.

---

[20]Figures are taken from Chennells, L., Dilnot A. and Emmerson, C., *The IFS Green Budget January 2000* (London, Institute for Fiscal Studies, Commentary 80, 2000).

GENETICALLY MODIFIED ORGANISMS (GMOs): CROPS AND FOOD

Serious public concern has arisen over the use of genetically modified food and crops.[21] Such crops have been developed as part of modern biotechnology, made possible through the discovery in the 1950s of the structure of deoxyribonucleic acid (DNA). The term 'genetically modified' (GM) may be defined as follows:[22]

The term 'genetic modification', when applied to food, refers to any artificial alteration in the genetic makeup of a food, animal or plant, or to the use of genetic engineering techniques in the production and manufacturing of food.

There is a variety of regulatory techniques available for GM crops and products, including overview by the courts (see *R v Secretary of State for the Environment and the Ministry of Agriculture, Fisheries and Food, ex parte Watson* [1999] Env LR 310. Labelling of products with GM content is required under EC Regulations 258/97 and 1139/98 and consents are required for releases and licences for crop trials. The release of GMOs may take place only through the granting of a consent by the Secretary of State under the Environmental Protection Act 1990 and the Genetically Modified Organisms (Deliberate Release) Regulations 1990 and 1995. See also the Genetically Modified Organisms (Contained Use) Regulations 1992 (SI 1992 No. 3217). The Regulations implement Directive 90/220/EEC providing for notification, consent and regulatory controls to protect human health. Consent is on a case-by-case basis and relies on guidance from scientific risk assessments.

The debate on GMOs is at the interface between setting standards through regulation, outlined above, and the public acceptance of the assurances provided by science. The House of Commons Environmental Audit Committee argued that the government should adopt a proactive strategy to reduce any potential environmental damage from GMOs. This strategy was rejected[23] in favour of a number of approaches implemented in the first half of the year 2000:

(a)   trials of GM crops to monitor any damage;

---

[21]See House of Commons, Third Report of the Agriculture Committee 1999–2000, *The Segregation of Genetically Modified Foods* (28 February 2000).
[22]See House of Commons Research Papers 93/55 and 99/38; Barclay, C., *Genetically Modified Crops and Food*, Research Paper 99/38.
[23]ENDS Report 298, p. 35.

(b)   the setting up of a global scientific body to advise on GM safety.[24] (this proposal was made at the G8 summit in July 2000);

(c)   inclusion of GMOs in EU environmental liability rules;

(d)   the establishment of the Agriculture and Environment Biotechnology Commission (AEBC), intended to increase public confidence in this area of science, chaired by Professor Malcolm Grant of the University of Cambridge.

Doubts remain about the safety of GMOs and the credibility of scientific evidence. There are significant uncertainties about issues such as the possibility of GMO crops becoming invasive, i.e., behaving like a weed, and any transfer of the engineered genes to wild relatives resulting in the creation of new GMOs with unknown characteristics. Risk assessments, on a case-by-case basis, form part of the licensing system and judgments are based on scientific criteria. The social context of the risk assessment (see Chapter 4) until relatively recently has been largely ignored, possibly fuelling public concerns. Here is an example of a well-structured regulatory system which none the less lacks public credibility in its standards.

CONCLUSIONS

The regulation of contaminated land and waste poses some of the most complex problems for environmental standard-setting. The need for regulation and the mix of regulatory techniques is well demonstrated by the problems of controlling waste and providing an appropriate regime for contaminated land. The general difficulty about regulation is well defined by Prosser:[25] 'Rationales for regulation then appear mixed: they are derived from economic principle, from (usually ill-defined) conceptions of the public interest, and from the idea that certain rights ought to prevail over market outcomes.'

As set out above, there is a plethora of regulatory techniques applied to land and waste and this has the potential to lead to contradictory policies. One example illustrates this point — the use of market-driven techniques such as contracts for remediation. Overlaying the market principles of free contracts are the procedures required by the EU for the licensing of waste management operations. The requirement of a licence has the effect of inhibiting contractors from engaging in remediation,[26] or worse that the

---

[24]ENDS Report 305, p. 6.

[25]Prosser, T., 'Regulation, Markets and Legitimacy' in J. Jowell and D. Oliver (eds)., *The Changing Constitution*, 4th edn. (Oxford, Oxford University Press 2000), at 232–3; Prosser, T., 'Theorising Utility Regulation' (1999) 62 MLR 196.

[26]ENDS Report 296, p. 5.

majority of companies engaged in remediation may be acting without a licence. This arises because of confusion over whether a licence is necessary, and also because a licence has safeguards that may make remediation an uncompetitive area where contracts may not provide sufficient incentives to make it attractive. The licence provisions requiring 'a fit and proper' person who is insured against financial loss may also prove problematic. The complexity and lack of clarity in interpretation of the requirements or of the need for a licence add a further dimension to an already difficult area of law. This may make it hard to attract commercial operators to engage in contracting, with the result that many contractors may act on the fringes of the law.

An example of a market-led instrument is the tax credit for landfill schemes.[27] There are doubts about whether monies earmarked for the scheme in local authorities will be spent on the development of a contaminated land strategy.[28]

The debate over GMOs illustrates the difficulties of providing a convincing science basis for the regulatory structure. This is a good example of public confidence in standards set by scientists being at a low ebb, thus rendering ineffective the regulation of GMOs to the extent that the public have continued doubts about their safety.

Regulating waste is an example of the complexity and variety of regulatory instruments that are available for regulating the environment. The result is a hotchpotch. Layer upon layer of legal controls exist that include a licensing regime and tough penalties for failing to comply with the regulations, including, where appropriate, the use of criminal sanctions. Taken together the result is a complicated structure which makes evaluation difficult and problematic. The EU has failed to provide an overarching strategy because member states wish to implement their own structures for control and the result is a mismatch of poorly coordinated strategies that remain largely untested in terms of their efficacy in improving the environment.

---

[27]ENDS Report 294, pp. 34–5.
[28]ENDS Report 305, p. 5.

CHAPTER NINE

Environmental Standards and Air

INTRODUCTION

Establishing air quality standards is a difficult challenge. There are many diverse air pollutants emitted by a variety of sources, from car exhaust gases to highly toxic fumes arising from industrial emissions. The effects of the pollutants may be both acute and chronic in terms of human health and the environment. Some atmospheric emissions have highly localised effects, others may cause adverse impacts across national boundaries, while still others exert their influence on a global scale. Assessment and prediction of the impacts of air pollutants is often fraught with problems and uncertainties. The challenge of setting standards for air quality and emissions, then, brings considerable legal and scientific demands. The history of establishing a clean air strategy based on standards in Britain started during the Victorian period. It forms a discrete contribution to the development of environmental protection and is also an example of how standard-setting may build up incremental improvements to the air quality in major towns and cities. In the 1980s, Britain made substantial gains in regulating emissions from industry and in developing clean air technology for domestic heating.

The European Union has provided a framework for the implementation of measures to improve air quality and many of the standards discussed in this chapter are part of a European initiative or form an international agreement. Setting targets for air quality is a common technique for improving that quality but this must be placed against a background that is less clear in terms of policy and objectives. As Kramer has noted[1] 'there is no coherent, overall Community air pollution strategy'. The explanation in part lies in the problem of tackling emissions from the main energy sources used in producing electricity and emissions from large industrial processes and there is the added difficulty that while economic activity may differ in each member state, the collective output in terms of pollutants may cross national boundaries. As Kramer points out, this makes finding a common solution very difficult. A further problem is that just as energy policy may impact on air pollutants, transport policy may impact on the pollution caused by motor vehicles. The Commission has taken a lead in the formation of policies in both areas, but there are difficulties in achieving a common response. The adoption of the catalytic converter for all new cars since 1993 is a rare example of finding a common technological solution throughout the EU, but it is less easy to be optimistic about finding a solution that could be easily implemented, for example, in renewable energy. Member states may be reluctant to introduce a requirement that might have economic consequences for investments in their indigenous energy industries.

Air standards, because of their transboundary nature, may reflect higher expectations than it is possible to meet through the formulation of energy or transport strategies which incorporate the air policy. Setting standards for air quality may, paradoxically, become a more effective way of developing an effective energy or transport policy than attempting to find a common policy for those areas.

Environmental standards relevant to the air are considered in four sections below. First, the development of an air quality strategy containing air quality standards and targets. The second section sets out the standards for a variety of different processes and installations as part of an air quality strategy. The third section covers emissions from vehicles and industry with a local impact on the environment and public health. The fourth section covers issues that relate to climate change and how this will impact on standard-setting. The analyses provided in the previous chapters on land and water are drawn together in considering various common environmental problems. Attempts to control, for example, acid rain, levels of stratospheric ozone-depleting chemicals, greenhouse gases concentrations and photochemical smog have come from setting standards. Lastly, we discuss the standards for noise and the steps adopted to prevent noise pollution.

---

[1] Kramer, L., *EC Environmental Law*, 4th edn. (London, Sweet and Maxwell, 2000), at 204

AIR QUALITY STANDARDS AND AIR QUALITY MANAGEMENT

Standards in their historical context

Effective air quality standards started to emerge in the nineteenth century, when it came to be recognised that air quality had an impact on public health. It is estimated,[2] for example, that the consumption of coal in Britain from 1800 to 1950 increased from 10 to 194 million tons with over a quarter of all coal used for domestic purposes. Sulphur dioxide emissions[3] rose from 0.25 to 6.00 million tons between 1800 and 1965 during a period when the standards of public health were low, in part as a result of poor quality of air combined with poor nutrition and health care. Life expectation at birth in England and Wales rarely changed for men and women in the nineteenth century, but significantly rose from the late 1950s. As Clapp concludes:[4] '... in comparison with modern Britain the life-table for 1838–54 depicts a heavy loss of human life, some of it almost certainly attributable to atmospheric pollution.'

The responses to problems of air quality were varied and included a combination of investigative and monitoring strategies. A smoke abatement policy was introduced for England and Wales, the Alkali Inspectorate was established under the Alkali Act 1863 to set controls on emissions, and the Public Health Act 1875 established standards for housing and sanitation (see also the Control of Pollution Act 1974 and the Health and Safety at Work etc. Act 1974). The Alkali Inspectorate adopted the principle of the Best Practicable Means (BPM) and the first statutory emission standard limiting hydrogen chloride (see the Alkali Act 1874).[5] The foundations for standard-setting followed a common pattern — a listing of specific processes and setting emission standards (Alkali etc. Works Regulation Act 1906). Establishing a link between air quality and health permitted remedial action to be taken (Public Health (Smoke Abatement) Act 1926), including listing additional noxious substances and processes to be added to by powers granted to the Secretary of State. Even now this pattern remains fundamental.

Today health care standards are more readily accepted and action taken, but the link between health and atmospheric pollution may often be difficult to establish. A range of medical problems, such as asthma and bronchitis, are aggravated or even caused by poor air quality, although

---

[2]Clapp, B. W., *An Environmental History of Britain* (Harlow, Longman, 1994), at 16–23.
[3]*Ibid.*, at 56–7.
[4]*Ibid.*, at 65.
[5]National Society for Clean Air, *1999 Pollution Handbook* (London, 1999), at 66.

how this occurs remains unclear. There has been substantial debate as to whether the causal link between air pollution and these illnesses is sulphur dioxide emissions or particulates. A number of large epidemiological studies were undertaken in the 1960s and 1970s in an attempt to clarify this, but comparisons between the studies were difficult since different air sampling procedures were used. This underlines a problem raised with regard to water sampling (see Chapter 7), that (monitoring) data may vary with sampling procedure. The data from the epidemiological studies, however, appear to suggest that particulates are the key causal agent in pollution-linked asthma and other respiratory illnesses.[6] Asthma, in particular, is one of the fastest growing diseases in the United Kingdom, affecting some 20 per cent of children. Significantly, there appears to be an additive affect (see Chapter 4) between these pollutants in exacerbating pulmonary conditions. In setting standards, such interactions between air-borne pollutants may be crucial.

Poor air quality can also have acute affects on plants and animals, and chronic exposure to atmospheric pollution over long periods can have an adverse effect on ecosystems, lowering both water and soil quality. There has been much concern in recent years about the impact of air pollution on the fabric of historic buildings and other structures, e.g., through acid rain formation. A range of air pollutants contributes to the greenhouse effect, in particular carbon dioxide emissions from power generation. The effects of global warming will be measured not only in terms of ecosystem damage and change, but also in terms of major social and economic impacts. Probable changes in agricultural productivity, climate, sea-level and disease distribution because of global warming may prove difficult to predict accurately or manage effectively. There are widespread concerns about depletion of the ozone layer induced by a variety of reactive chemicals, which are air pollutants.

The response at national, EU and international level is to set targets and standards for air quality and emissions and this involves both proactive and reactive forms of standard-setting. Air quality standards set by Community Directives are seen as the most effective to improve air quality. At national and international level there is much discussion of alternative economic instruments, such as setting national emission ceilings, the adoption of tradable air pollution certificates and using clean technology in the developing world to forestall future problems.

---

[6]Elsom, D. B., *Atmospheric Pollution: A Global Problem*, 2nd edn. (Oxford, Blackwell) provides a brief discussion of the health effects of low-level atmospheric pollution (at 25–29).

Standards for air pollution should be seen in the general context of instruments and techniques for regulating air quality. In the UK there have been some initiatives associated with developing strategies for the prevention of air pollution: inspection of processes is required under the Health and Safety at Work etc. Act 1974; limits on emissions are provided under Part I of the Environmental Protection Act 1990; and there are smoke control systems under the Clean Air Acts 1956–1968. Examples of strategies for the prevention of air pollution include the following:

(a) *Reducing energy usage.* The Home Energy Conservation Act 1995 provides for the drawing up of local energy conservation reports in relation to residential accommodation. Local authorities in Scotland, England and Wales and the Housing Executive in Northern Ireland can be designated as energy conservation authorities. Section 2 of the Act provides that it is the duty of every energy conservation authority to prepare a report setting out measures 'that the authority considers practicable, cost-effective and likely to result in significant improvement in the energy efficiency' of residential accommodation in its area. Significantly, the report should include an assessment of the cost of energy conservation and an assessment of the extent to which carbon dioxide emissions (a major contributor to global warming) into the atmosphere would be decreased as a result of the measures. The 1995 Act also provides that the energy conservation report must contain an assessment of the impact of reduced emissions into the atmosphere of oxides of nitrogen and sulphur dioxide.

(b) *The regulation of stubble burning.* Section 152 of the Environmental Protection Act 1990 empowers the Secretary of State to make regulations banning farmers from this practice on agricultural land. Stubble burning produces various emissions, especially carbon dioxide and particulates. (See the Crop Residues (Burning) Regulations 1993 (SI 1993 No. 1366).)

(c) *The setting of minimum standards of emissions for road vehicles* (see s. 41 of the Road Traffic Act 1988 and EU Directives on the standard for new vehicles (Directive 91/441, Directive 88/76 and Directive 94/12)) *and the setting of standards on vehicle fuels such as lead free petrol* (see Directive 75/116/EEC and Directive 87/219/EEC; see also the Motor Fuel (Sulphur Content of Gas Oil) Regulations 1990 (SI 1990 No. 1097) and the Motor Fuel (Lead Content of Petrol) Regulations 1981 (SI 1981 No. 1523)). Alkyl lead compounds such as tetraethyl lead and teramethyl lead are used as anti-knock additives in petrol. As a result of combustion in the engine, up to

70 per cent is emitted in car exhausts to be deposited locally or dispersed over considerable distances. There are two key reasons for control: (i) health concerns linked to airborne lead; and (ii) catalytic converters, which reduce other car emissions, do not work properly with leaded petrol.

An air quality strategy

A new national strategy for air quality was introduced in 1997, under Part IV and s. 80 of the Environment Act 1995, which provide for:

(a) air quality standards;
(b) the aims and objectives of controlling air pollutants; and
(c) measures to be taken to enforce the objectives.

Part IV of the Act requires that a periodic review of the national air quality strategy, including standards and objectives, is undertaken. The same requirement falls on local authorities who are required to establish a system of Local Air Quality Management (LAQM). This provides for standards to be set at a local level, including review and assessment, and for an action plan for improvements to pursue air quality objectives.

Section 87 of the Environment Act 1995 provides the Secretary of State with regulation-making powers. The Air Quality (England) Regulations 2000 (SI 2000 No. 928) address seven of the eight pollutants contained in the 1997 national air quality strategy with ozone omitted due to the transboundary nature of the problem and the difficulty of adopting effective local action. The Air Quality (England) Regulations 2000 (SI 2000 No. 928) replace the 1997 Regulations and contain a designated period for implementation and a number of prescriptive standards (see Table 9.1). Generally the proposal is to set tighter targets than in the past. Again, ozone is not included in the list as it is proposed that action should be taken as part of a national strategy. In its draft consultation document,[7] the DETR admits that particle targets set in the past had been largely unachievable, and in the light of this new targets in line with the European Union targets have been agreed.

---

[7] *The Air Quality Strategy for England, Scotland and Northern Ireland* (Cm 4548).

Table 9.1 Proposed draft standards with date by which the standard is expected to be achieved

Pollutant	Standard	Measurement	Date
Benzene	16.25 µg/m³ (5ppb)	running annual mean	31 December 2003
1,3 Butadiene	2.25 µg/m³ (1ppb)	running annual mean	31 December 2003
Carbon monoxide	11.6 mg/m³ (10ppm)	running 8 hour mean	31 December 2003
Lead	0.5 µ/m³	annual mean	31 December 2004
	0.25 µg/m³	annual mean	31 December 2008
Nitrogen dioxide	200 µg/m³ (105ppb)	1 hour annual mean	31 December 2005
	40 µg/m³ (21ppb)	1 hour annual mean	31 December 2005
		(not to be exceeded > 18 times/ year)	
Particles (PM$_{10}$)	50µg/m³	14 hour annual mean	31 December 2004
	40µg/m³	14 hour annual mean	31 December 2004
		(not to be exceeded > 35 times/ year)	
Sulphur dioxide	350 µg/m³ (132 ppb)	15 min, 1 hour, 14 hour mean	31 December 2004
		(not to be exceeded > 24 times/ year)	
	125 µg/m³ (47 ppb)	15 min, 1 hour, 14 hour mean	31 December 2004
		(not to be exceeded > 3 times/ year)	
	266 µg/m³ (100ppb)	15 min, 1hour, 14 hour mean	31 December 2005
		(not to be exceeded > 35 times/ year)	

The proposals set out in Table 9.1 serve to reinforce certain principles in adopting this form of standard-setting:

(a) Problems over setting and reaching attainable standards for particulates[8] (PM$_{10}$) lead to a review of the standard and its amendment.

(b) In developing a new air quality standard for particulates, scientific evidence and uncertainty as to the harmful effects of different levels of particulates are in dispute.[9] The absence of scientific

---

[8]ENDS Report 304, pp. 14–15.
[9]*Ibid.*

consensus may inhibit the progression of common standards for particulates.

(c) Continuous monitoring of standards is required. The government's Expert Panel on Air Quality Standards is likely to require further revisions in the light of future Community developments. Moreover, as scientific uncertainty is resolved on the adverse effects of gaseous pollutants, standards may have to be reassessed. Responsive air quality standards are essential.

(d) There may be additional complexity in reaching commonly agreed sets of standards. The Scottish Executive may continue with the 1997 standards rather than adopt the new proposals.[10]

(e) There may be difficulties in implementing standards between different levels or tiers of government. In particular, the system of air pollution control falls under the remit of local authorities.

The role of local authorities

An important part of the new national strategy is the introduction of air quality management areas under ss. 83 and 84 of the Environment Act 1995. This permits local authorities to set limits on local pollution. Currently, a review is undertaken by the Environment Agency of the statutory guidance for processes that fall under the local air pollution control arrangements. In particular, the requirement to adopt the best available techniques not entailing excessive costs (BATNEEC) is being considered in preference to the principle of best available techniques. There is some debate whether the two terms make any practical difference at the operational level. However, the EU has made a significant contribution in developing new directives, especially in the area of solvents and sulphur.

Local authorities have a number of responsibilities for the regulation and control of the air quality within their areas. These include the enforcement of statutory nuisance legislation, enforcement of the Clean Air Act 1993 that covers smoke, grit, dust and fumes, enforcing noise legislation and ensuring a consistent policy for their region. There is a Memorandum of Understanding (February 1997) between local authorities and the Environment Agency for the common development of strategies that fall within their shared responsibilities and local authorities are also under a duty to carry out a consultation process with the Secretary of State, other local authorities and the Environment Agency, as well as to receive representations from local business interests.

---

[10]ENDS Report 300, p. 38.

Local authorities play an important role in IPPC. This covers over 2,000 processes throughout the major industry sectors under the Prescribed Processes and Substances Regulations 1991 (SI 1991 No. 472). Included in IPPC is an assessment of the total impact of releases from processes to air, water and land. The Pollution Prevention and Control Act 1999 provides amendments to the Environmental Protection Act 1990 and is intended to extend cover to over 6,000 installations across England and Wales.

The division of responsibility between the local authority and Environment Agency is as follows:[11]

Regime A — An integrated permitting regime. Emissions to air, land and water of the potentially more polluting processes. (Environment Agency)
    Regime A1 — Emissions to air, land and water of potentially more polluting processes. (Environment Agency)
    Regime A2 — Emissions to air, land, and water of processes with a lesser potential to pollute. (Local authority)
Regime B — Local air pollution control under the Pollution Prevention and Control Act 1999. (Local authority)
Regime B — Air regulation. (Local authority)

Common to the setting of standards is the need to establish effective monitoring techniques (see Chapter 7) and monitoring systems. For air quality this is achieved through the use of monitoring stations at over 200 sites under an Enhanced Urban Network since 1995, the successor to the early development in 1961 of the National Survey of Air Pollution. The success of air quality standards depends on the efficacy of their monitoring. In the past criticisms of the quality of monitoring systems (particularly as to the location and accuracy of monitoring sites) has impugned their credibility and accurate and reliable monitoring requires considerable technical development and research to establish the most appropriate procedures. The technical problems may be formidable,[12] but in addition there are a number of crucial questions that go to the siting of monitoring stations, which will substantially influence the levels of pollutants measured. Consideration must be given to issues such as:

(a)   geographic location — residential, city centres, at road intersections, rural locations, etc.;

---

[11]DETR, *Pollution, Prevention and Control*, 29 June 2000.
[12]Harrison, R. M. (ed.), *Pollution: Causes, Effects and Control*, 2nd edn. (Cambridge, Royal Society of Chemistry, 1993) provides information on methods to measure levels of air pollutants.

(b) position — next to a road, at the edge of the pavement furthest away, at adult or child's height; and

(c) frequency of measurement — minutes, hourly, daily, varying with season or climatic conditions, local topography.

Any of these might well differ with the particular pollutants, since their chemistry and longevity in the air vary. In addition, they are differentially influenced by weather conditions and exert any adverse effects in different ways. Effective monitoring is a demanding achievement.

STANDARDS FOR DIFFERENT PROCESSES AND INSTALLATIONS

An example of the contribution of the European Union to the setting of standards is to be found in the strategy to reduce discharges of pollutants from major sources. There are a number of parts to the strategy:

(a) Proposed national emission ceilings for critical atmospheric pollutants for each member state.

(b) A proposed Council Directive on the sulphur content of specific fuels. This includes COM (98) 385, with the setting of minimum standards and the ratification of the UNECE Sulphur Protocol (COM (97) 88).

(c) Revision of the 1988 Large Combustion Plant Directive (88/609/ EEC). The Directive applies limits on the emissions of certain pollutants from combustion plants that are rated at a minimum of 50 megawatts (MW) thermal input. There are exemptions for certain plants. The aim is to reduce emissions of sulphur dioxide and oxides of nitrogen by setting national ceilings for member states. There are three phases (from 1990 to 2003) for implementing the Directive. There is a UK programme for reducing emissions published by the DETR.[13] The quotas that are set in the UK are subject to revision to ensure that the UK meets the targets of the Directive. Changes such as the use of different fuels may have implications for the target. Her Majesty's Inspectorate of Pollution (now the Environment Agency) set new targets to take account of the current situation.[14]

(d) Air quality standards are part of the IPPC strategy for the environment (see Prescribed Processes and Substances Regulations 1991 (SI 1991 No. 472)). EC Directive 84/360 requires member

[13]See Department of the Environment, *Programme and National Plan for Reducing SO$_2$ and NOx Emissions from Large Combustion Plants* (1990)
[14]See ENDS Report 245, p. 29).

states to provide prior authorisation for industrial plant in various industries such as energy, metal processing and production, manufacturing industries in terms of non-metallic mineral products, chemicals, waste disposal and others. The principles employed in deciding on the authorisation include BATNEEC and the fact that the plant concerned does not emit significant amounts of pollutants, including sulphur and nitrogen and their compounds; carbon monoxide; organic compounds excluding methane (e.g., volatile organic compounds (VOCs)); chlorine and fluorine and their compounds; dust; asbestos; and glass and mineral fibres.

(e) There are a number of Directives on municipal waste incinerators, including Directive 89/369/EEC on the prevention of air pollution from new (authorised from 1 December 1990) municipal waste incineration plants. There is also Directive 89/429/EEC that applies to plant before 1 December 1990, and this includes a time-table for new municipal waste incineration plants. There are proposals for a Directive on the Incineration of Hazardous Waste (OJ No. C 130/1, 21 May 1992). Any proposed incinerator plants first require to be authorised and limits are set on the legally permitted emissions. Directive 87/217/EEC on Pollution caused by Asbestos requires member states to ensure that asbestos releases into air, water and land are reduced at source and prevented. The principles involved in setting standards fall under BATNEEC, reinforced by the Trade Effluents (Prescribed Processes and Substances) Regulations 1989 (SI 1989 No. 1156).

Vehicle emission controls and transport policy

As noted above, both member states and the EU have found it impossible to formulate a common transport policy. In July 2000, the government in the United Kingdom introduced a long-awaited White Paper on Transport Policy, setting out an increase in expenditure on public transport, particularly rail. The use of by-pass schemes around some major towns and cities and upgrading some major sections of motorways where traffic delays are common were also included in the White Paper. There is, therefore, the beginning of an integrated transport policy.[15]

The contribution of road use to air quality is undoubted, but the link between the levels of traffic pollution and the effects on public health is more contentious.[16] It is proving scientifically demanding to establish not

---

[15]ENDS Report 291, p. 35.
[16]ENDS Report 300, p. 5.

only acute effects but also chronic effects from long-term exposure to atmospheric pollutants and the variables and uncertainties associated with the epidemiological toxicology studies are substantial. Currently, the United Kingdom's reduction in carbon dioxide levels is slow, and it is doubtful if the target of 20 per cent reduction between 1990 and 2010 will be met.[17] Vehicles, of course, contribute to carbon dioxide emissions and the European Commission aims to reduce emissions from road transport by up to 70 per cent by the year 2010 (COM (96) 248). There are concerns that the standards of air quality set by the government as sustainable targets may be inconsistent with the direction taken in regulating road vehicles as it is accepted that significant increases in traffic are inevitable, and that setting targets for road use 'might be a blunt instrument'. The setting of fuel charges at about 6 per cent above the rate of inflation (the fuel escalator), intended to help meet the CO_2 target, has proved to be unpopular and has been scrapped.[18] The proposal to set traffic targets has been rejected as being too heavy-handed.[19]

The strategy contained in the Transport Act 2000 is to give local authorities powers to make:

(a) congestion charges and parking levies, the revenue to be hypothecated to transport policies;
(b) bus strategies, to have regard to congestion, air, noise and pollution as part of joint partnerships with business.

Regulating road transport for emissions, in particular for nitrogen oxides, carbon dioxide, carbon monoxide, hydrocarbons and particulates, is part of the standard-setting structure for vehicle construction, use and emission control. There is a plethora of standards to be found in Directive 93/59/EEC on vehicles, supplemented by Directive 94/12/EEC, contained in the Construction and Use Regulations 1986 as amended (SI 1995 No. 2210). There are UK and EC standards on the measurement of smoke emissions from diesel engined vehicles and a standard BS AU 141, now legally binding on the UK. The Road Traffic Regulation Act 1984 has been supplemented by the Road Traffic (Vehicle Emissions) (Fixed Penalty) Regulations 1997 (SI 1997 No. 3058) to cover the emissions from engines; and in cases of drivers leaving their engines running unnecessarily, a fixed penalty is set.

---

[17]ENDS Report 302, p. 3.
[18]ENDS Report 298, p. 5.
[19]ENDS Report 300, p. 38.

Standard-setting regulations, as outlined above, depend on a coherent transport policy if they are to make any significant reduction in air pollution.

Agricultural good practice

In 1992, the government introduced a Code of Good Agricultural Practice for the Protection of Air. The Code sets out the relevant legislation, standards and gives guidance on how best practice may be established and the steps required to ensure good standards for reducing ammonia and greenhouse gases. This is an example of standard-setting targeted at a special group with good advice being expected to lead to improvements to the agricultural sector as a whole.

Control of noxious emissions and dark smoke

The Clean Air Act 1993 contains the main provisions on air pollution and the control of dark smoke. The 1993 Act replaced and consolidated the Clean Air Acts 1956 and 1968 and the Control of Smoke Pollution Act 1989. Here standards are set through the use of guides, circulars and guidance issued by the DETR. The 1993 Act prescribes the height and construction of chimneys and creates an offence for dark smoke to be emitted from a chimney of any building or any fixed boiler or industrial plant, or from any industrial or trade premises. Dark smoke is defined according to the Riglemann Chart which acts as a type of calibration curve and provides local authority environmental health officers with the standard means to measure and monitor dark smoke emissions. The Chart is calibrated from 0 to 5, and the standard for dark smoke is set at 2. In addition there is a plethora of regulations and exemptions: the Dark Smoke (Permitted Periods) Regulations 1958 (SI 1958 No. 498); the Clean Air (Emission of Dark Smoke) (Exemption) Regulations 1969 (SI 1969 No. 1263); the Clean Air Act (Emission of Grit and Dust from Furnaces) Regulations 1971 (SI 1971 No. 162); the Clean Air (Measurement of Grit and Dust from Furnaces) Regulations 1971 (SI 1971 No. 161); and the Clean Air (Height of Chimneys) (Exemption) Regulations 1969 (SI 1969 No. 411).

Liability is placed on the occupier of a building, or the person who is in possession of a boiler, for the use of a chimney. In industrial or trade premises there is strict criminal liability on the occupier of the premises, or on any person who causes or permits the emissions. Otherwise the offences are mainly summary ones, and there is a requirement under s. 51 of the 1993 Act to notify the occupier of the premises, or the person in possession of the boiler or plant, in writing within four days of the alleged offence. Statutory exceptions to strict liability may be found in s. 1(4) of the Act and, broadly, these are based on lighting up a furnace, or the failure to prevent smoke emissions that are not reasonably foreseen. There is also, under s. 2(4) of the 1993 Act, a defence if the defendant can show that the alleged emission was inadvertent, and that all practicable steps had been taken to prevent or minimise the emission of dark smoke.

Further exceptions are provided in a number of regulations (see the Dark Smoke (Permitted Periods) Regulations 1958 and the Clean Air (Emission of Dark Smoke) (Exemption) Regulations 1969) which specify exemptions in the lighting of a furnace, or where the emission was due to some failure of apparatus that could not be foreseen or to the use of unsuitable fuel when suitable fuel was unobtainable. In industrial and trade premises, it is for the defendant to bear responsibility for showing that no dark smoke was emitted where material is burned on the premises.

Regulation of smoke and emissions of grit and dust is covered by the Clean Air Act 1993. Section 4 requires that new furnaces should be smokeless and there are limits on the rate of emission of grit and dust (see s. 5 of the 1993 Act and the Clean Air (Emission of Grit and Dust from Furnaces) Regulations 1971). There are regulations for the fitting of grit and dust arresting plant, and also certain exemptions which may be granted at the discretion of the local authority and subject to appeal to the Secretary of State for Environment (see the Clean Air (Arrestment Plant) (Exemptions) Regulations 1969 (SI 1969 No. 1262)).

Sections 10 and 11 of the Clean Air Act 1993 provide for the measurement of grit, dust and fumes emitted from furnaces. There are also powers for the control of the heights of chimneys under s. 14 of the Act (see Clean Air (Height of Chimneys) (Exemption) Regulations 1969 (SI 1969 No. 411)). The tendency to utilise tall stacks (chimneys) for emissions to the atmosphere while helping to protect local environments has been blamed for dispersing the pollutants and the effect may be to transfer adverse impacts to regions distant from the original source. There are proposals to deregulate and repeal certain parts of the Clean Air Act 1993 as part of an overall deregulation strategy.[20]

In addition to the regulation of emissions such as grit and dust, there are also smoke control areas that are subject to smoke control orders under s. 18 of the 1993 Act. Procedures for making and enforcing orders for the prohibition of smoke in such areas are covered by ss. 18 to 22 of the 1993 Act and powers are vested in the Secretary of State to require the creation of smoke control areas by a local authority. Setting standards is part of the

---

[20]See Department of the Environment, *A Proposal to Repeal Provisions of the Clean Air Act 1993* (July 1993).

ndards Regulations 1989 (SI 1989 No. 317) and there are
f orders that apply to fireplaces in domestic dwellings (see
_ Clean Air Act 1956) and regulations for smokeless fuels (see
_Jinoke Control Areas (Authorised Fuels) Regulations 1991 (SI 1991 No.
1282) and the Smoke Control Areas (Authorised Fuels)(Amendment)
Regulations 1992 (SI 1992 No. 72)). These regulations provide local
authorities with powers and obligations in smoke control areas over
domestic and industrial premises.

Climate Change and Ozone Depletion

This area of the law is not static and new developments in terms of scientific
understanding lead to new Directives. The EU has introduced Regulation
91/594/EEC[21] on substances that may contribute to the depletion of the
ozone layer in the stratosphere and this covers various chlorofluorocarbons
(CFCs), halons, carbon tetrachloride and 1,1,1 trichloroethane. There are
restrictions in the UK on the importation, supply and storage of non-refillable
containers containing CFCs for use in refrigerants or air-conditioning
machinery. All these compounds contribute to the chemical reactions that
reduce ozone concentrations in the stratosphere, although the actual reaction
varies somewhat with the class of compound.[22] There are major concerns
about the health (e.g., skin cancers and cataracts) and ecosystem effects of
ozone depletion due to the resultant rise in UV radiation reaching earth.[23]

Responses to global warming and climate change[24] have varied through
consideration of a wide range of economic and fiscal instruments to meet
targets for the reduction of carbon dioxide and other greenhouse gases.
There is now the planned introduction of a climate change levy[25] from
April 2001 as part of the United Kingdom's response to global warming.
In 1994, the UK's strategy was set out in *Climate Change — the UK's
Programme,* which sought to provide incentives to reduce greenhouse gas
emissions. The levy is intended to cut 2 per cent off business emissions of
carbon dioxide by 2010 and is part of an economic instrument to
implement the UK's obligations under the Kyoto Protocol. Negotiations
are ongoing to reach agreements between key energy-intensive industries
and the government. A proposal from the European Commission for a
carbon or energy tax has failed to be agreed by member states.

---

[21][1991] OJ L 76/1.
[22]See McEldowney, J. and McEldowney, S., *Environment and the Law* (Harlow,
Longman, 1996), where the above analysis is explored in more detail.
[23]*Ibid* and see Elsom, *op. cit.* n. 6, at 132–44.
[24]Elsom, *op. cit.* n. 6, at 145-68.
[25]ENDS Report 290, p. 19.

There is also the possibility of a trading scheme for greenhouse gases as part of a programme of reduction of gases throughout the European Union. A trading scheme consists of a market in emissions. Those countries with a surplus may sell to those countries with a deficit and there may be the possibility of stockpiling future emissions to meet further reductions in emissions targets.

NOISE

Regulating noise through standards has proved one of the most problematic areas. Environmental health departments receive large numbers of complaints about noise, the scale varying from domestic premises, industrial and commercial premises, through to industrial sites and appliances.[26] The European Union has been slow to take action, but through noise standards for vehicles and aircraft a series of Directives have attempted to provide noise emission standards throughout the EU. There is an internationally accepted standard for the measurement of noise. See Table 9.2.[27]

Table 9.2 International standard for measurement of noise

Noise level (db)	Human perception
0	Threshold of hearing
10	Leaves rustling
30	Quiet bedroom at night
40	Average living room
50	Living room with distant traffic noise
60	Busy office
70	Conversational speech
75	Major road with heavy traffic
88	Heavy lorry on busy road
90 +	Potential loss of hearing from prolonged exposure
100	House near airport
125	Jet aircraft taking off
140	Threshold of pain.

[26]See McEldowney and McEldowney, *op. cit.* n. 22, chap. 13.
[27]Taken with modifications from Kerse, C. S., *The Law Relating to Noise* (London, Oyez, 1975), and *This Common Inheritance* (Cm. 1200). See also Van Wynsberghe, D., Noback C. R. and Carola, R., *Human Anatomy and Physiology*, 3rd edn. (New York, McGraw Hill Inc., 1995).

The general approach to noise in the United Kingdom is to rely on the use of the common law to provide remedies in public or private nuisance. Local authorities have statutory powers to investigate reasonable complaints about noise and Part III of the Control of Pollution Act 1974, supplemented by the Environmental Protection Act 1990, provides for various controls on noise. In terms of regulating the environment, the powers of the local authority are investigative, preventative and remedial. Investigation powers are provided for under s. 79 of the 1990 Act, and a noise abatement notice may be served on the offender under s. 80 of the 1990 Act. Statutory powers have been gradually supplemented, creating a list of criminal offences associated with noise. Part III of the Environmental Protection Act 1990, the Noise and Statutory Nuisance Act 1993 and the Noise Act 1996 make night-time noise an offence and provide a way for the police to stop noise from continuing through the use of confiscation powers. Noise in a public street and on construction sites may be regulated and burglar alarms may be regulated under the Noise and Statutory Nuisance Act 1993. Also regulated under the 1993 Act are noisy parties and public entertainment is covered by the Local Government (Miscellaneous Provisions) Act 1982. There are also a number of miscellaneous statutory regulations for the control of noise. Controls on noise at work are provided under the Health and Safety at Work etc. Act 1974 and noise in industrial and construction sites under the Control of Pollution Act 1974. Aircraft noise is regulated under the Civil Aviation Act 1982.

Recent research[28] highlights some of the main problems with the existing structure for noise regulation in the United Kingdom. On the enforcement of noise law, there appear to be weak strategies with variable enforcement policies throughout local authorities surveyed in the United Kingdom. One difficulty is that the detection, enforcement and overall regulatory strategy are so intertwined that the regulatory body is 'in effect both judge and jury as to the efficacy of the law'.[29] The approach is described as 'half-hearted': 'The way in which noise law is enforced in the United Kingdom would seem to indicate that there is not a strong commitment on the part of local authorities to combat neighbourhood noise.'[30]

A further finding in the research indicates that in the absence of a clearly focused policy containing clear objectives and the means to achieve them, the law is ineffective. Thus the conclusion to be drawn from this analysis

---

[28]See McManus, F., 'Noise Law in the United Kingdom — a very British solution?' (2000) Legal Studies 264.
[29]*Ibid.*, at 290.
[30]*Ibid.*, at 285.

is that the absence of coherent policy objectives leads to 'poor quality law, the main hallmarks of which are ambiguity and overall lack of coherence, which constitute a profound impediment to the law's effectiveness'.[31]

CONCLUSIONS

Air quality standards are a good example of the strengths and weaknesses of standard-setting strategies. A plethora of economic instruments — such as the climate change levy, tradeable emissions standards and taxation on vehicle fuel — has been adopted in addition to the normal range of standards used by regulatory bodies. Standards are used as targets even where it is doubtful that the targets may be achieved, or, as in the case of particulates, where it is unclear if tougher standards will make any significant difference to the protection of public health. Standards for air quality depend on accurate monitoring and the correct siting of testing stations. Countries with a good track record may nevertheless appear to suffer if air standards in adjoining countries are poor or badly regulated. The nature of air standards is that to be effective they must be transboundary. This point is amply demonstrated by the Chernobyl disaster, which showed the general systemic weaknesses in providing adequate responses to the problem. Standard-setting, to be effective, must operate where there is common agreement.

We have seen from earlier chapters that public opinion is an important element in the development of good standard-setting. The Royal Commission has made this point throughout its report on setting standards. The concerns of the public have been met, for example, on the effects of airborne lead from vehicle emissions on the intellectual development of children. There is in fact no firm scientific evidence to support such a link, and other health impacts may be more likely. Reduction in lead emissions through the imposition of a variety of standards has occurred in response to factors other than public opinion alone (see above), but nonetheless concerns have been addressed and increased confidence in the regulatory process achieved.

In the absence of an effective or coordinated energy or transport policy at national or EU level, there is a sense that standards may be a substitute for such a policy and this may give the impression of achievement while the reality may be very different. The absence of national standards for ozone is an indication of the problems and limitations on standard-setting as a substitute for problem-solving through environmental policies that are sustainable.

---

[31]McManus, *op cit.* n. 28.

Air quality standards are ultimately dependent on government policy. Transport and energy policies have been led by international agreements to achieve reductions in carbon dioxide and other emissions and, in that way, standard-setting may become the key to implementing policy decisions. Paradoxically, it is only through effective policies that standards may be efficiently implemented.

The example of noise regulation and control, where effective law enforcement is difficult to measure, standards are variably applied and controls are left in the hands of the regulators, highlights a further problem. The inevitable lack of uniformity and consistency in approach leaves environmental law weak and ineffective.

Lastly, there is the question of public confidence and scientific knowledge.[32] No matter how well designed regulations may be, or how carefully they may be implemented, the regulatory structure of environmental law depends not only on 'sound science' but also on the public's perception of risk. In that context, underlying the public's confidence in standards is the public's perception of what is good or bad science.

---

[32]See Elworthy, S. and Holder, J., *Environmental Protection Text and Materials* (London, Butterworths, 1997)

CHAPTER TEN

Evaluating the Future: Sustainable Development and Environmental Standards

This chapter draws together the main analyses presented in the book. There are three strands to the analysis. First, there is an analysis of scientific developments and the future of standard-setting in the environment. This covers the way in which the science of toxicity testing, techniques to determine harm to ecosystems, risk assessment and modelling are likely to develop in the future. The positive sides to future possibilities such as 'Life-cycle 2', clean technologies, as part of the precautionary principle, are considered and future collaboration between scientists working within different specialisms in determining safe levels of environmental releases is also discussed.

Secondly, the future direction of regulation and the increasing use of legal structures are examined. The debate on the Utilities Act 2000 set out the importance of increased regulatory powers over environmental issues granted to energy regulators, and this is an indication of the importance of integratory regulation of the environment and energy. Lastly, standard-setting is appraised as part of a general trend towards the use of more variable economic instruments. The use of taxation, licences and financial incentives is considered. The findings of the Royal Commission are examined, as is the use of standards and indicators in the implementation of the United Kingdom's sustainable development strategy.

THE FUTURE OF STANDARD-SETTING AS A REGULATORY TECHNIQUE

Regulating the environment through standards is set to form the future development of environmental protection and there is a variety of reasons why this is likely. First, in the broader context of the European Union, the plethora of rights enjoyed by citizens will undoubtedly increase the role of the courts. Verifiable and openly accountable standards are necessary to achieve proportionality throughout the many agencies and regulatory bodies. In terms of an overall strategy to incorporate the European Union, its four Treaties and the miscellany of legislation into a form of written Constitution, the application of standards at local level fits the pattern of juridical developments.

Secondly, although many standards are numerically based, there are wide ranges of standards that include economic and fiscal instruments that are policy-driven. Pragmatically, standards may be made flexible, and in that sense they may provide both proactive as well as reactive systems of control. Standards may be used to monitor and detect harm, pollution and unlawful discharges and, equally, standards may be proactive in setting a benchmark to prevent harm and avoid pollution. The intrinsic nature of standard-setting is the expectation that standards rest on verifiable, even quantifiable, data that provide objectivity and reassurance and public demands for increased accountability and scepticism of professional judgments that are subjective lead to a critical appraisal of environmental regulation. The disposal of the Brent Spar oil installation has lessons for science. The then government had given permission for the oil company, Shell, to dispose of Brent Spar by sinking it in deep water after appropriate risk assessments had been submitted and reviewed. Greenpeace objected, publicising a risk assessment that indicated there was considerable risk of environmental harm to the deep sea ecosystem if this disposal route was adopted. Shell changed the selected route for disposal as a reaction to public pressure. In fact Greenpeace subsequently admitted that their risk assessment had been in error, primarily because it was based on inaccurate assumptions about the amount of toxic waste on the platform. Nonetheless, Brent Spar is now being decommissioned on land. This is technically demanding and undoubtedly a more expensive route of disposal and, in addition, there is an increased exposure of workers to risk and potentially greater environmetal risks associated with land decommissioning. Public belief and perception is capable of doubting even sound science, as Richard Macrory concludes:[1]

---

[1]Macrory, R., 'Setting Environmental Standards and the Royal Commission Report' in Neil Faris and Sharon Turner (eds), *Public Law and the Environment* (London, UKELA, 1999).

... the 1997 MORI survey indicated that 44% had confidence in government environmental scientists compared to 83% in scientists working for NGOs. Industry scientists commanded slightly higher confidence than government, while the Environment Agency (England and Wales) came somewhere between Government and NGOs.

Doubts and uncertainties about the reliability of science have emerged from the BSE crisis, public concerns about GMOs, safety concerns about the Sellafield reprocessing plant and recent revelations about medical malpractice. These are object lessons that scientists would be ill-advised to ignore. The public understanding of science has become a major goal in recent years with a review of the contribution of scientists to this public understanding found in the Wolfendale Report published in 1995.[2] The Committee on the Public Understanding of Science (COPUS), a joint initiative of the Royal Society, the Royal Institution and the British Association, is seen as one key component in providing support and disseminating best practice in achieving the public understanding of science. Initiatives in this area are undoubtedly important, but the response should go further to transparency and openness. In the case of risk assessments and the science on which these are based, there should be full transparency and this should go not only to the degree of confidence about the data and levels of determined effects, but also to an open discussion of realistic uncertainties. The UK has a mature electorate well able to assess risks and benefits if provided with clear, full and frank information. The House of Lords Select Committee on Science and Technology[3] in a recent report on science and society emphasised guidelines produced by the Government Chief Scientific Adviser in 1997 on communicating uncertainty and risk: '... Their main theme is openness: where scientific advice is uncertain, this should be admitted from the start. We warmly commend these guidelines. Suppressing uncertainty is bound to diminish public trust and respect'.

There is growing interest in how standards may be more transparent in providing information for the evaluation of the performance of public bodies. Benchmarking and educational information on schools and universities contribute to the debate about how effectively public money is spent and the use of environmental audit as part of sustainable development strategies is one way in which standards may be adapted to

---

[2]See Department of Trade and Industry, *Committee to Review the Contribution of Scientists and Engineers to the Public Understanding of Science, Engineering and Technology* (the Wolfendale Report, 1995), at 1–9.

[3]House of Lords Select Committee on Science and Technology, Third Report, *Science and Society* (February 2000).

enable monitoring of the environment. Targets and performance indicators may be used to judge how effectively environmental policies have been adopted or implemented with standards then performing a number of distinct functions:

(a)   a reporting function in establishing the most effective strategy;
(b)   a monitoring function in addressing the question of what has been achieved and how effective future strategies are likely to be;
(c)   an assurance function in establishing degrees of risk and harm; and
(d)   an accountability function in ensuring that there is transparency in the formulation and implementation of environmental policy.

There is, by analogy with public sector auditing,[4] a vision of environmental standards being tested, targets and performance indicators set and outcomes assessed.

The third reason why standards are important for the protection and monitoring of the environment arises from the nature of the environment worldwide. Population growth, high levels of human consumption, industrialisation and increasing effects on the global environment such as global warming, ozone depletion and loss of biodiversity,[5] all have impacts across international borders for the world as a whole. Standard-setting provides data for comparative analysis and, where necessary, common policies. Environmental standards that attempt to address global problems may provide the most effective way to respond to the growing concerns about the world's environment and international treaties have been established that in effect may represent the first tentative attempts to set standards for countries in terms of limiting and regulating activities that contribute to environmental problems with global ramifications. Conventions on Biodiversity and Climate Change arose from the United Nations Conference on Environment and Development held at Rio, Brazil, in 1992 and under the Framework Convention on Climate Change, the Climate Change Programme set out how emissions of greenhouse gases might be controlled. The London Conference on the Montreal Protocol in July 1989 established stringent controls on chlorofluorocarbon (CFC) production and use, a major contributor to ozone depletion in the stratosphere. Recently, the head of the UK Food Safety Agency has proposed that there should be an international body to oversee (and set standards for) the use and safety of genetically modified foods.

[4]See Hollingsworth, K., 'Environmental monitoring of government — the case for an environmental auditor' (2000) 20 LS 241.
[5]Bailey, R. (ed.), *Earth Report 2000* (London, McGraw Hill, 2000).

196

REFORMING STANDARDS AS PART OF SUSTAINABLE DEVELOPMENT

The Royal Commission has identified a number of broad directions in which standards may be developed. The main thrust of its recommendations are summarised below, together with additional recommendations for reform:

(a) *Procedures for setting standards*   A number of distinct elements are required to ensure consistency and objectivity. These may be identified:

   (i)   Data must be carefully assessed after rigorous and full investigation.

   (ii) Public opinion and value judgments must be taken into consideration in the question of whether a standard is appropriate or not.

   (iii) There should be an analysis of the best technical options.

   (iv) An assessment of risk and uncertainty should be carried out and, where appropriate, an economic appraisal.

   (v)   The systems of accountability must be open and sufficiently transparent to provide public assurance.

   (vi) Quality testing of standards should be carried out to ensure that resources and implementation strategies are undertaken.

(b) *Uniformity and consistency in standards*   Setting standards from a diverse number of sources and for a variety of reasons invariably raises the question of how standard-setting procedures might be improved. One suggestion which goes much further than the Royal Commission recommendations might be to consider a single regulatory body for standard-setting, together with a statutory code of procedure for setting standards. There are three strategies for the improvement of the existing system of standard-setting, as follows:

   (i)   There should be a simplification of standards and, where appropriate, a rationalisation of them. Policy tests for standards should share a common formulation, and whenever possible standards should be integrated into a coherent form that allows a rationalisation of the procedures and processes.

   (ii) The multiplicity of standards places an undue burden on business and industry and a single statutory code might provide a useful point of reference. If the existing standard-setting arrangements are unduly complex and confusing they are at best likely to be misunderstood or at worst ignored, defeating the whole point of standard-setting. The aims and objectives of standard-setting are in part to provide assurance to the general public, as well as to ensure a safe and secure environment and a major simplification of the procedures and processes provides a more attractive and user-friendly regime.

(iii) Peer review and scrutiny of standards requires an open and transparent approach to standard-setting and a single regulatory body might be formed to ensure that standard-setting itself follows a code of best practice. An alternative would be to consider the arguments recently advanced for the setting up of an environmental auditor,[6] a proposal that envisages the monitoring of sustainable development strategies of government departments and the carrying out of environmental audits. The proposal offers an attractive and well-considered option that might encourage greater public trust in the development of environmental standards linked to environmental policy. There is already a useful model for the adoption of such a regulatory body, namely the Comptroller and Auditor General and his function through the National Audit Office to provide a form of public scrutiny over public expenditure. The advantages of such a proposal are:

(1) the Environmental Audit Committee of the House of Commons may adopt a role similar to that of the Public Accounts Committee in the scrutiny of public money;

(2) Parliamentary accountability will improve the visibility and understanding of environmental standards;

(3) the use of a Parliamentary form of accountability provides transparency and supervision of government policy;

(4) environmental standards may be linked to performance indicators about improvements to the environment.

SCIENTIFIC DEVELOPMENTS AND FUTURE PERSPECTIVES

The Royal Commission has identified a number of issues regarding the current perception that the scientific understanding of a problem must be the starting point for setting solutions that include the appropriate

---

[6]See Hollingsworth, *op. cit.* n. 4.

standards. There are a number of inherent problems with a wholly scientific approach to standard-setting. These are:

(a) The scientific knowledge of the problem may not meet public expectations. A good example of this is the BSE crisis and vCJD, where scientific understanding is still limited. For example, the incubation period for the disease, whether all infected by the agent will develop disease symptoms, how many of the population are infected, are all associated with considerable uncertainties. In addition, it is not clear if other animals used in the human food chain are infected. Even the development of tests for the human form of the disease has not kept pace with public expectations. Indeed, even though there has been substantial investment in developing a test for this prion disease, no techniques have been successfully developed as yet beyond morphological examination of the brain at autopsy. The extent of the human form of the disease, and whether it will lead to an epidemic, is largely a matter for speculation rather than scientific certainty. Similarly, the risk of harm from GMOs is a matter of intense scientific debate. In this case the new molecular technologies are moving forward at a rapid pace, providing the scientific community with a considerable challenge in establishing scientific understanding of any potential effects on ecosystems or where GMOs are consumed as part of the human diet. In this area, as with many others, techniques to pool scientific knowledge rapidly and effectively are essential.

(b) Policy-making and science require a rigorous separation. This allows policy-makers to make decisions based on their best interpretation of the available science. Governments may rely on scientific data, but unless this is transparent public confidence may be lost. There is an analogy with the government's decision to allow the Bank of England to set interest rates. Minutes of the Economic Advisory Body that meets to advise the Governor of the Bank of England are made public after a short period of delay for any market-sensitive information to become obsolete. This procedure has invested the government's economic policy with greater authority than hitherto, and thus promoted confidence in that policy. In the same way, standard-setting might receive greater public support if a strategy for more openness were adopted.

(c) Standards should be reviewed on a regular basis. Flexibility in standard-setting is required to take account of new developments and the latest scientific findings. The uncertainty related to the potential human and ecosystem effects of endocrine disrupting compounds is one example where flexibility for the future may be required. Review should go not only to the standards themselves, but also to techniques in ecotoxicology, human toxicology and risk assessment. There should be flexibility to incorporate new techniques that offer improvements on those currently available in assessing, monitoring and controlling risks that are addressed through standard-setting.

(d) Public consultation and the methodology for obtaining public opinion and gauging public concerns should be improved. A range of methods should be used to provide information to the public and link complex scientific research to the needs of ordinary people. Possible techniques for engaging the public have been proposed, including consultations at local and national level, opinion polls, consultative panels, focus groups and citizens' juries, stakeholder dialogues and internet dialogues.[7]

(e) As outlined in previous chapters in the book, regulating the environment sets a demanding challenge for the various legal, economic and scientific instruments that are available as part of the system of regulation. There is a strong case for simplification of the system of regulatory control. Codification of procedures and standards may also assist in developing a transparent and accountable system of regulation.

CONCLUSIONS

Environmental standards form a diverse but distinct area of regulating the environment and their significance is likely to grow in coming years. As outlined in Chapter 5, both proactive and reactive techniques are much in evidence in the development of environmental regulation in the United Kingdom. An assessment of the different forms of regulation in terms of their cost and effectiveness is needed, which includes analysing the virtues of self-regulation as well as 'command and control' forms of regulation. Politicians are conscious that public concerns about the environment cover issues from food to transport. Standard-setting covers a wide variety of economic instruments and setting environmental objectives is a key element of a revenue policy[8] that taxes relevant goods or activities in such a way as to reflect the costs of the environmental damage they cause. Examples include:

---

[7]House of Lords Select Committee on Science and Technology, *op. cit.* n. 3.
[8]See *The IFS Green Budget: January 1998* (London, Institute for Fiscal Studies, 1998).

(a) *Transport* — vehicle fuel duties, vehicle excise duties, the taxation of company cars, the taxation of parking spaces at work, the taxation of fuel provided free for private motoring;

(b) *Energy taxation* — value added tax on domestic fuel, and the promotion of energy saving materials;

(c) *Water pollution* — proposals for using fiscal instruments to control pollution;

(d) *Waste* — landfill taxes.

The debates over proposals in the Utilities Act 2000 reflect the higher agenda given to environmental issues. The proposed new Gas and Electricity Markets Authority is intended to have regard to guidance on social and environmental matters from time to time proposed by the Secretary of State. This form of general economic regulation targeted at consumers invites consideration of the standards that may be set to implement an energy policy that encourages competition but insists on environmental protection. A variety of different indices may be thought relevant to implementing the aims of the Bill and these include:

(a) the objectives set by the United Kingdom's international commitments to reduce greenhouse gases and the emission of carbon dioxide by 20 per cent by the year 2010.[9]

(b) a new obligation to supply renewable electricity (the details of this requirement are to be a matter for secondary legislation);

(c) a plethora of obligations, ranging from energy efficiency to standards for incineration, and from renewable energy sources to the existing non fossil fuel obligation arrangements.

We have seen that the European Union provides an important source for standards. The form of the standards may be provided through setting targets and this is a common theme, especially in developing an energy policy. The European Commission has proposed the expansion of renewable energy sources through a Draft Directive[10] in May 2000 which sets targets by 2010 for environmental sustainability. This is indicative of specific targets for waste, packaging, sewage discharges, air quality, biodiversity and so on.

Standards must be directly related to 'sound science' and should be kept under constant review and a number of recent examples explain how the process of standard-setting is monitored:

---

[9]ENDS Report 305, p. 35.
[10]ENDS Report 304, p. 51.

(a) The Environment Agency has set new limits for the emissions of sulphur dioxide from coal and oil-fired power stations.[11] This represents a more flexible system of control and takes account of existing and new power stations.

(b) A new system of control has been introduced from 1 April 2000 for remediating contaminated land sites based on identifying the most hazardous sites.

(c) The Air Quality (England) Regulations 2000 (SI 2000 No. 928) have introduced a revised air quality strategy that generally tightens controls but also takes into account interim arrangements in the light of new evidence of the long-range transport of secondary particles from continental Europe.[12]

There may be difficulties in developing new standards because of the lack of scientific evidence to support them. Since 1995, the Government's Expert Panel on Air Quality Standards has recommended a new standard for fine particles[13] with the intention that the relevant standard should be reviewed and measured as PM_{10}. However, it has not been possible to establish a link between exposure to various levels of particles and health and research into hospital emissions proved inconclusive.

The regulation of the environment is complex and difficult. There are attempts to bring coherence to the regulatory structure but, in the absence of a move to codification and simplification, this is likely to prove unfulfilled. Standards may require greater cooperation between industry and the government; and to ensure their implementation a flexible approach[14] may be preferable to an over-regulated one. Equally, standards may become part of the sustainable development culture in a particular industry. This is seen in the development of environmental accounts assessing the impact of the company on the environment and providing for a percentage of the company's profits to be spent on environmental measures. This form of voluntary self-regulation is a sign that standard-setting is beginning to impact on the consumer who is environmentally aware. Environmental accounts provide the raw data to assess the consequences of industrial activity on the environment and specific industries may act in anticipation of future regulation and through voluntary sustainability agreements self-regulate their activities. It is likely that this trend will continue for the future.

---

[11] ENDS Report 300, p. 9.

[12] ENDS Report 303, p. 39 and ENDS Report 300, pp. 37–8.

[13] ENDS Report 250, pp. 17-21 and ENDS Report 304, pp. 14–15.

[14] ENDS Report 304, pp. 15–16 details the flexible mechanisms employed in implementing the Kyoto Protocol on controlling greenhouse gases.

Select Bibliography

INTRODUCTION

This bibliography is in two parts: Part I advises the reader of the various sources necessary for an understanding of environmental regulation; Part II contains the main reading list on the subject.

PART I

The Twenty First Report of the Royal Commission, *Environmental Pollution: On Setting Environmental Standards* (Cm 4053, October 1998), provides a background explanation for the understanding of standards in the environment and for general issues of liability. A valuable analysis is given by V. Barnett and A. O'Hagan, *Setting Environmental Standards* (Chapman and Hall, 1997). A foundation for the study of environmental policy is contained in *This Common Inheritance: Britain's Environmental Strategy* (Cm 1200, 1990). There are two books that deserve specific mention in the context of regulating the environment. These are Neil Gunningham and Peter Grabosky, *Smart Regulation* (Clarendon Press, 1998) and D. Vogel, *National Styles of Regulation* (Cornell University Press, 1986).

The reader is directed to a number of sources for particular areas or specialisms. On the role of the courts, see P. McAuslan, 'The role of courts and other judicial type bodies in environmental management' (1991) 3 JEL

195; and House of Lords Select Committee on the European Communities, 3rd report, *Remedying Environmental Damage* (HMSO,1993). On public law and constitutional law, see Colin Munro, *Studies in Constitutional Law*, 2nd edn. (Butterworths, 1999); A. W. Bradley and K. D. Ewing, *Constitutional and Administrative Law*, 12th edn. (Longman, 1997); J. F. McEldowney, *Public Law*, 2nd edn. (Sweet and Maxwell, 1998); M. Sunkin and G. Phillipson, *Public Law* (Butterworths, 1998); Wade and Forsyth, *Administrative Law*, 7th edn. (Oxford University Press, 1994); Michael Superstone and James Goudie (eds) *Judicial Review* (Butterworths, 1992). Discussions on nuisance liability include F. H. Newark, 'The Boundaries of Nuisance' (1949) 65 LQR 480. Also see Ogus and Richardson, 'Economics and the Environment: A Study of Private Nuisance' [1977] CLJ 284; J. P. S. MacLaren, 'Nuisance law and the Industrial Revolution — Some Lessons from History' (1983) 3 Oxford Journal of Legal Studies 155; and Kevin Gray, 'Equitable Property' (1994) *Current Legal Problems* 157. On the use of the criminal law in enforcing environmental regulations, see the Law Reform Commission of Canada, *Crimes Against the Environment*, Working Paper No. 44; *Pollution Control in Canada: The Regulatory Approach in the 1980s*, A Study Paper; *Sentencing in Environmental Cases*, Study Paper.

The various reports of the Royal Commission on Environmental Pollution provide an important source of scientific and legal information and analysis. The main reports are as follows: 1st Report (Cm 4585, 1971); 2nd Report, *Three Issues in Industrial Pollution* (Cm 4894, 1972); 3rd Report, *Pollution in Some British Estuaries and Coastal Waters* (Cm 5054, 1972); 4th Report, *Pollution Control: Progress and Problems*, (Cm 5780, 1974); 5th Report, *Air Pollution Control: An Integrated Approach* (Cm 6371, 1976); 6th Report, *Nuclear Power and the Environment* (Cm 6618, 1976); 7th Report, *Agriculture and Pollution* (Cm 7644, 1979); 8th Report, *Oil Pollution and the Sea* (Cm 8358, 1981); 9th Report, *Lead in the Environment* (Cm 8852, 1983); 10th Report, *Tackling Pollution — Experience and Prospects* (Cm 9149, 1984); 11th Report, *Managing Waste: The Duty of Care* (Cm 9675, 1985); 12th Report, *Best Practicable Environmental Option* (Cm 310, 1988); 13th Report, *The Release of Genetically Engineered Organisms to the Environment* (Cm 720, July 1989); 14th Report, *Genhaz — a System for the Critical Appraisal of Proposals to Release GMOs into the Environment*, (Cm 1557, June 1991); 15th Report, *Emissions from Heavy Duty Diesel Vehicles*, (Cm 1631, September 1991),16th Report, *Freshwater Quality*, (Cm 1966, June 1992); 17th Report, *Incineration and Waste*, (Cm 2182, May 1993); 18th Report, *Transport and the Environment*, (Cm 2674, October, 1994); 19th Report, *Sustainable Use of Soil* (Cm 3165, February 1996); 20th Report, *Transport and the Environment Since 1994* (Cm 3752, September 1997); 21st Report, *Setting Environmental Standards* (Cm 4053, October 1998); 22nd Report, *Energy — The Changing Climate* (Cm 4749, June 2000). Other important reports that deserve mention are: *Monitoring Environmental Assessment and Planning* (HMSO, 1991); *This Common Inheritance: Britain's Environmental Strategy* (Cm 1200) (HMSO, 1990); *Biodiversity — The UK Action Plan* (Cm 2428); and *A Guide to Risk Assessment and Risk Management for Environmental Protection* (HMSO, 1995).

There are a number of useful regulations to consult as examples of standard-setting in the areas of environmental assessment. Miscellaneous regulations applicable to environmental assessment include: SI 1988 No. 1241 (trunk roads and motorways);SI 1989 No. 167 (electricity power stations); SI 1990 No. 367 (overhead electricity power lines, oil and gas pipelines);SI 1988 No. 119 (mandatory Annex 1 assessments); SI 1989 No. 1207 (afforestation projects); SI 1988 No. 1336 (port and harbour projects); SI 1988 No. 1218 (marine salmon farming projects);SI 1988 No. 1221. In Scotland, SI 1994 No. 2010 provides an extension of the environmental assessment rules to Scotland. There are also a number of international agreements, such as: OECD, *Guidelines in Respect of Procedures and Requirements for Anticipating the Effects of Chemicals on Man and in the Environment*, 7 July 1977 (C(77)97 (Final)); 1991 Espoo Convention on Environmental Impact Assessment in a Transboundary Context (ENDS Report 207, pp. 34–5); UNEP, *Environmnetal Auditing* (report of the United Nations Environment Programme) (1989).

There are a number of useful sources in specialised journals: *Journal of Environmental Law* (Oxford University Press), *Environmental Law Review* (Vathek), *Environmental Law and Management* and *Water Law and Utilities Law Review*, both published by Chancery Law Publishing and the *International Journal of Biosciences and Law* (published by ABA). Journals for legal practitioners that provide useful information include: the *Environmental Law Series* (Cameron Markby), *European Legal Developments* (Baker and MacKenzie), *Green and Clean in Europe* (Allen and Overy), and *Environmental Law* (journal of the UK Environmental Law Association, UKELA). A number of relevant environmental law books are available: Stuart Bell and Donald McGillivray, *Environmental Law* (Blackstone Press, 2000); John McEldowney and Sharron McEldowney, *Environment and the Law* (Longman, 1996); David Hughes, *Environmental Law*, 3rd edn (Butterworths, 1996); Owen Lomas and John McEldowney (eds) *Frontiers of Environmental Law* (Chancery Law Publishing, 1991); Churchill, Gibson and Warren, *Law, Policy and the Environment* (Journal of Law and Society, 1991). Useful specialised studies include: G. Richardson, A. Ogus and P. Burrows, *Policing Pollution — A Study of Regulation and Enforcement* (Oxford University Press, 1983); S. Elworthy, *Farming for Drinking Water: Nitrate Pollution of Water — An Assessment of a Regulatory Regime* (1994). Environmental law may also be found in a number of specialised loose-leaf encyclopaedias: see *Garner's Environmental Law* (Butterworths);

The Encyclopaedia of Environmental Law (Sweet and Maxwell). There are also related encyclopaedias, for example, Bailey and Tudway, *Electricity Law and Practice* (1992–). International environmental law is examined in Birnie and Boyle, *International Law and the Environment* (Oxford University Press, 1992) and on European Community Law see A. Kiss and D. Shelton, *Manual of European Environmental Law* (Cambridge, Grotius Publishers, 1993).

Keeping up-to-date in matters environmental is particularly important in this area of the law. See ENDS Report (published by Environmental Data Services Ltd) that provides a monthly digest of current developments and integrates law with science.

There are a large number of texts that deal with the fate, effects, monitoring and control of chemicals and substances in the environment. In terms of the fate of substances and their ecological and human effects in a number of different media, see C. F. Mason, *Biology of Freshwater Pollution*, 3rd edn. (Longman, 1996); S. M. Haslam, *River Pollution: an Ecological Perspective* (Wiley, 1992); D. M. Elsom, *Atmospheric Pollution: A Global Problem*, 2nd edn. (Blackwell, 1994); R. M. Harrison (ed.), *Pollution: Causes, Effects & Control*, 2nd edn. (Royal Society of Chemistry, 1993). A. M. Mannion and S. R. Bowlby (eds), *Environmental Issues in the 1990s* (Wiley, 1992); T. O'Riordan, *Environmental Science for Environmental Management* (Longman, 1994); and N. F. Gray, *Drinking Water Quality: Problems and Solutions* (Wiley, 1994). Books examining topics highly focused on ecotoxicology, toxicology and risk include: P. Calow (ed.), *Handbook of Ecotoxicology*, vol. 1 (Blackwell, 1993); P. A. Erickson, *Environmental Impact Assessment* (Academic Press, 1994); C. D. Klaassen (ed.), *Casarett and Doull's Toxicology — the Basic Science of Poisons*, 5th edn. (McGraw-Hill, 1996); H. F. Hemond, *Chemical Fate and Transport in the Environment* (Academic Press, 1994); I. C. Shaw and J. Chadwick, *Principles of Environmental Toxicology* (Taylor & Francis, 1998); F. Moriarty, *Ecotoxicology: The Study of Pollutants in Ecosystems*, 3rd edn. (Academic Press, 1999); and P. Calow (ed.), *Handbook of Environmental Risk Assessment and Management* (Blackwell Science, 1998).

A variety of scientific journals provide articles presenting basic information on ecosystems, providing benchmarks for assessments. Many of these journals also contain articles relevant to anthropogenic effects on the environment and man. A few examples include *Nature*; *Science*; *Water Research*; *Water Science and Technology*; *Marine Biology*; *Functional Ecology*; *International Journal of Environmental Studies*; and *British Journal of Experimental Biology*. Other journals deal specifically and solely with pollution, topics in ecotoxicology, human toxicology and risk assessment. These include: *Marine Pollution Bulletin*; *Toxicology and Industrial Health*; *Environmental Carcinogenesis and Ecotoxicology Reviews*; *Regulatory Toxicology and*

Pharmacology; Risk Analysis; Journal of Human and Ecological Risk Assessment; Public Health Reports; Fundamental and Applied Toxicology; Ecotoxicology and Environmental Safety; Environmental Management; The Science of the Total Environment; Ecotoxicology; Environmental Pollution; Environmental Toxicology and Safety; Environmental Toxicology and Chemistry; and *Chemosphere.*

Various scientific societies produce reports or magazines that contain useful information. For example, *Chemistry and Industry,* produced by the Society for Chemistry and Industry, and the *Society of Environmental Toxicology and Chemistry News.* The Royal Society produces a range of useful reports and statements in relevant areas, including: *Endocrine Disrupting Chemicals* (Document 06/00, June 2000); *Towards sustainable consumption: A European perspective* (May 2000); *Nuclear Energy — The Future Climate* (joint report by the Royal Academy of Engineering and the Royal Society, Statement 10/99, June 1999); *Review of data on possible toxicity of GM potatoes* (Royal Society Statement 9/99, June 1999); and *Genetically modified plants for food use* (Statement, September 1998). The Royal Society of Chemistry also publishes material in the area, for example: Harrison, R. M. (ed.), *Pollution: Causes, Effects and Control* (1990); and Harrison, R. M. (ed.), *Understanding our Environment: An Introduction to Environmental Chemistry and Pollution* (1992).

A number of UK organisations produce summaries and reports of relevant research. These include the Natural Environmental Research Council (NERC), the Medical Research Council (MRC), the BBSRC, and the Social Science Research Council (SRC). Many relevant government reports, discussion documents, etc. from the Ministry of Agriculture, Fisheries and Food; the Department of Environment, Transport and the Regions; and the Department of Health can be accessed through the UK government internet site, www.open.gov.uk, as can relevant Parliamentary reports, etc. Mission statements and information on the Environment Agency, together with reports and statistics, can be found at www.environment-agency.gov.uk. There are a number of useful databases under the auspices of these organisations and others, including GIS data at www.esri.com/data/online/index.html, NERC environmental data at www.nerc.ac.uk/environmental-data#DATACENTRES, and data on the terrestrial environment at www.nmw.ac.uk/ite/edn2.html. Base-line aquatic data on the river habitat survey are at www.environment-agency.gov.uk/gui/dataset3/3frame.htm, and on river flow at www.environment-agency.gov.uk/gui/dataset4/4frame.htm. The European Environment Agency provides data sets at www.eea.dk/fib.htm. The World Bank also has an environmental database intended to monitor environmental progress at www.esd.worldbank.org/env/publicat/

mep/mep.htm. There is the Chemical Abstract database providing information on 22 million substances at http://info.cas.org/casdb.html.

There is a variety of international institutions that produce reports including scientific analysis and data on health and environment, and which contribute in terms of developing techniques in standard-setting and risk assessment. The Scientific Committee on Problems of the Environment (SCOPE), under the auspices of The International Council of Scientific Unions (ICSU), reviews and publishes information on the health and environmental effects of man's activities, and on environmental monitoring procedures. There has been a series of publications arising under this mandate, under the general heading SCOPE. Other international organisations producing exceptionally useful and detailed reports include: the Organisation for Economic Cooperation and Development (OECD); the World Health Organisation (WHO); the United Nations (UN); the United Nations Environment Programme (UNEP); the World Bank; and the Asian Development Bank. Useful sources of information in the USA include publications by the US Environmental Protection Agency (USEPA); the Office of Science and Technology (OSTP); the US Food and Drug Administration (USFDA); the National Academy of Sciences (NAS); The American Society for Testing and Materials; and the National Research Council (NRC).

PART II

Abel, P. D., *Water Pollution Biology*, 2nd edn. (Taylor Francis, 1996).

Adams, J., *Risk* (UCL Press, 1995).

Alder, J. and Wilkinson, D., *Environmental Law and Ethics* (Macmillan, 1999).

Armstrong, M., Cowan, S., and Vickers, J., *Regulatory Reform* (MIT, 1998).

Ashworth, W., *The Genesis of Modern British Town Planning* (1954).

Attfield, Robin, *The Ethics of the Global Environment* (Edinburgh University Press, 1999).

Bailey, R., *Earth Report 2000* (McGraw-Hill, 2000).

Baldwin, R. (ed.) *Law and Uncertainty: Risks and Legal Processes* (Kluwer Law International, 1997).

Baldwin, R., Scott, C., and Hood, C., *A Reader on Regulation* (Oxford, Oxford University Press, 1998).

Baldwin, R. (ed.), *Regulation in Question: The Growing Agenda* (London School of Economics, 1995).

Baldwin, R., *Rules and Government* (London, London University Press, 1995).

Barnes, R. S. K. and Hughes, R. N., *An Introduction to Marine Ecology* (Blackwell Scientific Publications, 1988).

Bates, J. H. and Benson, C., *Marine Environment Law* (Lloyds of London Press Ltd, 1993).

Bates, J. H., *United Kingdom Marine Pollution Law* (Lloyds of London Press Ltd, 1995).

Beck, U., *Risk and Society* (Sage, 1992).

Beckerman, W., 'Sustainable Development: Is It a Useful Concept?' (1994) 3 *Environmental Values* 191.

Beesley, M. (ed.), *Regulating Utilities: The Way Forward* (London Institute of Economic Affairs, 1994).

Begon, M., Harper, J. L. and Townsend, C. R., *Ecology: Individuals, Populations and Communities*, 3rd edn. (Blackwell, 1996).

Bell, S., and McGillivray, D., *Environmental Law*, 5th edn. (Blackstone Press, 2000).

Birnie, P. and Boyle, A., *International Law and the Environment* (Oxford University Press, 1992).

Birtles, W., 'A Right to Know: The Environmental Information Regulations 1992' [1993] JPL 625.

Bishop, M., Kay, J. and Mayer, C., *The Regulatory Challenge* (Oxford University Press, 1995).

Biswas, A. K. and Agarwala, S. B. C., *EIA for Developing Countries* (Butterworths, 1994).

Bolin, B., Döös, B. R., Jäger, J. and Warrick, R. A. (eds) Scope 29, *The Greenhouse Effect, Climate Change and Ecosystems* (Chichester, John Wiley & Sons, 1991).

Bowers, J., *Sustainability and Environmental Economics* (Longman, 1997).

Boyle, A. and Freestone, D., *International Law and Sustainable Development* (Oxford University Press, 1999).

Bradley, K., (ed.) *Environmental Impact Assessment A Technical Approach* (London University Press, 1991).

Burridge, R. and Ormandy, D., *Controlling Minimum Standards in Existing Housing* (LRI, University of Warwick, 1998).

Cairney, T. (ed.), *Contaminated Land: Problems and Solutions* (Blackie Academic and Professional, 1993).

Calabrese, E. J. (ed.), *Biological Effects of Low Level Exposures: Dose Response Relationship* (CRC Press, 1994).

Caldwell, L. K., *Science and the National Environmental Policy Act: Redirecting Policy through Procedural Reform* (London, 1982).

Callies and Grant, M., 'Paying for Growth and Planning Gain: An Anglo-American Comparison of Development Conditions, Impact Fees and Development Agreements' (1991) 23 *The Urban Lawyer* 221.

Calow, P. (ed.), *Handbook of Ecotoxicology*, vol 1 (Blackwell, 1993).

Calow, P., *Controlling Environmental Risks from Chemicals: Principles and Practice* (Wiley, 1997).

Calow, P. (ed.), *Handbook of Environmental Risk Assessment and Management* (Blackwell Science, 1998).

Carnwarth, R., 'Environmental Enforcement — The Need for a Specialist Court' [1992] JPL 799.

Carnwarth, R., 'The Planning Lawyer and the Environment' (1991) 3 JEL 57.

Clark, M., and Herington, J. (eds), *The Role of Environmental Impact Assessment in the Planning Process* (Mansell, 1988).

Clark, R. B., *Marine Pollution* (Clarendon, 1989).

Clayton, K. and O'Riordan, T., 'Coastal Processes and Management.' in O'Riordan, T. (ed.), *Environmental Science for Environmental Management* (Longman Scientific & Technical, 1995).

Daintith, T. and Page, A., *The Executive in the Constitution* (Oxford University Press, 1999).

Diamond, J., *Guns, Germs and Steel* (Norton and Company, 1997).

Dodds, F., *The Way Forward Beyond Agenda 21* (Earthscan, 1997).

Elsom, D. M., *Atmospheric pollution. A Global Problem*, 2nd edn. (Blackwell, 1994).

Erickson, P. A., *Environmental Impact Assessment* (Academic Press, 1994).

Faris, N. and Turner, S., *Public Law and the Environment* (UKELA, 1999).

Freedman, B., *Environmental Ecology. The Impact of Pollution and Other Stresses on Ecosystem Structure and Function* (Academic Press, 1989)

Gerrard, S., 'Environmental risk management' in O'Riordan, T. (ed.), *Environmental Science for Environmental Management* (Longman Scientific & Technical, 1995).

Gibbons, J., 'The Common Agricultural Policy' in McDonald, F. and Dearden, S. (eds), *European Economic Integration* (Longman, 1992).

Gibson and Warren, *Law, Policy and the Environment* (Blackwell, 1991).

Gilpin, A., *Environmental Impact Assessment* (Cambridge University Press, 1995).

Goldin, I., and Alan Winters, L. (eds), *The Economics of Sustainable Development* (Cambridge, 1995).

Goudie, A., *The Human Impact on the Natural Environment*, 4th edn. (Blackwell, 1993).

Gouldson, A. and Murphy,J., *Regulatory Realities* (Earthscan, 1998).

Grant, A. and Jickells, T., Marine and estuarine pollution in O'Riordan, T. (ed.) *Environmental Science for Environmental Management* (Longman, 1995).

Grant, W., *Autos, Smog and Pollution Control* (Edward Elgar, 1995).

Gray, Kevin, 'Equitable Property' in Freeman, Oliver and Sanders (eds), *Current Legal Problems* (Oxford University Press, 1994).

Gray, N. F., *Drinking Water Quality: Problems and Solutions* (John Wiley, 1994).

Gunningham, N. and Grabosky, P., *Smart Regulation Designing Environmental Policy* (Oxford, Clarendon Press, 1999).

Haagsma, A., 'The European Community's Environmental Policy: A Case-study in Federalism' (1989) 12 *Fordham International Law Journal* 311.

Haigh, N., *Manual of Environment Policy: The EC and Britain* (Longman, 1994).

Hannigan, J. A., *Environmental Sociology* (Routledge, 1995).

Hant, K., and Jansen, Alf-Inge, *Governance and Environment in Western Europe* (Longman, 1998).

Harlow, C., and Rawlings, R., *Law and Administration*, 2nd edn., Law in Context (Butterworths, 1997).

Harrison, R. M. (ed.), *Pollution: Causes, Effects and Control* (The Royal Society of Chemistry, 1990).

Harrison, R. M. (ed.), *Pollution: Causes, Effects & Control*, 2nd edn. (The Royal Society of Chemistry, 1993).

Harrison, R. M. (ed.), *Understanding our Environment: An Introduction to Environmental Chemistry and Pollution* (The Royal Society of Chemistry, 1992).

Haslam, S. M., *River Pollution: an Ecological Perspective* (Chichester, John Wiley & Sons, 1994).

Heine, G., Prabhu, M. and Alvazzi del Frate, A., *Environmental Protection — Potentials and Limits of Criminal Justice* (Freiburg, 1997).

Hemond, H. F., *Chemical Fate and Transport in the Environment* (Academic Press, 1994).

Hester, R. E., and Harrison, R. M., (eds), *Waste Treatment and Disposal* (The Royal Society of Chemistry,1995).

Hewitt, K., *Regions of Risk,* (Longman, 1997).

Hilson, C., *Regulating Pollution* (Hart Publishing, 2000).

Hindmarsh, R., *et al.* (eds), *Altered Genes Reconstructing Nature: The Debate* (Allen and Unwin, 1998).

Holder, J., and others (eds), *Perspectives on the Environment* (Avebury, 1993).

Holdgate, M. W., *A Perspective of Environmental Pollution* (Cambridge University Press, 1979).

Holman, C., *Air Pollution and Health* (London, Friends of the Earth, 1991).

Horan, N. J., *Biological Wastewater Treatment Systems. Theory and Operation* (Chichester, John Wiley & Sons, 1990).

Hoskins, W. G., *The Making of the English Landscape* (Morrison & Gibb, 1995).

Howarth, W., 'Reappraisal of the Bathing Water Directive' [1991] 2 *Water Law* 92.

Howarth, W., *Water Pollution Law* (Shaw and Sons, 1988).

Hughes, J. M. R. and Goodall, B., 'Marine Pollution' in Mannion, A. M. and Bowlby, S. R. (eds), *Environmental Issues in the 1990s* (Wiley, 1992).

Hughes, D., *Environmental Law*, 3rd edn. (Butterworths, 1997).

Hutter, B., *Compliance: Regulation and Environment* (Clarendon Press, 1997).

International Commission on Radiological Protection *1990 Recommendations of the International Commission on Radiological Protection*, (1991) ICRP Publication 60, Annals of the ICRP 21: 1–3.

Jewell, T. and Steele, J., 'UK Regulatory Reform and the Pursuit of Sustainable Development' (1996) 8 JEL 283.

Johnson, S. P. and Coercelle, G., *The Environmental Policy of the European Communities* (1989).

Kiss, A. and Shelton, D., *International Environmental Law* (Dordrecht, 1991).

Kiss, A. and Shelton, D., *Manual of European Law* (Grotius Publications, 1993).

Kiss, A. and Shelton, D., *Manual of European Environmental Law* (Grotius Publications, 1993).

Klaassen, C. D (ed.), *Casarett and Doull's Toxicology — the Basic Science of Poisons*, 5th edn. (McGraw-Hill, 1996).

Kramer, L., 'The implementation of environmental laws by the European Communities' (1991) *German Yearbook of International Law* 9.

Kramer, L., *EEC Environmental Law*, 4th edn. (London, Sweet and Maxwell, 2000).

Kramer, L., *European Environmental Law Casebook* (London, Sweet and Maxwell, 1993).

Lammers, I. G., *Pollution of International Watercourses* (1984).

Landes, D., *The Wealth and Poverty of Nations* (Abacus, 1999).

Langford, T. E., *Electricity Generation and the Ecology of Natural Waters* (Liverpool University Press, 1983).

Lomas, O. and McEldowney, J. F (eds.), *Frontiers of Environmental Law* (Chancery, 1991).

Lovelock, J., *The Ages of Gaia.* (Oxford University Press, 1988).

Lowry, J. and Edmonds, R., *Environmental Protection and the Common Law* (Hart Publishing, 2000).

Lynch, J. M. and Wiseman, A., (eds.), *Environmental Biomonitoring* (Cambridge University Press, 1998).

MacEwan, A. and MacEwan, M., *National Parks: Conservation or Cosmetics?* (George Allen and Unwin, 1982).

MacEwen, A. and MacEwan, M., *Greenprints for the Countryside* (George Allen and Unwin, 1987).

Macrory, R. and Hollins, S., *A Source Book of European Community Environmental Law* (Clarendon Press, Oxford, 1995).

Mannion, A. M. and Bowlby, S. R. (eds), *Environmental Issues in the 1990s* (Wiley, 1992).

Mason, C. F., *Biology of Freshwater Pollution*, 3rd edn. (Longman, 1996).

McAuslan, P., 'Planning Law's Contribution to the Problems of an Urban Society' (1974) 37 MLR 134.

McAuslan, P., *The Ideologies of Planning Law* (Pergamon Press, 1980).

McEldowney, J. F., *Public Law*, 2nd edn. (Sweet and Maxwell, 1998).

McEldowney, J. and McEldowney, S., *Environment and the Law* (Longman, 1996).

McEldowney, S., Hardman, D. J. and Waite, S., *Pollution: Ecology and Biotreatment* (Longman, Essex, 1993).

McLaren, J. P. S., 'Nuisance Law and the Industrial Revolution — Some Lessons from Social History' (1983) 3 Oxford Journal of Legal Studies 155.

McLeay, S., *Accounting Regulation in Europe* (Macmillan Press, 1999).

Mooney, H. A. and Bernadi, G. (eds) *Introduction of Genetically Modified Organisms in the Environment* (John Wiley & Sons Ltd, 1990)

Moore, V., *A Practical Approach to Planning Law*, 4th edn. (Blackstone Press, 2000).

Moriarty, F., *Ecotoxicology. The Study of Pollutants in Ecosystems*, 3rd edn. (Academic Press, 1999).

Mostafa K. Tolba, (ed.), *The World Environment 1972–1992: Two Decades of Challenge* (Chapman and Hall, UNEP).

National Society for Clean Air, *1999 Pollution Handbook* (NSCA, 1999).

Ogus, A. I., 'Regulatory laws: Some lessons from the past' (1992) 12 LS 1.

Ogus, A. I., *Regulation: Legal Form and Economic Theory* (Oxford University Press, 1994).

O'Riordan, T., *Ecotaxation* (Earthscan, 1997).

O'Riordan, T., (ed.), *Environmental Science for Environmental Management* (Longman, 1995).

Pearce, D., Barbier, E. and Maikandya, A., *Sustainable Development: Economics and Environment in the Third World* (Earthscan, 1994).

Pearce, D. W. (ed.), *Blueprint 2: Greening the World Economy* (Earthscan, 1991).

Pearce, D. W. and Warford, J., *World Without End: Economics, Environment and Sustainable Development* (Oxford University Press, 1992).

Porteus, A., 'Hazardous wastes in the UK — an overview', in Porteus, A. (ed.), *Hazardous Waste Management Handbook* (Butterworths, 1985).

Power, M., *The Audit Explosion* (DEMOS, 1994).

Power, M., *The Audit Society: Rituals of Verification* (Oxford University Press, 1997).

Prosser, T., *Law and the Regulators* (Clarendon Press, 1997).

Purdue, M., 'Defining Waste' [1990] JEL 259.

Ramade, F., *Ecotoxicology* (John Wiley, 1987).

Reece, H., (ed.), *Law and Science* (Oxford University Press, 1998).

Rehbinder, E. and Stewart, R., *Environmental Protection Policy* (New York University Press, 1995).

Richardson, G., Maloney, W. and Rudig, W., 'The Dynamics of Policy Change: Lobbying and Water Privatisation' (1992) 70(2) *Public Administration* 157.

Richardson, G., Ogus, A., and Barrows, P., *Policing Pollution* (Oxford University Press, 1983).

Rowland, F. W. and Isaksen, I. S. A. (ed.), *The Changing Atmosphere* (John Wiley & Sons, 1988).

Samiullah, Y., *Prediction of the Environmental Fate of Chemicals* (Elsevier Applied Science, 1990).

Shaw, I. C. and Chadwick, J., *Principles of Environmental Toxicology* (Taylor & Francis, 1998).

Shorrocks, B. and Coates, D. (eds), *The Release of Genetically-engineered Organisms* (Shrewsbury, British Ecological Society, Field Studies Council).

Smith, R., *The Fontana History of the Human Sciences* (Fontana Press, 1997).

Somsen, H., *et al.*, (eds), *Environmental Yearbook* (Oxford University Press, 2000).

Somsen, H., *Protecting the European Environment* (Blackstone Press, 1996).

Soussan, J. G., 'Sustainable Development' in Mannion, A. M. and Bowlby, S. R. (eds), *Environmental Issues in the 1990s* (John Wiley and Sons, 1992).

Speilerberg, I. F., *Monitoring Ecological Change* (Cambridge University Press, 1991).

Steele, J., 'Remedies and Remediation: Foundational Issues in Environmental Liability ' (1995) 58 MLR 615.

Stewart-Tull, D. E. S. and Sussman, M., *The Release of Genetically Modified Microorganisms — REGEM 2* (Plenum Press, 1992).

Tolba, M, *et al, The World Environment 1972–1992* (Chapman and Hall, 1992).

Turner, K. R., Pearce, D. and Bateman, I., *Environmental Economics* (Harvester, 1994).

Vogel, D., *National Styles of Regulation* (Cornell University Press, 1986).

Wadham, J. and Mountfield, H., *Human Rights Act 1998* (Blackstone Press, 1999).

Westlake, K., 'Landfill' in Hester, R. E. and Harrison, R. M. (eds), *Waste Treatment and Disposal* (The Royal Society of Chemistry, 1995).

Weston, J., *Planning and Environmental Impact Assessment in Practice* (Longman, 1997).

White, F. and Hollingsworth, K., *Audit, Accountability and Government* (Oxford University Press, 1999).

Winter, G., 'Perspectives for Environmental Law — Entering the Fourth Phase' 1 JEL 42.

Wood, C., *Environmental Impact Assessment* (Longman, 1996).

Woolf and McCue, 'Who regulates the regulator?' The great debate' (1993) 4 Util LR 199.

Woolf, A., *Quotas in International Environmental Agreements* (Earthscan, 1997).

Wurzel, R., 'Environmental Policy' in Lodge, J. (ed.), *The European Community and the Challenge of the Future*, 2nd edn. (London, Pinter, 1993).

Yang, R. S. H., *Toxicology of Chemical Mixtures: Case Studies, Mechanisms, and Novel Approaches* (Academic Press, 1994).

Reports

Brundtland, G., *Our Common Future: Report of the World Commission on Environment and Development* (Oxford University Press, 1987).

Civil Service Year Book — available as an annual publication from HMSO.

Coal and the Environment, Cmnd 8877 (HMSO, 1983).

Convention on Civil Liability for Oil Pollution Damage (1969).

Department of Environment, *Neighbouring Noise Working Party, Review of the Effectiveness of Neighbour Noise Controls* (DoE, 1995).

Department of Environment, *Countryside Survey 1990: Main Report* (DoE, 1993) .

Department of the Environment, *Economic Instruments for Water Pollution* (DoE, 1997).

Department of the Environment, *Air Quality: Meeting the Challenge* (1995).

Department of the Environment, *Climate Change — The UK's Programme* (HMSO, 1994).

Department of the Environment, *Freshwater Quality: Government Response* (DoE, February, 1995).

Department of the Environment, *Improving Air Quality — A Discussion Paper on Air Quality Standards and Management* (DoE, 1994).

Department of the Environment, *Ozone in the United Kingdom 1993: Third Report of the United Kingdom Petrochemical Oxidants Review Group, Air Quality Division* (DoE, 1994)

Department of the Environment, *Contaminated Land*, Cm. 1161 (HMSO, 1990).

Department of the Environment, *Sustainable Waste Management: A Waste Strategy for England and Wales, Consultation Draft, January 1995* (DoE, 1995).

Department of the Environment, *Recycling Waste*, Management Paper No. 28 (HMSO, 1991).

Drinking Water Inspectorate, *Drinking Water 1994* (HMSO, 1995).

GESAMP (Group of Experts on the Scientific Aspects of Marine Pollution), *The State of the Marine Environment*. (Blackwell Scientific, 1990).

Grey, D. R. C, Kinniburgh, D. G., Barker, J. A. and Bloomfield, J. P., *Groundwater in the UK. A Strategic Study. Issues and Research Needs* (Groundwater Forum Report FR/GF 1).

House of Lords Select Committee on the European Communities, *20th Report on Agriculture and the Environment* (Session 1983–4 HL 247).

Law Commission, *Report on the Consolidation of Certain Enactments relating to Clean Air* (1992) Law Comm. No. 209; Scot. Law Comm. No. 138.

National Rivers Authority (NRA), *Water Pollution from Farm Waste 1989* (NRA South West Region, 1990).

NRA, *Low Flows and Water Resources* (NRA, 1993).

NRA, *Policy and Practice for the Protection of Groundwater* (NRA, 1992).

OECD, *Report of the OECD Workshop on Environmental Hazard/Risk Assessment*, Environment Monograph No. 105 (OECD, 1995).

OECD, *OECD Guidelines for the Testing of Chemicals, Plus the 9th Addendum* (OECD, 1998).

OFWAT, *Paying for Quality: The Political Perspective* (OFWAT, 1993).

OFWAT, *Paying For Water: A Time for Decisions* (OFWAT, 1991).

OFWAT, *Future Charges for Water and Sewerage Services: The Outcome of the Periodic Review* (OFWAT, 1994).

PPG24, *Planning and Noise* (HMSO, 1994).

Report of the Noise Review Working Party (HMSO, 1990).

Royal Commission on Environmental Pollution, 16th Report, *Freshwater Quality*, June 1992 (Cm 1966) (HMSO, 1992).

Royal Commission on Environmental Pollution, 21st Report, *Environmental Pollution: On Setting Environmental Standards* (Cm 4053) (October 1998) (HMSO, 1998).

Rural England (Cm 3016) (HMSO, 1995).

Stewart, M., 'Modelling sewage treatment costs', Office of Water Services Research Paper No. 4 (January 1994).

Stewart, M., 'Modelling water costs', Office of Water Services Research Paper No. 2 and Warwick Economic Working Paper No. 9416 (1994).

Stewart, M., 'Modelling water costs', Office of Water Services Research Paper No. 3 (January 1994).

The Government's White Paper, *Review of Radioactive Waste Management Policy* (Cm 2919) (HMSO, 1995).

This Common Inheritance (Cm 1200) (HMSO, 1990).

UK Annual Report, *This Common Inheritance* (Cm. 2822) (HMSO, 1995).

UK Groundwater Forum, *Groundwater in the UK: A Strategic Study* (UK Groundwater Resources, June 1995).

UK Sustainable Development: the United Kingdom Strategy (HMSO, 1994).

UNDP, *Human Development Report 1992* (Oxford University Press, 1992).

United Nations Economic Commission for Europe (UNECE), *Policies for Integrated Water Management*, E/ECE/1084 (1985).

United Nations, *Agenda 21: The United Nation's Programme of Action from Rio* (United Nations, 1992).

WHO, *Guidelines for Drinking-water Quality*, vol. 2 (World Health Organisation, 1984).

WHO, *Health Hazards from Nitrates in Drinking-water* (World Health Organisation, 1985).

World Bank, *World Development Report 1992* (Oxford University Press, 1992).

Index